# Sociology AS

## The Complete Companion

AQA

Patrick McNeill

•

Jonathan Blundell

•

Janis Griffiths

Published in 2003 by:

Nelson Thornes Ltd
Delta Place
27 Bath Road
CHELTENHAM
GL53 7TH
United Kingdom

03 04 05 06 07 / 10 9 8 7 6 5 4 3 2 1

A catalogue record for this book is available from the British Library

ISBN 0–7487–7212–X


Commissioning Editor: Rick Jackman

Production Editor: James Rabson

Project Manager: Fiona Elliott

Cover Designer: Nigel Harriss

Designer and typesetter: Patricia Briggs

Picture Researcher: Sue Sharp

Production Controller: Amanda Meaden

Illustations by Harry Venning and Oxford Designers and Illustrators

Printed and bound in Italy by Canale

## Acknowledgements

The authors and publisher would like to thank Steve Chapman
for his invaluable advice and assistance in the development of
this resource.

The authors and publisher would like to thank the following for
permission to reproduce material in this book:

The Child Support Agency for the table on page 49; Denscombe
(2002) for the graph on page 89; The Guardian for text excerpts on
pages 41, 53, 59, 61 and 99; © Her Majesty's Stationery Office for
the tables on pages 34, 36, 41, 48 and 103, and the graphs on
pages 34, 44, 50, 51 and 125; The Independent for the text excerpt
on page 57; The Observer for the text extracts on pages 39 and 51;
Sociology Review for the table on page 40, the graph on page 49,
and the text excerpts on pages 47, 83 and 97; The Times
Educational Supplement for the text excerpt on page 93.

The authors and publisher would like to thank the following
organisations for permission to reproduce illustrations as follows:

Advertising Archive for the image of the Surf advert on page 38;
© Andes Press Agency/Carlos Reyes-Manzo for the image on
page 15; Apple for the image of a computer on page 9; Associated
Press for the image on page 29; Associated Press, HO for the image
on page 62; Associated Press, POOL for the image on page 59;
Bubbles Photo Library for the image on page 78; Bubbles/Frans
Rombout for the images on page 70; © Bubbles/Loisjoy Thurston
for the image on page 10, the image of father and child on page 38,
and the image on page 84; Bubbles Photo Library/Katie Van Dyck
for the image on page 55; Mark Campbell/Photofusion for the image
on page 4 and the image of a shopping crowd on page 114; Corbis
for the image on page 73; © Paul Doyle/Photofusion for the image
on page 26; Education Photos/John Walmsley for the image of
sociology students on page 6; Colin Edwards/Photofusion for the
image on page 56; Mary Evans Picture Library for the image on
page 42; Hulton Archive for the image on page 42, the image of
Ziggy Stardust on page 46 and the image on page 95; © Pam
Isherwood/Photofusion for the image on page 43; Ute
Klaphake/Photofusion for the image of Harrow school on page 74;
Carlos Reyes-Manzo/Andes Press Agency for the images on pages
49, 76, the image of school children on page 114, and the image
on page 115; Brian Mitchell/Photofusion for the image of primary
school girls on page 71; G. Montgomery/Photofusion for the image
on page 88; Maggie Murray/Photofusion for the image of the
comprehensive school on page 74 and the images on page 87
and 102; The Press Association for the image on page 98; Betty
Press/Panos Pictures for the image on page 105; Christa
Stadtler/Photofusion for the image of the C of E school on page 71;
Topham Picturepoint for the image of an atomic bomb on page 12;
TophamPicturepoint/Universal Pictorial Press for the image of Vinnie
Jones on page 46; © Trip/H Rogers for the image of a French village
on page 6 and the images on pages 16; © Trip/M Jelliffe
for the image of an African village on page 6; and Harry Venning for
the cartoons on pages 31, 32, 36, 44, 53, 72, 75, 76, 80, 82, 84, 90,
92, 96, 101, 116, 118, 121, 122 and 124

# Contents

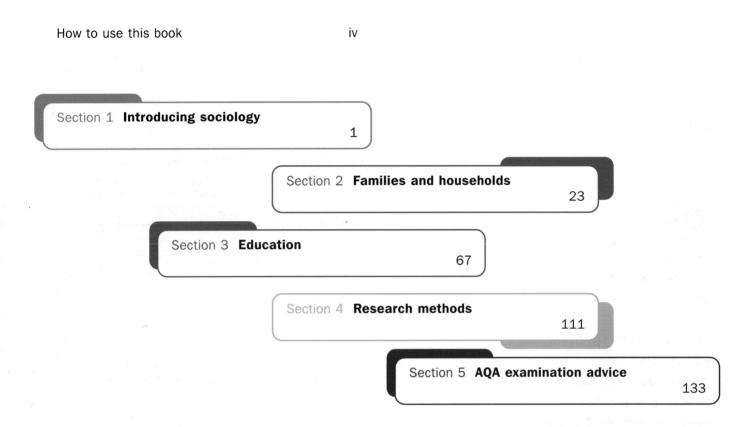

# How to use this book

This book is designed to encourage active learning, i.e. to help you to think about and respond to what you are reading. The material is presented in double-page spreads that include a range of special features.

 This sign in the margin introduces a short note, comment or question relating to the main text.

## Important studies

These are short summaries of key pieces of sociological research.

### Research issue

These describe issues that sociological researchers who study the topic must think about.

### Coursework advice

This is advice for students who have the opportunity to do some sociological research as part of their course.

### Watch out

These are warnings about things to avoid when you are taking your sociology exam.

Glossary terms: Some words are printed in **bold**. These are particularly important sociological terms and are defined for you on the page and in the Glossary at the end of the book.

### Think it through

These are activities and exercises designed to help you think about what you have been reading. They help you develop some of the skills that you will need in the exam but they are not set out in the same way as exam questions.

### Round-up

These are short summaries of the material on the double-page spread.

At the beginning of each section, you will find a **mindmap**. This is a way of presenting an overview of the section in a visually appealing way. We suggest that you produce your own mindmaps as you work through the sections.

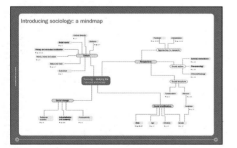

At the end of each section, you will find:

- a **summative review** – this summarises the section.
- **self-assessment questions** – these are designed to help you test how much you have learned. It would be a good idea to get together with some fellow-students to write more of these questions and to test each other on them.
- a **timeline** – this is designed to give you a picture of key developments in the history of sociology.

The final section in the book includes an explanation of the AQA examination papers, plus examples of exam answers, with advice and comments written by senior examiners. These answers have been written specially for this book and are not 'real' examples.

# Section 1 Introducing sociology

# Introducing sociology: a mindmap

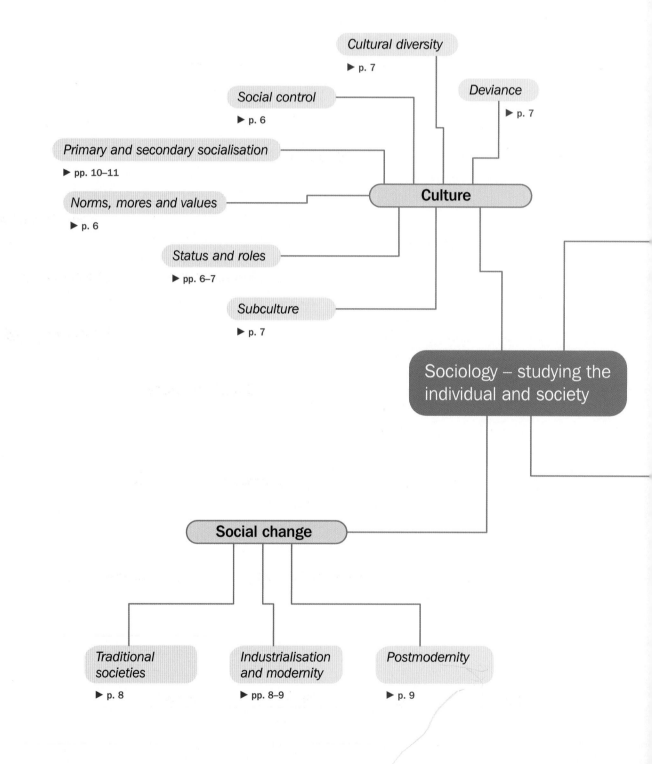

Cultural diversity
► p. 7

Social control
► p. 6

Deviance
► p. 7

Primary and secondary socialisation
► pp. 10–11

Norms, mores and values
► p. 6

**Culture**

Status and roles
► pp. 6–7

Subculture
► p. 7

Sociology – studying the individual and society

**Social change**

Traditional societies
► p. 8

Industrialisation and modernity
► pp. 8–9

Postmodernity
► p. 9

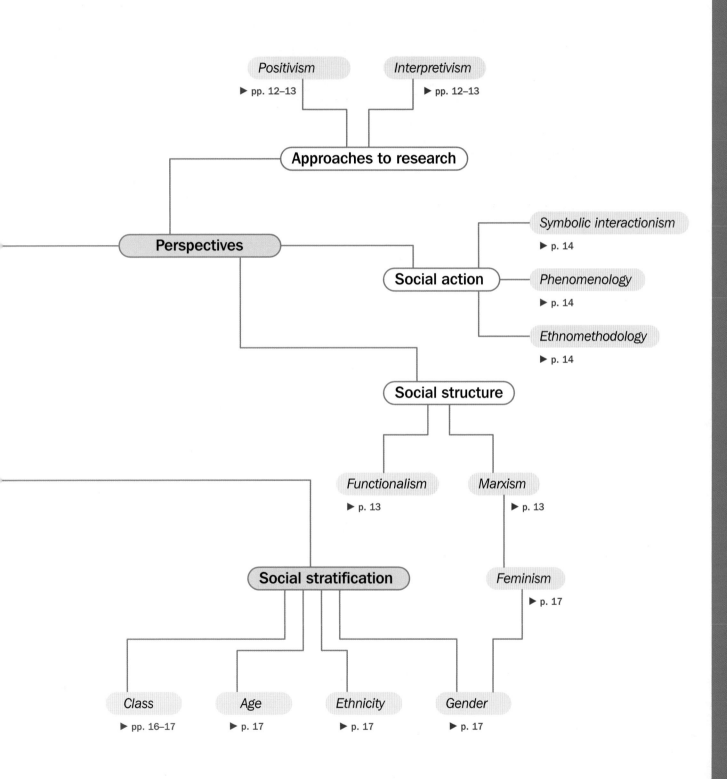

Positivism
▶ pp. 12–13

Interpretivism
▶ pp. 12–13

**Approaches to research**

**Perspectives**

Symbolic interactionism
▶ p. 14

**Social action**

Phenomenology
▶ p. 14

Ethnomethodology
▶ p. 14

**Social structure**

Functionalism
▶ p. 13

Marxism
▶ p. 13

**Social stratification**

Feminism
▶ p. 17

Class
▶ pp. 16–17

Age
▶ p. 17

Ethnicity
▶ p. 17

Gender
▶ p. 17

# What is sociology?

Sociology is the study of people in society

The simplest answer to the question posed above is that sociology is 'the study of people in society'. But what do we mean by 'society' and what is distinctive about sociology as a way of studying people in society?

We can start by making two statements about sociology.

1 *Sociology is an academic subject that is taught in schools, colleges and universities.* Most British universities have a sociology department. The first professor of sociology was Emile Durkheim at the Sorbonne in Paris in 1902. Usually, however, sociology is said to have begun about seventy years before this, with the writings of Auguste Comte – a Frenchman who developed some of the key ideas of what later became sociology.

✳ The period from 1750 to 1850 is often called the 'Age of Revolutions' because there was so much social and political upheaval in Europe and America.

2 *Sociology is a way of trying to understand society, and is linked to changes in society.* Comte lived in the century following the French and American revolutions, when ideas about liberty, equality and democracy led to the overthrow of the old political order and the creation of new societies. Since then sociology has been divided between those who see its purpose as being simply to describe society, without offering judgments, and those who want to understand society in order to change it.

✳ The early sociologists often tried to understand the new modern society that was emerging around them by comparing it with society in the past.

## What do sociologists study?

You can get some idea of the wide range of topics that are studied by sociologists by looking at the specifications from the awarding bodies (AQA and OCR). Topics include:

HEALTH  SOCIAL STRATIFICATION  WORLD SOCIOLOGY  SOCIAL POLICY

FAMILIES AND HOUSEHOLDS  MASS MEDIA  WEALTH, WELFARE AND POVERTY  RELIGION

POPULAR CULTURE  POWER AND POLITICS  EDUCATION  PROTEST AND SOCIAL MOVEMENTS

YOUTH AND CULTURE  CRIME AND DEVIANCE

## What do sociologists do?

Empirical: Based on observation or experiment rather than on theory.

Like all scientists, sociologists carry out research. The aim of the research may be simply to describe a social context, or it may be to explain it. Description may be the first step towards explanation. Either before they start their research, or while they are doing it, a sociologist will work out a possible explanation of some aspect of social life, and then do **empirical** research to test their idea (known as a 'hypothesis'). The evidence from the research may lead to the hypothesis being accepted, modified, or rejected. Theory and research go together; they are both essential.

## Structure and action

Some students find it hard to accept that sociology seldom offers clear answers. There is disagreement in all of the natural and social sciences, but it is particularly difficult to reach firm conclusions in sociology because of the complexity of the subject matter – people. Research findings can be interpreted in different ways and sociologists often do not agree amongst themselves. However, the nature of these disagreements often makes it possible to group sociologists together using labels that indicate the approach they favour. For example, one major division is between those who focus on social structure and those who focus on social action. This has resulted in two main approaches to sociology, which are explained in greater detail on pp. 12–15.

### Macro and micro approaches

In brief, the 'social structure approach' tends to focus on the large (macro) scale of social life; for example, on the education or legal systems, or on how these systems are connected. By contrast, the 'social action approach' focuses on the small (micro) scale. Taking this approach, a sociologist interested in education might study and analyse social interaction in a single classroom.

---

### Watch out

**Remember that any way of dividing sociology into two or more 'perspectives' is a simplification. Sociologists occupy a whole range of positions on a continuum, from those who are concerned with macro structural questions to those who study the smallest micro details of social interaction, and individual sociologists may change their views during their careers. Be careful not to oversimplify these divisions.**

---

 For an explanation of research methods, and of the concepts of validity and reliability, see p. 118.

Globalisation: The processes by which societies and cultures around the world become increasingly interdependent economically, culturally and politically.

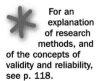 *There are literally hundreds of websites about sociology. A good site to start from is:* www.atss.org.uk

## Research methods

Sociologists use a wide range of research methods. Almost any source of information about people in society can be helpful, provided that its reliability and validity can be assessed.

The main methods used by sociologists are social surveys (including question-naires), interviews, ethnographic methods (including participant observation), and analysis of secondary data.

Social surveys can be used to study large numbers of people, by asking questions either of all of them or of a representative sample. Ethnographic methods are more appropriate when studying a small number of people, usually in a group. Secondary data are data already available from other sources such as government surveys.

## Explaining social change

One of the biggest problems sociologists face is in explaining how societies, and people's lives within societies, change over time. Sociology began as a way of trying to make sense of the dramatic upheavals in politics, work and social life in the late eighteenth century and early nineteenth century. Some sociologists were opposed to what they saw happening, and hoped that societies could remain stable despite the changes. Other commentators hoped for that stability to be overturned, because stability meant that wealth and power would continue to be held by a small minority. They wanted revolutionary change rather than gradual, evolutionary progress. Their concern with inequalities of wealth and power remains at the heart of much sociology today.

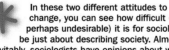 In these two different attitudes to change, you can see how difficult (and perhaps undesirable) it is for sociology to be just about describing society. Almost inevitably, sociologists have opinions about what they study.

The pace of social change has quickened and sociology is as relevant as ever. Some of the changes in British society are the result of changes that are happening on a global scale. **Globalisation**, which describes the many ways in which people now find their lives connected to others around the world, has become a central concern of sociologists over the past ten years.

## Value freedom

Can sociologists be completely objective, not allowing their opinions and feelings to influence their work? How far should sociology be concerned with changing the social world, and how far with just understanding it? Here again, there is a division of opinion. Some sociologists argue that it is their duty to be as objective as possible; sociology should be like natural science, where the scientific researcher is not influenced by their values (in theory, at least). This is much harder in sociology, because it is about people. An alternative view is that sociologists should accept that they are bound to be influenced by their values, so they should be open about these, leaving the reader to judge how far their work has been influenced by their values.

## Social policy

Some sociology has the aim of improving society and social welfare in the belief that through greater understanding we can develop more enlightened policies on health, education, crime, etc. Sociology that has this practical aim is called 'applied sociology'. For example, a sociologist might try to find out which methods of responding to juvenile crime are more likely to reduce it. The findings might lead to a change in government policy.

## Jargon

The language of sociology can be off-putting. Sociologists sometimes use unnecessary jargon (words that would not be understood by non-sociologists – a sort of private language), and seem to be stating the obvious in a complicated way. This is a common failing of academics in every subject! However, some of the jargon is useful, because – once you have learned it – it helps you express complex ideas with fewer words.

## Round-up

**Sociology is an academic subject, in which sociologists study many aspects of social life using a wide variety of theories and research methods. Because of its subject matter, sociology is often linked to attempts to improve aspects of social life. Sociologists face particular issues relating to value freedom.**

# What do all societies have in common?

Social life can only be maintained if there is a certain degree of social order, based on acceptance by the majority of at least some basic rules for behaviour. If this order did not exist, there would be no society. This basic agreement forms a large part of a society's culture. Sociologists have analysed these aspects of social life using a set of related concepts: norms, mores, rules, values, attitudes, statuses and roles.

## Norms

**Norms** are the unwritten and usually unspoken rules of everyday life, referring to specific situations. Young children are taught some norms during socialisation, but we all learn new norms constantly throughout our lives as we encounter new situations. Norms are usually learned through observing the behaviour of others and how others react to what we do. Sanctions against people who break norms vary from silent disapproval through verbal rebuke to physical punishment.

## Mores

Mores (pronounced 'more-rays', coming from the Latin for 'manners' or 'customs') are a stronger form of norms. They have a moral aspect and are about upholding standards of behaviour that are widely felt to be the 'right thing to do'. Because of this moral aspect, the sanctions against people who break mores are often stronger than against those who deviate from norms.

## Rules

Rules – and laws – are stronger than norms and mores and there are specified sanctions for breaking them. Schools and other institutions have rules and have the power to punish those who break them. Laws apply to the whole of society, and many people (judges, the police, lawyers, etc.) are employed to identify and deal with those who break the law. Rules and laws are formal, usually written down, and those who break them are normally aware of the consequences of being caught doing so. Sanctions can range from a warning to fines, imprisonment or even execution.

## Values

**Values** are the beliefs and moral views that are deeply held by most of the people in a society, and so can be taken as typical of that culture. Values lie behind norms. If you know the values of a society, you may be able to work out what the norms are likely to be in a particular situation.

## Attitudes

Attitudes are not as deeply held as values. A society can tolerate a wide variety of attitudes, but not of values. For example, people in Britain have a wide variety of attitudes towards political parties and their policies, but there is the underlying value, shared by the majority, that a democratic political system (one in which there are parties with different policies) is the best system.

## Status

**Status** means a position in society. Everyone has several statuses, and together these are referred to as a 'status set'.

Some statuses are based on characteristics that the person is born with, for example, position within a family, age, sex and ethnicity. These are 'ascribed statuses'. They cannot be changed by an individual, although collectively people may be able to challenge disadvantages arising from that status. For example, women have challenged the lower status of females.

Other statuses are 'achieved' by individuals, sometimes by competing against others – for example, by passing an examination, or getting a job.

Norm: A rule of behaviour in everyday life.

Values: The beliefs and morals that underlie norms.

Status: A position in society.

## Think it through

1 What are the roles in this situation?

2 What norms, mores, and rules apply to the students?

3 Are the norms or mores different for different groups (e.g. for males and females)?

4 What values underlie these norms and rules?

5 What sanctions might be applied to someone who breaks the norms, or the rules?

There are almost always some common elements to be found between different societies

## Roles

With each status there is a set of expectations – norms that the person with that status is expected to follow. This is a **role**. Just as everyone has a status set, so everyone also has a role set. Roles can sometimes clash; for example, students who have part-time jobs are sometimes asked to work extra hours when they should be studying. This is 'role conflict', between the roles of student and employee.

## Cultural diversity

Cultures vary from one society to another. The differences cover every aspect of social life: language, religious beliefs and practices, food and drink, clothing and decoration, cultural practices such as art, music and dance, uses of technology, and so on.

In many parts of the world, and especially in cities, there are societies made up of people from diverse cultural backgrounds. In London, for example, there are people from many different ethnic groups, speaking different languages and following different beliefs. This is the result of global migration, fuelled in the past by slavery and colonialism and today by globalisation, war, disasters and political repression. London can therefore be described as 'multicultural'. Some societies have a single dominant culture, and are 'monocultural'. Japan is an example of a modern industrial society that is still fairly monocultural.

Cultures borrow freely from each other and even cultures thought of as 'traditional' are continually evolving.

### Research issues

Researchers studying other cultures and subcultures often aim to gain an insider's view by joining a social group and observing the participants 'from the inside' and on their own terms (see pp. 122–3 on 'participant observation').

The processes of globalisation are spreading Western (and particularly American) culture around the world. Some sociologists have seen this as 'cultural imperialism', in which local cultures are swamped by Western culture with its values of **individualism** and consumerism. However, the transfer of culture is a two-way process and Western culture has itself absorbed and been changed by aspects of many different cultures. Many people in Britain, for example, eat food prepared in the style of a wide range of different cultures.

## Subculture

In modern societies, different social groups may have different cultures and ways of life. For example, people living in rural areas may have a different way of life from those in urban areas. A social group with its own particular values and way of life is a subculture.

## Deviance

**Deviance** refers to actions that break the norms and values of a society. 'Crime' refers to actions that break laws. Some deviant acts are criminal. However, some criminal acts are so common (e.g. speeding on the motorway) that it could be argued that they are not deviant. There is a continuum from eccentricity through mildly anti-social behaviour and deviance to seriously anti-social behaviour and crime.

Norms, values and laws vary between societies, so what is counted as crime and deviance may also vary.

## Important studies

The Channel 4 film *Baka* (1988) showed the way of life of the Baka people who live in the rainforest of southern Cameroon. Aspects of Baka culture include the following.

• Everyone belongs to a clan, and members of a clan cannot marry each other.
• There is no marriage ceremony, but the man must give gifts to his wife's parents.
• Parents share equal responsibility for looking after children.
• Status depends on age – old people, both men and women, are very highly regarded.
• Children sometimes play all day but, even from about four years of age, are also expected to help with preparing food and looking after babies and infants.
• The Baka do not read or write but have many stories, songs and rituals.

**Role:** The set of norms and expectations that go with a status.

**Deviance:** The breaking of norms, mores, values or rules.

**Individualism:** An emphasis on individual people – e.g. in terms of happiness and success – rather than on groups, communities or societies.

### Watch out

We are all members of a culture. It therefore follows that in studying other cultures or subcultures, we look at them from our own cultural point of view. There is a danger here of ethnocentrism, of assuming that our own culture is 'normal' and that it provides a sort of benchmark against which other cultures can be judged.

## Round-up

Social order, based on sharing of aspects of culture, is essential for the smooth running of society. There are wide differences between cultures. Within modern societies there are often distinct subcultures as well as the majority culture. The breaking of cultural expectations and rules is called 'deviance'.

# How have societies changed?

## Sociology and the modern world

As you have seen, sociology had its origins in the attempts by people in the early nineteenth century to make sense of the massive social changes that were taking place in Western Europe and elsewhere. However, although sociology emerged in a particular kind of society, it can still be applied to the study of other types of society.

### The myth of 'traditional society'

One way in which early sociologists tried to make sense of their own societies was by contrasting the emerging modern way of life with how life was assumed to have been in the past. 'Modern' societies were contrasted with 'traditional' societies. The differences between these two concepts, modern and traditional, formed the basis of much early sociology.

It was suggested that there had been changes in:

- scale – from small to large
- the basis of economies – from being based on agriculture to being based on industry
- where people lived – from most of the people living in the countryside to most living in towns and cities
- people's relationships with others – in the modern world, more relationships are impersonal and fleeting; this was sometimes seen as a change from 'community' to 'society'.

The picture of a 'traditional society' that is implicit in this list of comparisons is not a flattering one. Traditional societies tend to come across as being rather primitive and stagnant – although some writers also see that they had important values (such as in family and community life) that are in danger of being lost in the modern world.

In fact, the idea of 'traditional societies' is misleading. It lumps together the vast range of societies that existed before about 1750 – from hunter-gatherer societies to the complex and urban-based empires of pre-modern Europe, Asia, Africa and the Americas. Supposedly 'traditional' societies usually turn out to have been dynamic (constantly changing), while apparently ancient customs are found to be of more recent origin. Well-known examples in our own society include many of our Christmas traditions, such as Christmas trees and cards, which date back only to the Victorian period. All societies are always in a process of change.

### Industrialisation

The Industrial Revolution refers to the transformation of Britain from a predominantly rural and agricultural society to a predominantly urban and industrial one. This transformation is usually dated from about 1750 (though its origins were much earlier) to 1850. Subsequently, other nations – Germany and the USA first, then others – went through a similar transformation. This change is referred to as '**industrialisation**'.

During the Industrial Revolution changes took place in each of the following areas.

- *Population* – the population grew rapidly; the death rate fell; people migrated from rural to urban areas where they became the new industrial working class. '**Urbanisation**' occurred (i.e. there was an increase in the proportion of a country's population living in cities).
- *Technology* – this was an astonishingly inventive period in which new methods such as the use of steam power greatly increased production.
- *Transport* – this included the canal system, much improved roads and the railways. Together these made it much easier both to take raw materials to industrial areas and to distribute manufactured goods.
- *Agriculture* – improved techniques led to rising yields. The resulting greater prosperity of farmers, who became a rural middle-class, made them an important market for new industries.
- *Industry* – this was transformed by new technology and large investments of capital.
- *Empire* – Britain expanded its trade and then its empire, in search of sources of raw materials and new markets. Potential competition to British industry – such as the thriving Indian textiles industry – was destroyed.

This enormous and rapid transformation provided the early sociologists such as Comte and Durkhein with much to try to understand and analyse. This was a period of great optimism and faith in progress. It created what we can call the 'modern world', or '**modernity**'. The idea that societies could be improved, even perfected, led to political ideologies such as communism – which was not just aimed at understanding the world, but also at changing it. This optimism survived the two world wars. After World War II, in Britain and other western countries, a Welfare State, protecting the most vulnerable, was created and there was state intervention in the running of industries. There was general acceptance of this arrangement by both right-wing and left-wing politicians, which is referred to as the 'post-war consensus'. It began to break down in the 1970s as the role of governments in providing welfare and in running industries was increasingly questioned.

**Industrialisation:** The set of changes by which a society moves from being predominantly rural and agricultural to being predominantly urban and industrial.

**Urbanisation:** The increase in the proportion of a country's population living in towns and cities.

**Modernity:** The period of history from the late eighteenth to late twentieth centuries, marked by a belief in progress through science and rationality.

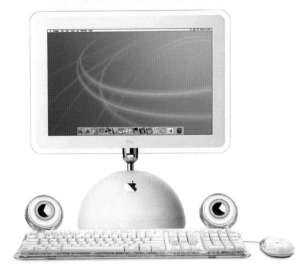

What do we mean by progress?

## Into postmodernity?

The mood of certainty and optimism associated with modernity was called more and more into question by events in the twentieth century. Advances in science and technology improved health and living standards, but also led to modern warfare, killings on an unprecedented scale and degradation of the environment. Moreover, the rising living standards of developed countries were achieved only through the exploitation of their colonies in what later became the 'Third World'. The pace of social change is continually accelerating, but we have no clear idea in what direction we are heading.

Some sociologists and others have suggested that the pace and scale of change means that the world is now very different even from only a few decades ago. They describe this as the change from living in modernity to living in **postmodernity**. Much of what we took for certain – gradual progress, better lives for our children, experts who could tell us what to do – has been lost. Some of the features of postmodernity have been said to be as follows.

- The mass media dominate our lives to the extent that we confuse media images with reality.
- Economies are now based on information and knowledge rather than manufacture of goods.
- Sources of identity such as class have become less important; people increasingly have multiple and cross-cutting identities. Identities are also increasingly based on lifestyle and consumption (which can be more easily changed).

Other writers, however, have argued that these changes have not been so sweeping, and that the period we are now living in is better described as 'late' or 'high' modernity.

### Think it through

Look at the images above. Draw a table with two columns and list in one column ways in which life today has improved compared with the life lived by our ancestors; in the other column list ways in which life is not as good. Which of the ideas that you have listed can be attributed to advances in science and technology?

## Important studies

Lyotard (1984) argued that we live in a postmodern world because the two major myths or 'meta-narratives' (big stories) of the modern world can no longer be believed. These are:

- the myth of liberation – that science and progress can make us more free. This myth has been destroyed by the way scientific knowledge has been used in great crimes such as the Holocaust and weapons of mass destruction
- the myth of truth – the status of knowledge and the idea that we can find out the 'truth' about things are now in question. This myth has been destroyed by theories that say that we can never know what is true and that all truths are relative.

**Research issue** Many descriptions of 'primitive' societies were written by military invaders, colonists and missionaries, and can be seen as helping to justify the so-called 'civilising' of the societies in question.

## Round-up

Sociology has always been interested in the changes that have led to the creation of the modern world. The most significant historical changes that students of sociology need to have some understanding of are industrialisation and its role in creating the modern world, and the emergence of the post-war consensus and its replacement by a diverse and uncertain postmodern world.

Postmodernity: The period of history after the modern period.

# How do we learn to be social?

## The biological and the social

What are the main influences on how people behave in society? For some writers, our behaviour can be explained by referring to biological factors (our 'nature'). For example, in recent years there have been claims that criminal behaviour, health, intelligence and sexual preference are linked to, even determined by, our genes and their DNA. This theory is known as **determinism**. Most sociologists, however, take the view that human behaviour can be explained by referring to social factors (our 'nurture' or upbringing).

| Ways in which sociology is affected by the nature–nurture debate | | |
|---|---|---|
| *Area of study* | *Possible biological factors* | *Possible social factors* |
| Educational achievement | Inherited intelligence | Class, ethnicity |
| Criminal activity | Inherited criminal personality | Class, family, culture and subculture |
| Gendered behaviour | Genetic differences between men and women | Patriarchal authority |

**Determinism:** The view that all events are fully determined (caused) by previous events. In the context of human social behaviour, it is contrasted with 'voluntarism'.

 The long-running 'nature vs. nurture' debate is about the importance of these different factors in relation to each other. It is undeniable that there are biological differences between men and women; the question is how far these influence the social behaviour of men and women.

## Primary socialisation

**Socialisation:** The processes by which people learn the norms and values of a society.

'**Socialisation**' is the process by which people learn to become members of a society. This involves:

- internalising the norms and values of the society (internalising means that although initially these norms and values exist outside the individual, he or she will eventually be able to accept them as being their own)
- learning how to perform social roles.

 Older textbooks often imply that primary socialisation takes place only within families. However, in Britain and other developed countries today, many pre-school-age children spend more of their time away from their families (for example, at playgroups and nurseries) than used to be the case.

'Primary socialisation' refers to the first and most important phase of socialisation in infancy and early childhood, which takes place mostly within the family. During this period, the child learns basic norms and values – for example, norms about eating behaviour, and the value placed on being 'good'. Adults reinforce their children's learning through positive and negative sanctions – smiles and words of approval for success and conformity, disapproval and possibly punishment for failing to behave as required.

 Theories suggesting that behaviour can be explained by inherited, biological factors are sometimes referred to as 'genetic determinism'.

Some socialisation takes place through the child observing and imitating. Some involves parents explicitly instructing their children. Children constantly try out different behaviour, to see what the response of their parents and others will be. Socialisation is not a one-way process in which children are slowly filled up with norms, values and roles; rather, children can and do reject and modify them. Both 'structure' and 'agency' (see pp. 14–15) are at work.

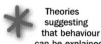 Sociologists sometimes refer to cases of supposedly 'feral' children as evidence of the crucial role of primary socialisation in enabling people to fulfil their human social potential. Visit www.feralchildren.com

## Important studies

Buss (1998) studied differences between how men and women choose their partners. Questionnaires were sent to over 10 000 people in 37 countries. The results showed that men chose women who were young and good looking, because these factors indicated fertility, while women chose men who had money or income and could therefore look after their wife and children. The genetic-determinist interpretation of this would be as follows.

- Men and women are programmed differently by their genes.
- In both sexes, the aim is for the genes to be passed on to the next generation.
- Men have evolved to be competitive and to seek as many mates as possible in order to have as many children as possible.
- Women have evolved to seek protection from a man while they raise children.

This interpretation can, however, be challenged by a social explanation. This might argue that women need a man with money because the opportunities for women to be financially independent are limited.

## Secondary and adult socialisation

After primary socialisation, the child begins to experience a wider range and variety of social situations and influences. The child is still learning norms, values and roles. This phase is called 'secondary socialisation'.

Socialisation continues throughout life as people encounter new situations and have to learn new norms, values and roles. The term 'adult socialisation' is used for the learning by adults of new roles for which earlier socialisation may not have fully prepared them, such as becoming a parent or starting a new job.

### Agents of socialisation

While the family is the main agent of primary socialisation, there is a range of agents of secondary socialisation.

- *Schools* – in schools we learn how to get on with other adults and children, how to conform to rules and how to become independent of parents; we also acquire knowledge and skills for later life.
- *Peer groups* – children are aware from an early age that there is a 'child' role, and they observe other children to try to learn what is expected of them.
- *Mass media* – these are of growing importance in modern times. Some media products have an explicit educational or socialising purpose, but all media contain messages of some kind that children will take in.
- *Religion* – this provides strong guidelines for behaviour and for many people remains a powerful source of values and mores.

## Socialisation and social control

All sociologists accept the need for socialisation. It is the mechanism by which societies ensure that there is continuity (but also some change) from one generation to the next. However, functionalists and Marxists differ in how they see socialisation.

- For functionalists, it is vital that all members of a society learn the same core values; this creates a 'value consensus', which acts to hold a society together and prevent discord and breakdown. All societies must have ways of socialising the next generation, although these may differ between societies. Everyone benefits from this.
- Marxists, on the other hand, see socialisation as involving the instilling into the population of the values of the ruling class. Only the ruling class benefits from this.

Socialisation requires individuals to accept a set of norms, values and roles. Failing to meet society's requirements can be defined as 'deviance' or crime and may lead to punishment. With socialisation goes social control.

Functionalists see social control as necessary and working to the benefit of all. For Marxists, however, social control is used by the powerful in society to force or persuade the less powerful to behave as they want them to. Marxists argue that what we have called the agencies of socialisation are used by the ruling class to propagate its ideology, a world-view that justifies existing inequalities. The power of these agencies – schools, the media, and religion – is such that the ruling-class ideology achieves **hegemony** and becomes widely accepted. It thus becomes difficult for other world-views (such as Marxism) to be heard or gain currency.

The French Marxist Louis Althusser (1971) argued that the ruling class in capitalist societies secured its power through the ideological state apparatuses (ISAs). These are the institutions that were not directly controlled by the state but which served the interests of the state – and thus the ruling class. In the past, religion was the main ISA, but Althusser maintained that schools had taken over this role. When the ISA fails to ensure that the working class accepts their position, the ruling class can turn to the repressive state apparatuses (RSAs) – police, armed forces – to deal with 'troublemakers'.

Social control: The ways in which societies control the behaviour of their members.

 Different sociologists adopt different perspectives on society. Two of the most influential perspectives within sociology have been functionalism and Marxism (both described in more detail on pp. 12–13).

 Agencies of socialisation can also be described as 'agencies of social control'.

The socialisation function of families and education is explained in greater detail in later sections of this book.

Hegemony: The dominance of an ideology in a society.

### Think it through

Watch some television programmes made for pre-school children, such as *Teletubbies*, *The Fimbles* and *The Tweenies*.

1 What might children learn from these programmes about the norms and values of our society? What might they learn about the roles that children are expected to take on in our society?

2 Now watch some programmes (e.g. early-evening soap operas) that, although not made for pre-school children specifically, they are likely to watch.

What might children learn from these programmes?

# Round-up

There is a continuing debate about the relative importance of social and cultural, as opposed to biological, factors in influencing human behaviour. Sociologists emphasise how, in order to be fully human, people have to learn to become members of a society through the process of socialisation. Socialisation is seen by functionalists as essential for the stability and continuity of societies, but for Marxists it involves the imposition of an ideology and the enforcement of conformity.

# How does society shape our lives?

As you learned earlier, there are two main approaches to sociology. One focuses on 'social structures' (the macro approach) and one on 'social actions' (the micro approach). These two approaches reflect different views about the nature of society and of social life, and can be summed up as follows.

- *The social structure approach* – by social structure, we mean all the institutions of society and the ways in which they shape our lives. We are born into families and communities, educated in schools, employed in business organisations, ruled by governments, and so on. These institutions existed before we were born and will survive long after we have died. Some sociologists are interested primarily in the way these institutions work, and the effects they have on us. This is the social structure approach. It focuses on how our lives are shaped by the social forces around us and puts less emphasis on how we can influence or change those forces. Emile Durkheim was one of the early sociologists to take this approach.

- *The social action approach* – other sociologists however, stress that social institutions are created and maintained by people. For example, a school is a social institution because of the actions and behaviour of the pupils, teachers and others who are involved in the life of the school. This means that, while social institutions may seem to control our lives, we can change them (together or perhaps alone). The institutions may seem to set rules or guidelines about how we live, but rules can be broken. Sociologists who take the 'social action approach' are interested primarily in how people interact, and in why we act as we do. By focusing on how people interact, and the meanings they give to their actions (how they explain them and what they mean to them), this approach pays less attention to how social behaviour is shaped by structural forces. Max Weber was one of the early sociologists to take this approach (see p. 16).

All three sociologists mentioned so far are men. Durkheim and Weber, together with Karl Marx, are often referred to as the 'founding fathers' of Sociology. In the nineteenth century, women were excluded from universities and thus from much academic life, though writers such as Mary Wollstonecraft made important contributions to social philosophy in the eighteenth and nineteenth centuries.

Max Weber (1864–1920). Durkheim and Weber, together with Karl Marx, are often referred to as the 'founding fathers' of sociology.

## Think it through

For functionalists, the institutions of society work together so that society is healthy and stable, in the same way as the systems of the body work together. If something goes wrong in one part, this will have effects elsewhere.

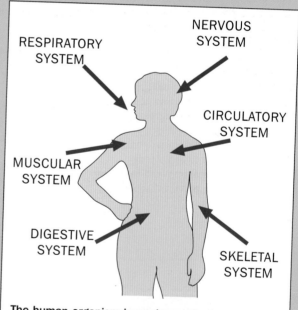

RESPIRATORY SYSTEM

NERVOUS SYSTEM

CIRCULATORY SYSTEM

MUSCULAR SYSTEM

DIGESTIVE SYSTEM

SKELETAL SYSTEM

The human organism is made up of related systems

1 In what way do the family and the education system work together?

2 In what way do the political system and the criminal justice system work together?

3 How would other social institutions, and society as a whole, be affected if the family ceased to function as it is supposed to?

## The social structure approach

This approach emphasises the extent to which human behaviour is constrained by social forces beyond our control; in simple terms, the extent to which we are slaves to society. Social structures and institutions seem to take on a life of their own and dominate our lives. Society has an existence above and beyond that of the individuals who comprise it. This approach is deterministic.

Two perspectives in sociology, functionalism and Marxism, take this social structure approach but each one has reached it for very different reasons.

### Functionalism

For functionalists, the institutions that make up the social structure work together, like the different parts of a body or machine, making up something that is more than the sum of its parts. Each part of the social structure fulfils a function that contributes to the overall well-being of the society, and enables it to function smoothly and survive. Society is based on a consensus, a basic agreement about the way things should be. This is known as **value consensus**.

### Marxism

For Marxists, the institutions of society also work together, but against the interests of most of the people. Marxists see modern industrial societies as divided into two classes as a result of the economic system, (capitalism). The class division is between:

- the bourgeoisie (the ruling class, who own the economic capital) and

- the proletariat (the working class, who own only their ability to earn a living).

The bourgeoisie's economic power enables them to control all aspects of society, and to use this control to maintain their dominance of the proletariat. The bourgeoisie is able, most of the time, to ensure that the proletariat accepts that the rule of the bourgeoisie (and the way things are) is just and fair.

Marxists agree with functionalists that there is basic agreement on values – but argue that the majority has been persuaded to accept a set of ideas, the dominant '**ideology**', which justifies the way things are and so acts against their interests. The dominant ideology is conveyed by the education system (see pp. 72–3), religious institutions, and so on. To support its interests and protect its power, the bourgeoisie has set up the State, which, in a democracy, appears to be neutral but in fact serves the interests of the ruling class.

Marxists argue that the conflict that is implicit in the way things are will eventually lead to revolution when the proletariat will overthrow the bourgeoisie and bring about a new, fair, social order.

Marxism has been a strong influence on European sociology (it was always much weaker in the USA). This influence has been undermined, but not completely ended, by the failure of the communist states that based themselves on Marxist ideas.

**Determinism** assumes that all events are fully determined (caused) by previous events. In the context of social life, it argues that human freedom of choice is therefore an illusion.

**Value consensus:** Agreement on a set of strongly held, fairly permanent beliefs about what is right or important.

**Functionalism** was the dominant form of sociology for the first half of the twentieth century. Today, however, it is often spoken of as being rather out of date and unable to explain the social conflicts and accelerated social change of the late twentieth century. Nevertheless, its insights continue to underpin much sociological and 'common-sense' thinking about society.

**Ideology:** A set of ideas and claims that together produce a fairly coherent world-view. In Marxist usage an ideology is always false (the ideology exists to serve the interests of a class rather than to explain reality.)

**Marxists** see the economic system as deciding the nature of the social system; this is an 'economic determinist approach'.

## Important studies

The basics of Marxism are set out in *The Communist Manifesto* by Marx and Engels, first published in 1848 (available in Penguin Classics). It is short, readable and still easily available, including on the internet.

### Watch out

Both functionalism and Marxism should be thought of as broad schools of thought, able to encompass differences of opinion. In summarising complex ideas, simplification is unavoidable. However, some of the common criticisms put forward in textbooks in relation to both functionalism and Marxism are based on oversimplifying and even caricaturing them. These views are not entirely opposed; for example, Marxists would agree that social institutions have functions, but they would not describe them in the same terms as functionalists.

### Research issue

When studying and trying to explain social structures and social change, sociologists compare one society with another. The 'comparative method' is the basis of most scientific explanation (see Research methods pp. 126–7).

## Round-up

Sociologists differ in the emphasis they place on the influence of social structures or of human agency in explaining social behaviour. The social structure approach takes two main forms – functionalism and Marxism. In their different ways, both functionalists and Marxists tend to see society as having an existence beyond the people who make up society, and as shaping our lives.

# How much choice do we have?

## The social action approach

In the previous section, you read about the social structure approach. As mentioned, this can be contrasted with the social action approach, which emphasises the extent to which people are conscious of their actions and how much individual social behaviour is the result of real choices (even though the range of choices may be limited by social contexts). The social action approach believes people give meaning to their actions and those of other people (they 'interpret' social actions) and make choices about how they will behave.

In this approach, people are often described as '**agents**' or actors, whereas in the structure approach they are more like puppets whose strings are being manipulated. 'Social actors' sometimes act alone (individual agency) and sometimes in groups (collective agency). The social action approach sees people not as slaves but as free – at least within certain limits. It is therefore a **voluntaristic** approach.

**Agency:** The ability of people, individually or collectively, to take decisions and to act.

**Voluntarism:** The assumption that individuals are agents, with some choice and control over their actions. Usually contrasted with determinism.

## Varieties of social action theory

Within the social action approach, as within the social structure approach, there are different perspectives.

### Symbolic interactionism

In your study of sociology you will come across 'symbolic interactionism'. This was developed by George Herbert Mead in the 1920s (Mead, 1934). He was interested in how people give meaning to their social actions on a one-to-one basis. He emphasised that we are constantly monitoring how we act, assessing how other people respond or will respond, and deciding on our next action. As we do this, our ideas about who we are (our self-concept and identity) are changing and developing all the time.

 The action approach is usually traced back within sociology to the German sociologist Max Weber (see p. 12). This makes it the younger of the two approaches, although its origins go back to much earlier philosophical views of the nature of social life.

 To some extent, all sociologists use the concept of social construction. It is something that distinguishes sociology from other disciplines. But the emphasis on social construction is much greater in the action approach.

### Phenomenology

Phenomenology places even greater emphasis on the extent to which all social phenomena, including society itself, are created by social interaction. The core idea is the concept of social construction. This term is used to describe how aspects of society that appear to be 'real', to exist independently of people, are in fact the result of social interaction. For example, you will read in Section 2 about the social construction of childhood. Childhood might appear to be a natural stage in the development of all humans – but who is described as a child, how children are treated and what is expected of them, varies enormously between different cultures and over time. So the idea of childhood can be said to be socially constructed.

A further example of social construction, which you will come across when you study sociological methods, is official statistics such as those of crime or health. Because decisions have to be taken about what to measure and how to measure it, these statistics do not simply reflect an objective reality. For example, whether or not a crime is recorded in the official crime statistics depends on whether it is reported to the police and whether the police decide to record it as a crime. It is these decisions that make it an official statistic, not the original action (see p. 117).

### Ethnomethodology

This took these ideas even further. Ethnomethodologists were especially interested in uncovering the unspoken 'rules' of everyday social interaction and observing the consequences if these rules are broken. For example, Garfinkel (1967) arranged for some of his students to behave in their own homes as if they were lodgers, and observed how this disrupted normal social interaction.

The social action approach therefore has a very different view of society from the social structure approach. In the structure approach, the institutions that make up society are powerful and real – dominating our lives. Yet those who take the action approach would say that these institutions only exist because we create and re-create them all the time. They would say that the structure approach makes the mistake of **reification** – it treats social institutions as though they exist independently of people, whereas, in fact, they are only the sum of the actions of many people. Society is made, and constantly re-made, by people interacting with each other.

**Reification:** When the results of human interactions seem to take on an independent reality of their own.

# Important studies

Goffman (1969) made important contributions to the study of small-scale social interaction in everyday life. He described everyday life using the analogy of drama. People are like actors in a play. We can follow the scripts set out for us by our roles, or we can improvise. We are constantly playing to an audience, being aware of how others respond to us and modifying our behaviour accordingly; Goffman calls this 'impression management'. Our clothes, other aspects of our appearance, our houses, cars and jobs are props that we use to put on our dramatic performances. There are even backstage areas where we can relax from our otherwise continuous performances.

The term 'social construction' was popularised by Berger and Luckmann, in their book *The social construction of reality* (1967). They showed how society was actively created by people. We live in a world that has been made by social interaction. At the same time, this socially constructed world seems to have an existence of its own and shapes our lives.

## Structuration

Of the many attempts to bring the structural and action approaches together, the most recent is that of Anthony Giddens. Giddens (1979) uses the term 'structuration' to refer to the way in which social structures not only limit how people can act but also make it possible for social action to take place at all. Social structure and social action cannot exist independently of each other. People can only make choices within social frameworks.

## Think it through

In contemporary British society, older people are encouraged to conceal grey hair, wrinkles and other signs of ageing. In other cultural traditions, however, less negative interpretations are placed upon physiological aspects of old age. For the Sherbro people of Sierra Leone, incoherent and incomprehensible speech by an aged person is perceived as a positive sign. Their incoherence indicates their close communication with ancestors, who are regarded as important arbiters of destiny (McCormack 1985, cited in Hockey and James, 1993). Similarly for the Venda-speaking people of Southern Africa, old age is regarded as a 'pleasure'. Signs of old age, such as greying hair or the birth of a grandchild, are welcomed as indications of a person's approaching contact with the 'real' world of the spirits (Blacking 1990, cited in Hockey and James, 1993). In cultures where the afterlife is accorded great significance, old people's proximity to death enhances rather than reduces their status (Pilcher, 1995).

1 'Old age is socially constructed'. Explain and discuss this statement, referring to this extract and using some of the terms you have read about in this section.

## Research issues

The social action approach is associated with ethnographic research methods, which produce qualitative data and which, if done well, have high validity. The main aim of these methods is to try to understand why people behave as they do by seeing things from their point of view, and understanding the meanings people give to their actions. To describe this, Weber used the term '*verstehen*', normally translated as 'understanding'.

# Round-up

The social action approach emphasises human agency, the extent to which we can choose how to act. It can be contrasted with the social structure approach, which emphasises how society seems to have an objective reality that dominates our lives. Several perspectives within sociology, including symbolic interactionism, adopt this view. A key concept in sociology, derived largely from the action approach, is social construction, which is used to explain how the social world is made by people rather than having a separate existence. The more recent structuration theory aims to show how structure and action are interdependent.

# How equal are we?

## Sources of inequality

One of the main interests of sociologists has always been social differences, for example in wealth, income, status or power. These kinds of differences are known as 'social inequalities'. When groups of people can be ranked hierarchically (that is, in order) for differences such as wealth and power this is called 'stratification'.

For most sociologists, at least until very recently, the main form of stratification in modern societies was social class. The equivalents for earlier societies were caste, **estates** and slavery.

Over the past few decades, gender, age and ethnic or racial differences (which previously had usually been taken as a part of class stratification or as being less important than class stratification) have come to be seen as being just as important as class – and perhaps even more so.

Social inequalities exist in many forms, both within and between societies and social groups

### Life chances

The importance of stratification can be measured by its impact on life chances. The following measures (among many others) can show differences between classes, between the genders and between ethnic groups:

- life expectancy
- levels of health and illness
- income
- wealth
- housing
- achievement in education
- the likelihood of being convicted of a crime or being the victim of a crime.

### Caste compared with social class

In understanding class it is useful to be able to compare it to other, earlier forms of stratification. The caste system in India was based on occupation, but both occupation and caste position were decided at birth. For example, the son of a priest would be destined to be a priest and to belong to the priestly caste. This means that caste is ascribed; it is not the outcome of individual effort or mobility. Occupation in the class system, by contrast, is not fixed at birth, and is an achieved position.

Both caste and class involve fairly strict hierarchies, but in the caste system it is almost impossible to move from one level to another while the class system allows some mobility – though how much is a matter of debate.

**Estates:** The system of stratification in the medieval period, with division between clergy, nobility and commoners.

The sociology exam requires you to be familiar with four main aspects of stratification: class, gender, ethnicity and age. Stratification can also involve groups that are different in other ways, such as ability and disability, or sexual preference.

## Social class

Social class is a commonly used term for a recognised form of stratification, but there are wide differences between the theories of class given by different sociologists.

- Functionalists see class as a necessary and inevitable aspect of modern societies. Social-class differences emerge out of differences in talent and ability that deserve different rewards. Differences in wealth and power are justified and act as an incentive to all.

- Marxists see social-class differences as arising out of exploitation – the ruling class (the bourgeoisie) own the means of production and exploit the working class (the proletariat) by not paying them the full value of their work and taking the surplus as profit. This basic clash of interests between the classes is 'class conflict', which will ultimately lead to revolution and the overthrow of the ruling class.

- Max Weber, whilst agreeing that social class is an important source of inequality and power, also argued that religion, ethnicity, gender, age, etc. were other sources of what he called 'status differences' (Weber, 1978). These differences may result in conflict but not in revolution. This view was very influential in sociology in the latter part of the twentieth century.

- In recent years, postmodernists have questioned the importance of social class and suggest that people no longer strongly identify with it. Instead, people are more likely to define themselves through their lifestyle – that is, through what they consume.

# Important studies

The French sociologist Pierre Bourdieu (1984) argued that class was still of great importance in modern societies, but he offered reasons as to why this was not always recognised. His concept of 'cultural capital' explains how class differences are made invisible, because they are routinely reproduced in ways that seem natural. For example, the 'right' accent, effortlessly acquired within the family, may give a middle-class person an advantage over someone who has in the same way acquired a regional accent. Class differences are strongest when people are least aware of them.

## Think it through

Like Marx, Weber recognised the existence of social class but he also highlighted status divisions within classes, based on education, skill, pay and consumption of goods as represented by lifestyle choices. Moreover he noted that membership of particular status groups which were unrelated to class sometimes conferred benefits on people and sometimes denied them access to rewards. For example, members of different ethnic minorities or religions, women and disabled people in the UK may be denied access to top jobs, whatever their social class position.

Adapted from: Woodward, K. (ed.) (2000) *Identity: Gender, class and nation*, Routledge/Open University, London

1 Identify three status differences that might exist within the medical profession.

2 Identify and explain three other sources of inequality in society other than social class.

3 Assess the view that status is the key to understanding inequality in society.

## Gender

Feminists argue that gender differences are an important division in society today and they draw attention to 'gender stratification'. They point out that modern societies are often **patriarchal** and that this is reflected in male domination of areas of social life such as employment and politics.

## Ethnicity

The term 'ethnicity' came into use in sociology when it was recognised that the idea of race was deeply flawed. Members of an ethnic group may share some attributes that can be considered racial (for example, skin colour) but ethnicity refers to shared *cultural* rather than physical or other characteristics. These cultural characteristics may include: language, religion, family and marriage patterns, a common historical origin and a sense of shared identity.

Most modern societies are multicultural, with, usually, a dominant ethnic majority and one or more minority ethnic groups. The cultural characteristics of the minority groups in such situations are not survivals from the past but are shaped by their existence in a multicultural society. If that society is marked by prejudice and discrimination, the result can be a defensive strengthening of aspects of culture that mark the minority group as different.

## Age

Stratification by age is a characteristic of many societies. In Britain and other Western countries today, there are fairly clear differences in the situation of different age groups. Children have a different legal status from adults. They are closely protected and seen as having rights while also having their freedom severely curtailed (for example, they may be obliged to attend school). Older people, on the other hand, can suffer prejudice and discrimination and old age has a low social status. So, both the old and the young are treated as being less competent as those in between. This is 'age stratification'.

In other societies, age groups may be just as clearly marked (for example, with very clear transitions, marked by rites of passage, from childhood to adulthood and to becoming an elder). Identity based on belonging to an age **cohort**, experiencing events such as **rites of passage** together, can be very strong.

**Patriarchy:** A system where men have social, cultural and economic dominance over women.

**Cohort:** A group of people who share a significant experience at a point in time, for example, being born in the same year, or taking A levels in the same year.

**Rite of passage:** A ceremony to mark the transition from one stage of life to another; for example, marriage ceremonies.

# Round-up

The main dimensions of stratification considered in AS and A level sociology are social class, gender, ethnicity and age. These provide a theme running through the course. In the past, social class was the dimension that attracted the most attention from sociologists. The acknowledgement of the importance of the other dimensions is relatively new. The idea that modern – or postmodern – societies are characterised by a range of cross-cutting social divisions calls into question the idea of stratification.

## Watch out

**Everyone has an ethnic identity. It is a common mistake to think that ethnicity refers only to minorities. In Britain, the white majority is also an ethnic group (or, more accurately, several ethnic groups).**

**Ethnicity cuts across class stratification. For example, members of a minority ethnic group in Britain today, such as Indian people, may belong to the middle class or to the working class.**

# Introducing sociology: summative review

## What is sociology?

The discipline of sociology can be traced back to the work of the French writer Auguste Comte in the first half of the nineteenth century. European societies of the time were going through a period of dramatic social and political change, including industrialisation and urbanisation. Revolutionary political ideas were developing, and people's knowledge and understanding of the world was changing as the natural sciences generated theories that challenged traditional and religious beliefs. The emergence of sociology can be viewed as an attempt to understand these changes.

Sociology has developed and changed since the time of Comte. Today, it includes a wide range of approaches and views about the nature of society and the most appropriate ways to carry out empirical research. However, overarching all these differences is a shared concern to understand society and the relationship between individuals and society. For some, the purpose of this understanding is to try to improve society through applied social policies.

## Societies and culture

All societies have a culture. A culture that is broadly shared by individuals in society provides the basis of social order and makes social life possible. Sociologists use a number of related concepts to describe this basic agreement between individual members of society – norms, mores, values, status and roles. Norms are the unspoken and unwritten guidelines for behaviour in everyday life. Mores, a stronger form of norms, are the guidelines for behaviour that people believe is essential in order to maintain standards of decency. Values are the beliefs underlying norms and mores. Status is the position that someone holds in society; it can be ascribed ('given' by society, such as social class at birth), or achieved (the result of an individual's efforts, such as occupation). Roles are the sets of norms and expectations linked to a particular status. We all have many roles, and we can usually switch between them without much difficulty.

Norms, mores, values, statuses and roles exist in all societies, and individuals learn about them through the process of socialisation, but they take a variety of forms. For example, all societies have norms and mores about what kinds of behaviour are appropriate for men and women, but these norms and mores vary both within and between societies, and over time. As a result, what is regarded as deviant also varies. This variance is called 'cultural diversity'.

## Sociology and social change

Sociology began as an attempt to explain how the world was changing, and social change is still a major concern of sociologists. The past two hundred years, during which sociology developed, can be described as the 'modern period', or 'modernity'. Early sociologists such as Durkheim contrasted modern societies with traditional or pre-industrial societies. While this approach helped to shed light on the changes that had happened, it tended to suggest, wrongly, that all traditional societies had a lot in common, that they tended not to change, and even that they were 'primitive' in contrast to the 'advanced' societies of Europe. However, the pace of social change was certainly faster in the modern period, and early sociologists were concerned about the implications of this. The modern period was characterised by a strong belief in progress and that it would be possible to create a better world through improved knowledge and the use of scientific methods and rational (rather than traditional) ways of thinking. There was a belief that the problems of social life, such as poverty, unemployment and poor health, could be overcome.

Some of the defining characteristics of modernity have been weakened over the past twenty or thirty years. For example, the belief in progress and the power of science has been undermined by continuing disasters, tragedies and epidemics. Science has led to many improvements in our lives, but it has also led to weapons of mass destruction and to environmental degradation. In other ways, such as the speed of communication and our access to information, the world has changed and continues to change at an ever-increasing rate. Advances in communication technology, including the world-wide web, have contributed to this. Some sociologists, such as Lyotard, have argued that we no longer live in an age of modernity but rather in 'postmodernity'. This is a new phase of history characterised by the acceptability of a plurality of beliefs and values, greater diversity of life styles, and greater uncertainty.

## Perspectives in sociology

Sociology is sometimes described as having within it two distinct perspectives. One is the 'social structure perspective', which is concerned with social systems and social institutions – the macro (society-wide) scale. From this perspective, people's lives appear to be shaped by external and independent social forces. This is a deterministic view, in which people's choice and free will is limited. People are born into pre-existing societies that shape most aspects of their lives. The alternative tradition, the 'social action perspective', is concerned with the micro level of small-scale social interaction. In this perspective there is much less emphasis on the large social institutions. It focuses on people and sees them as having some freedom of choice and action; it is a more voluntaristic view.

These perspectives are linked to methodological approaches. Sociologists taking a structural perspective are concerned to establish social facts and laws. Their chosen research methods will aim to approximate the positivist methods of the sciences (while acknowledging that this is not fully achievable because of the subject matter of sociology, as opposed to that of the natural sciences). The emphasis is on reliability. In contrast, sociologists who take a social action perspective (sometimes called 'interpretivists') are more concerned to describe the meanings that people give to their actions; they use research methods that produce more valid data but rely more on the personal and social characteristics of the researcher. Positivist methods tend to produce quantitative data (in the form of statistics) while interpretivist methods tend to produce qualitative data (in the form of verbal descriptions).

Functionalism and Marxism are two perspectives within the social structure approach. Functionalism dominated sociology during the early and mid-twentieth century, especially in the USA. Functionalists are interested in the functions of social institutions – that is, how they contribute to the stability and continuity of societies. They emphasise how social institutions and forces tend to operate for the good of all, holding societies together through a common value system and enabling societies to survive over time. Marxists are also concerned with social institutions, but see their purpose as the perpetuation of the power of a ruling class. For Marxists, the existence of classes in conflict with each other is the most important feature of all societies. The same forces that seem benign to functionalists seem to Marxists to be ways in which a minority maintains its power and wealth through manipulation of values. Marxist ideas continue to have influence in sociology despite the collapse of communism, the political system based on Marxist ideas.

The alternative social action perspective has produced a number of schools of thought, including phenomenology, ethnomethodology and symbolic interactionism. These sociologists study the detail of social life and the everyday social interaction of people in groups, aiming to show how these interactions create the social reality of the people involved and how people exercise choice and agency in their social actions.

From the 1970s onwards, feminist sociology has challenged all these approaches – seeing all previous sociology as embodying patriarchal assumptions. Their views led not only to a new emphasis on researching the social experience of women but to a more fundamental challenge to the whole approach of 'malestream' sociology. Feminist sociologists tend to favour the interpretivist approach to methodology, since its ethnographic methods give women a voice they had previously been denied.

These debates are presented in a simplified form for students. Most sociologists today draw on a wide range of traditions and research methods, according to the relevance and helpfulness of the concepts and theories for what they are studying. Most sociologists would accept that, while people exercise some degree of choice about how they behave, they do so within a social structure or framework that constrains their choices.

## Social stratification

Sociologists in all traditions have recognised the importance of the fact that people belong to social groups with different degrees of power, wealth and status in society. The main aspects of stratification studied at A level are:

- social class
- gender
- ethnicity, and
- age.

However, there are other aspects, such as ability and disability. Social class is the central concept of Marxism but it is also important in other perspectives (although recently some postmodern sociologists have suggested that it is no longer important). Feminists have emphasised the importance of gender, seeing the most fundamental division in all societies as being between men and women rather than between classes. The importance of ethnicity has also been increasingly recognised. The different aspects of stratification are interrelated, so that social inequality today presents a complex picture.

# Introducing sociology: self-assessment questions

## Multiple-choice questions

*Questions 1–18 each have one correct answer and two incorrect answers.*

1 Who was the first professor of sociology?
   a Durkheim
   b Comte
   c Marx

2 Who is usually credited with having been the first sociologist?
   a Durkheim
   b Marx
   c Comte

3 Which of the following is normally an achieved status in modern society?
   a Gender
   b Ethnic identity
   c Occupation

4 Which of the following was an ethnomethodologist?
   a Mead
   b Goffman
   c Garfinkel

5 Which of the following is associated with a conflict view of society?
   a Durkheim
   b Goffman
   c Marx

6 What is meant by 'cultural imperialism'?
   a Several cultures existing together
   b The spread and dominance of one culture
   c How individuals learn their culture

7 Which of the following was a writer on postmodernity?
   a Marx
   b Garfinkel
   c Lyotard

8 Which of the following is a characteristic of postmodernity?
   a Industrial economy
   b Collapse of belief in science and progress
   c Competing political ideologies

9 What is meant by 'primary socialisation'?
   a The socialisation of very young children within the family
   b Social control
   c Socialisation of adults

10 Which sociologists see social control as working to the benefit of all?
   a Marxists
   b Feminists
   c Functionalists

11 Which of the following refers to guidelines for behaviour in specific situations?
   a Norms
   b Values
   c Mores

12 Which sociologist is credited with having founded the action tradition?
   a Durkheim
   b Weber
   c Marx

13 What analogy did Goffman use to describe social life?
   a Acting in a play
   b Society as an organism
   c Puppets on strings

14 What is meant by structuration?
   a How societies shape people's lives
   b How structure and action work together in shaping social life
   c The creation of new social structures

15 Who used the concept 'impression management'?
   a Mead
   b Goffman
   c Weber

16 Which of the following was not one of the 'founding fathers'?
   a Wollstonecraft
   b Durkheim
   c Marx

17 Which book sets out the basic ideas of Marxism?
   a *The Rules of Sociological Method*
   b *The Communist Manifesto*
   c *Mind, Self and Society*

18 Which of the following is a way in which caste is different from class?
   a It is based on occupation.
   b It is hierarchical.
   c It is based on ascribed status.

19 **Match the concepts to the explanations**

  a Micro

  b Macro

  i The kind of sociology that focuses on small-scale social interaction

  ii The kind of sociology that focuses on social structures and institutions

20 **Match the concepts to the explanations**

  a Structural approaches

  b Action approaches

  i Concerned with the motivations of individuals and groups

  ii Concerned with the influence of social systems and institutions

21 **Match the concepts to the explanations**

  a Ideological state apparatus

  b Repressive state apparatus

  i The ways in which the state can control people by manipulating values and ideas

  ii The ways in which the state can control people by force

22 **Match the sociologists to their descriptions**

  a Giddens

  b Mead

  c Weber

  i Used concept of 'verstehen'

  ii Founder of symbolic interactionism

  iii Used concept of 'structuration'

23 **Match the concepts to the perspectives**

  a Feminism

  b Marxism

  c Functionalism

  i Patriarchy

  ii Value consensus

  iii Class conflict

24 **Match the concepts to the sociologists**

  a Bourdieu

  b Althusser

  c Berger and Luckmann

  i Social construction of reality

  ii Ideological state apparatus

  iii Cultural capital

25 **Which is the odd-one-out? Why?**

  a Marx

  b Mead

  c Durkheim

# Introducing sociology: a timeline

- Sociology developing in USA; Mead and symbolic interactionism; Chicago School
- Growth in anthropology (study of non-industrial societies) based in Britain
- European interest in Marxism

- Auguste Comte introduces modern sociology

- Industrial Revolution
- Rapid growth in scientific knowledge
- Growth of cities
- Expansion of European empires in Africa, Asia and South America

- World War I (1914–1918)
- Russian Revolution (1917) based on Marxist principles
- Women gain right to vote
- 1920s Economic depression; high unemployment; political and social unrest
- Independence movements in some colonial states, e.g. India
- Rise of Fascism in Germany, Italy and Spain
- Spanish Civil War

| 1800 | 1850 | 1900 | 1914 5 6 7 8 9 1920 1 2 3 4 5 6 7 8 9 1930 1 2 3 4 5 6 7 8 9 1940 1 2 3 4 5 6 7 8 9 |

- Consolidation of British Empire
- Growth in civil and legal rights of working people; development of trade unions
- New social, religious and political ideas
- Mass education begins
- Origins of women's movement; suffragettes

- Marx and Engels writing (Marx dies 1883)
- Weber (social action) and Durkheim (functionalism) writing
- Growth of sociology in France and Germany

- World War II and its aftermath
- Welfare state established
- Ending of British Empire
- 'Cold War'
- Most women return to domestic work
- Increase in birth rate
- Growth in suburbs and new towns
- McCarthyism (right wing) in USA
- Increased immigration to Britain

- Dominance of functionalism in UK and USA (Talcott Parsons)
- Increase in social surveys
- Community (ethnographic) studies
- C Wright Mills (Marxist) writing in USA

- Sociology less radical/political; more research is government-funded
- Growth of post-modernism; interest moves from social inequality to issues of identity
- Sociology established in schools, especially post-16
- Attempts to bring structural and interpretive perspectives together – Giddens' structuration

- Conservative (Thatcherite) governments; increase in social inequality
- Decline of traditional industries and growth of service sector
- Rise of New Right thinking
- Collapse of Soviet Union
- Globalisation; huge growth in mass media and digital (computer) technology; growth of transnational corporations

| 1950 1 2 3 4 5 6 7 8 9 1960 1 2 3 4 5 6 7 8 9 1970 1 2 3 4 5 6 7 8 9 1980 1 2 3 4 5 6 7 8 9 1990 1 2 3 4 5 6 7 8 9 2000 1 2 3 |

- Britain becomes more 'liberal'
- Birth-control pill frees women to work
- Rise of youth culture
- Challenges to traditional class and gender barriers
- Feminism, anti-racism and Marxism develop

- Marxism, neo-Marxism, feminism and interpretivism challenge functionalist sociology
- Sociology becomes popular in UK universities

- New Labour targets child poverty, social inequality, unemployment, crime and education
- Decline of Tory party
- Devolution; regional politics more important in Wales and Scotland

- Sociology has influence on government policy; Giddens and the Third Way

# Section 2 Families and households

# Families and households: a mindmap

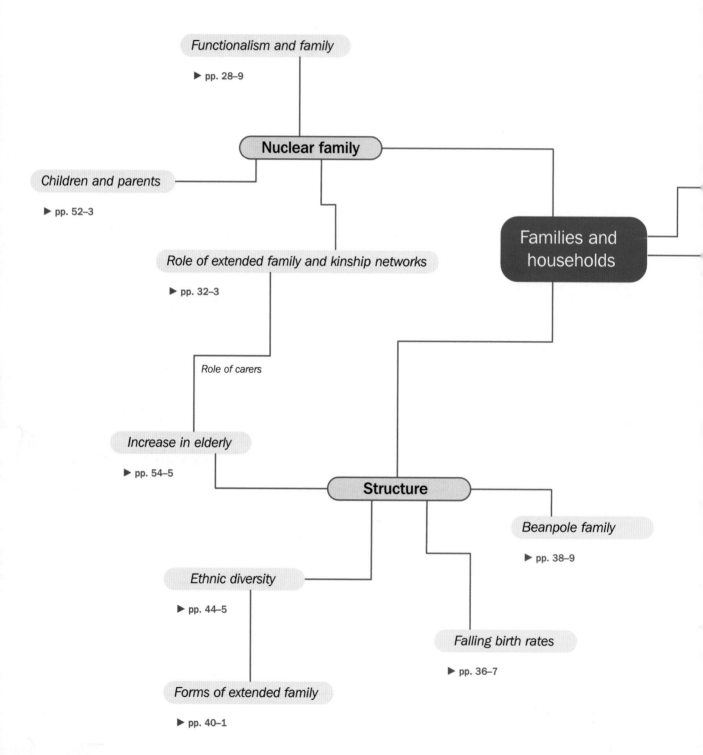

Functionalism and family

▶ pp. 28–9

Nuclear family

Children and parents

▶ pp. 52–3

Role of extended family and kinship networks

▶ pp. 32–3

Role of carers

Families and households

Increase in elderly

▶ pp. 54–5

Structure

Beanpole family

▶ pp. 38–9

Ethnic diversity

▶ pp. 44–5

Falling birth rates

▶ pp. 36–7

Forms of extended family

▶ pp. 40–1

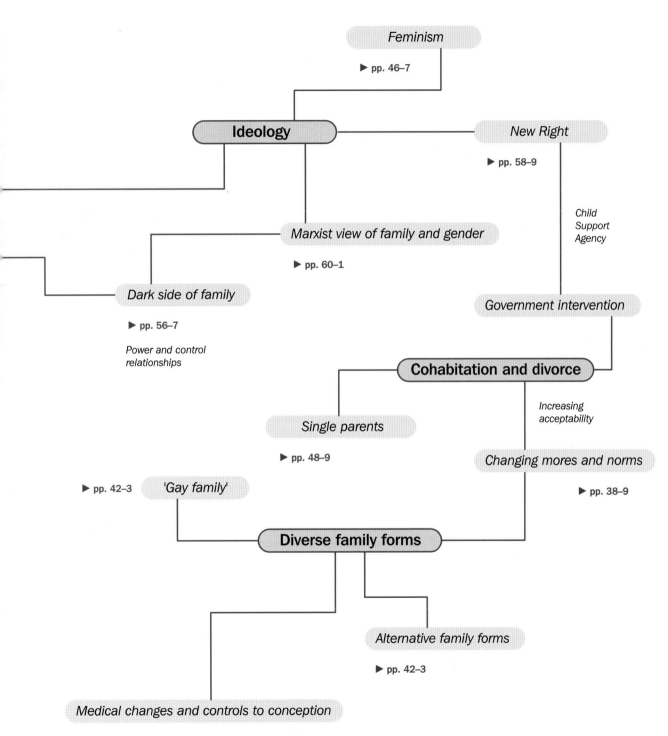

Feminism

▶ pp. 46–7

Ideology

New Right

▶ pp. 58–9

Child
Support
Agency

Marxist view of family and gender

▶ pp. 60–1

Dark side of family

▶ pp. 56–7

Power and control
relationships

Government intervention

Cohabitation and divorce

Increasing
acceptability

Single parents

▶ pp. 48–9

Changing mores and norms

▶ pp. 38–9

▶ pp. 42–3    'Gay family'

Diverse family forms

Alternative family forms

▶ pp. 42–3

Medical changes and controls to conception

▶ pp. 36–7

# What is the difference between a family and a household?

**Family:** A group of people to whom we may be biologically related and to whom we feel a sense of kinship.

Sociologists usually agree that there is no such thing as human nature and believe that people are the result of their culture rather than biology. However, it is worth noting that in one respect all humans do seem to be alike. They tend to form groups and choose to live with others like themselves. One of the most basic of human groups is the **family**. Very few people will have been raised without being members of some form of family unit. This means that the family is a universal cultural concept; all societies have some concept of family.

In biological terms the family is a group of individuals who share genetic material. Families often have physical characteristics in common and family members may resemble their parents or relatives very closely. We may even share habits of mood or behaviour with our relatives. However, it is at this point that sociology becomes involved in the nature–nurture argument: if we behave in a way that is similar to other family members, did we learn this behaviour or did we inherit it in our genetic material?

**Household:** An individual or a group of people who share a home and some meals, e.g. a family (perhaps with servants), students in a shared home or people in a community group such as a commune.

In contrast to the term family, a **household** refers to a single individual or members of a group who share a home without the special social obligations that being a family member has for the individual. A family may live as a household but a household is not necessarily a family. In Britain in the past, the household was a common social arrangement in which servants and employees would often live with a biological family unit. There would also have been considerable flexibility in social arrangements, so that parents with too many children to raise would pass on their babies to their childless brothers and sisters for adoption. Nowadays, households may consist of people who share accommodation – students, or single individuals such as the elderly, or couples and unmarried younger people.

The issue for sociologists is to define what is meant by a family and to look at ways in which people tend to organise themselves into those sets of special relationships that we know of as family

**Kinship:** The sense of duty we feel towards family members.

The term 'family', however, has a social meaning above and beyond a domestic arrangement. We often feel emotionally close to a set of individuals. Even if we do not actually like their company, we are obliged by a sense of duty to try to love and respect them. This special sense of obligation, or duty, is called **kinship**. We all have both an individual and a cultural concept of those whom we consider to be family. However, in modern Britain, we tend to have a fairly limited sense of family; for example, people may have biological relationships in that they are cousins, but they may never actually meet each other or make contact. Other cultures, such as Chinese or Asian people, have more complex arrangements of obligations and duties between family members and have special words to define relationships such as 'mother's brother' or 'father's brother' – words that are more specific than the English language term 'uncle'.

**Nuclear family:** Parents and children in a single household.

**Extended family:** Nuclear family plus grandparents, uncles, cousins, etc.; may share a home or keep in close contact.

The tightly formed unit of family that consists of just parents and children in a single domestic unit is known as the **nuclear family**. According to *Social Trends* in 2001 this arrangement accounted for 23% of households in modern Britain. The term **extended family** is used to describe those relations who may live close to or with parents and children. In some cultural groups brothers and sisters will share a household. This is called a horizontal extended family. In other cultural groups the elderly are very much part of family life and there will often be a number of generations living in the household. This is known as a vertical extended family.

> *Household composition has become more varied in recent decades, and increasing numbers of people are living alone. In Spring 2001 almost three in ten households in Great Britain comprised one person living alone, more than twice the proportion in 1961. The proportion of households consisting of a couple with dependent children fell from 38% in 1961 to 23% in Spring 2001, while the proportion of lone parent households with dependent children tripled, accounting for 6% of all households in both 1991 and 2001.*

Social Trends 32, 2002

# Important studies

George Murdock (1949) wrote one of the best-known texts in the early study of the family. He concluded that all societies, no matter how variable their family structure, had at their core a nuclear family consisting of a cohabiting heterosexual couple and their own or adopted children. His definition of family structure was very rigid, and there are criticisms of his study because it was based on readings of other texts rather than on his own fieldwork.

The Census of 2001 presents a very different picture of modern British society, suggesting that a more flexible approach to understanding family and household is needed in Britain. There has been an increase in the number of single-person households but, with modern communications, this does not mean that such people are socially isolated. People are living in more varied social arrangements: they may live alone or with a partner, and then get married. If they then divorce and remarry, they are part of a sequence of nuclear families. In addition, as Britain has become more culturally varied, other patterns have emerged. Indian families tend to form households with an average of 3.6 people and Pakistani/Bangladeshi households average 4.5 people. Some of these contain members of three generations. In contrast, households headed by a Black person are substantially more likely to be lone parents with their children.

## Think it through

### Households

Over the past 30 years, household size has declined from an average of 2.91 persons in 1971 to 2.48 in 1991, then more slowly to 2.30 in 2000. There have also been marked changes in household consumption, with increases in the proportion of one-person households, and of households headed by a lone parent. The proportion of elderly people living alone has remained stable since the mid-1980s, but among those aged 25–44, the proportion increased from 5% in 1985 to 12% in 2000. The proportion of households containing a married or cohabiting couple with dependent children declined from 31% of all households in 1979 to 25% in 1991 and then decreased more gradually to 21% in 2000.

### Families with dependent children

Changes in family composition show the same pattern as those in household composition. Thus, there has been a steady decline in the proportion of families with dependent children headed by a married or cohabiting couple and a corresponding increase in the proportion headed by a lone parent. Whereas couple families accounted for 92% of all families in 1971, they comprised 78% of families in 1993 and 74% in 2000. Most of the growth in lone-parent families has been among lone mothers, lone-father families accounting for between 1 and 3% of all families throughout the lifetime of The General Household Survey.

Source: *Living in Britain: The General Household Survey*, 2000/2001, HMSO, London, p. 5 (www.statistics.gov.uk)

1 Explain the difference between a family and a household.

2 Suggest three different forms of household structure that are commonly found in modern British society.

3 Evaluate the suggestion that both household and family structure are undergoing significant change in modern British society.

# Round-up

**Family members are related to each other, have a sense of kinship, and usually live in a household. Households may include only one person, or a group of people who may not be related but share domestic arrangements. In the twenty-first century, there is an increasing variety of household types.**

# Why do we live in families?

## The functionalist view of family life

Despite continual criticisms of family life, people still carry on forming families and many appear to enjoy family life. It is this that has led some **functionalist** sociologists, such as Talcott Parsons, to look for reasons why the family is so popular as a social institution. He looked at the **functions** of the family both for the individual and for society, and viewed it as an essential institution for society as well as a cultural universal.

*Functionalism: Theories that explain social institutions in terms of the functions they perform for the society.*

When Talcott Parsons studied American families in the early 1950s (Parsons and Bales, 1955), he concluded that the family had two major functions or purposes. These are:

- the stabilisation of the adult personality
- reproduction (or **procreation**) and the **socialisation** of the young.

*Procreation: The process of having children; the process of creating new members of society.*

*Socialisation: The process of learning how to behave in a way that is appropriate to your culture or society.*

Parsons had a very positive view of the family. However, it is clear that families have a variety of other functions besides reproduction and social stability.

The popularity of family and marriage is such that there are strong moves from many homosexuals to form couples and to create the families that heterosexual couples enjoy

---

## ADDITIONAL FUNCTIONS OF THE FAMILY

- Families have more functions than Parsons claimed. For instance, families contribute to our **ascribed status** – the standing or status we have in society – over which we have no control. Obviously, membership of the Royal Family offers high status. We also have a family name, and this may indicate our ethnic or geographical origin; for instance, names beginning with O' (such as 'O'Reilly') are often Irish.

- The existence of the family is a means of regulating sexual activity because it sanctions some sexual relationships (such as those between heterosexual couples) and makes others taboo (such as those between close relatives). There can also be a negative element to this in that homosexuality for either gender is thereby not seen as fully normal in our society.

- Western society is economically and socially complex. People may be socially and economically dependent on their family until they are in their mid-twenties or beyond. Students, for instance, may need economic support for job training in professional roles such as medicine or teaching.

---

## Critics of the functionalist view of the family

*Ascribed status: Social standing or status allocated at birth.*

Critics of the family, such as Marxist and feminist writers, also see the family as supporting society but regard this as a bad thing because they believe society itself to be unequal and unfair.

Marxists and feminists point out that most family relationships benefit men rather than women. They argue that men have power within the family because they are likely to have higher wages than women or children. This reflects the power relationships of society, in which men dominate the political and economic world. This domination by men is known as **patriarchy**.

*Patriarchy: Domination by males in society.*

For a reflection of Parsons' view of the purpose of family in stabilising the adult personality and in social reproduction, you could look at any Disney cartoon from the 1950s or 1960s. These show a very traditional view of family and sexual roles. One example would be *The Aristocats*. Males are usually shown as wild until tamed by the love of a good female. The female gains satisfaction from caring for children and males. Note that while Disney-style cartoon images tend to reinforce traditional family roles and values, contemporary cartoons such as *The Simpsons* and *South Park* show a more negative and modern view of family life, while still reinforcing some traditional family values.

# Important studies

In the 1950s, Talcott Parsons wrote a number of books and articles on the modern American family; he is the originator of what has come to be known as the '**fit thesis**', which suggests that family forms evolve to suit the needs of industrial society. Families have evolved into nuclear-family forms so that men have become breadwinners and women look after the emotional needs of the family. This, he argues, is because it is good for society as well as for individuals. However, this can be criticised from a number of viewpoints, particularly that of feminism – which points out that the nuclear family form is not always a good one for women because they end up socially and economically powerless in the face of male domination.

In a study of family relationships in families with teenage children, Langford, Lewis, Solomon and Warin (2001) discovered a positive picture of family life. They found that family members valued family life highly, seeing life without family as being lonely and sad. For many people, family is a 'taken for granted' assumption. It is something that they do not question. Interestingly, and in contrast with feminist writing on the family, Langford *et al.* discovered that women were more likely to be positive about family life than their husbands or children.

Melanie Phillips, a well-known journalist and commentator, is a modern writer associated with New Right thinking. In a number of articles in *The Times* and other newspapers, she has suggested that family life is in decline, partly due to what she calls a 'flight from parenting'. In other words, people are becoming less willing to accept the demands and responsibilities of being a parent. She believes that the traditional family is the building-block of our society. People who are born into traditional families have more stable personalities and a closer identification with each other. She feels that family life is in decline because people are no longer willing to participate in traditional family life.

> Fit thesis: A functionalist theory suggesting that families evolve to suit the needs of industrial society.

## Think it through

The passage below is adapted from the opening words of the Church of England wedding ceremony, first written in 1552.

> Dearly beloved, we are gathered together here in the sight of God, and in the face of this Congregation, to join together this man and this woman in holy Matrimony; ...is not by any to be enterprized, nor taken in hand, unadvisedly, lightly, or wantonly, to satisfy men's carnal (*sexual*) lusts and appetites, ...but reverently, discreetly, advisedly, soberly, and in the fear of God...
>
> First, It was ordained for the procreation of children, ...
>
> Secondly, It was ordained for a remedy against sin, and to avoid fornication [*sex, which was not allowed under the rules of Christianity*]; that such persons as have not the gift of continency [*being able to go without sex*] might marry...
>
> Thirdly, It was ordained for the mutual society, help, and comfort, that the one ought to have of the other, both in prosperity [*good times*] and adversity [*bad times*]...

1 What three reasons exist for families and marriage according to this version of the wedding ceremony?

2 Outline the similarities and differences between this view of marriage and that of writers in the functionalist tradition.

3 Suggest three factors that explain why many people choose to form traditional families.

4 Evaluate the suggestion that the traditional Christian view of marriage and the family is no longer relevant in modern British society.

# Round-up

Despite heavy criticism from feminists and Marxists, who take a conflict view of family relationships, families seem to fulfil many social and emotional needs. Attitudes towards what makes a 'normal' family have changed significantly over the past 50 years and family forms are now more flexible so that many people retain a positive view of what families can offer to society and themselves.

# What image do we have of the perfect family?

**Familial ideology:** The view that the traditional family is 'better' than any alternatives.

Families have a social meaning that is rather more than an arrangement of people related by biological inheritance or by marriage. There is also a common view, or **familial ideology**, which suggests that certain types of family arrangements and expressions of human sexuality are 'better' than others. This type of thinking is frequently tied in with religious belief and morality, and it can be argued that this ideology of family is Christian, European and middle-class. This ideology is important because it forms government policies and politics. During the 1980s, the governments of Britain and the USA regularly called for a sense of 'traditional family **values**'.

Homosexuality is often viewed as inferior to heterosexuality. This is illustrated by government guidelines in Britain on the teaching of sex in schools, which advocate using the context of a loving family relationship and that homosexuality should be viewed as abnormal.

**Values:** The set of beliefs and morals that people consider to be of importance.

**Stereotypes:** Oversimplified images of groups of people. These images often rely on generalisations.

The common concept of the 'perfect family' in Western society is often known as the 'cereal-packet norm'. The term originates from the days when breakfast cereals were advertised with pictures of families on the front. These families were almost inevitably a nuclear family of father, mother and two children, the older of whom would usually be a boy. These **stereotypes** survive in various media representations of family, often in advertising for food products such as gravy powder or for family investment items such as housing and large saloon cars. Examples of these traditional families are much less frequently seen in the media than they were in the 1950s and 1960s, which may be a reflection of changes in family structure in modern society.

## What evidence is there that some types of family are seen as better than others?

| For | Against |
| --- | --- |
| Products are marketed to families and so food products such as pies and cakes come in packs of four. | Increasingly, advertising on television portrays non-traditional families. |
| Laws governing family and marriage allow only heterosexual couples the right to marry. | There has been a liberalisation of laws so that non-married partners have many of the rights of married couples. |
| The Child Support Agency was created to encourage fathers to contribute financially to their children's lives after family break-up. | The Child Support Agency does not restrict its activities to those who have been married, but targets unmarried fathers as well. |
| Media images of the family often revolve around a couple and their children. This is evident in situation comedies and in soap operas. | Television has shown some acceptance of non-traditional images such as gay sexuality and pre-marital sex. |
| Many politicians have made statements claiming that single mothers are a problem for society. | Some Members of Parliament have openly acknowledged their active homosexuality, which was illegal in Britain until the late 1960s. |

**Coursework advice**

Using content analysis as a method, you could watch a number of domestic comedies or soap operas on television to study the various families shown. Trace the family trees of the characters that are represented as regulars on the programmes. How many of these programmes have a nuclear family at the centre of the action? You might like to discuss with your group the question of whether families such as *The Simpsons*, *The Royle Family*, or the families in *EastEnders*, suggest an affectionate or a critical view of family relationships.

Add your own ideas to the list in the table above. Do you find it easier to add evidence to the 'For' side of the argument or to the 'Against' side?

 www.fnf.org.uk – *Families need fathers – is a compaigning website that supports the rights of fathers in the event of relationship breakdown.*

The nuclear family

# Important studies

Jon Bernardes, author of *Family studies: An introduction* (1997), argues that the traditional view of the family is a 'young, similarly aged, white, married, heterosexual couple with a small number of healthy children living in an adequate home. There is a clear division of responsibilities: the male is primarily the full-time breadwinner and the female primarily the care-giver and perhaps a part-time or occasional income earner.' He argues that this model does not reflect the reality of variations of family form in either history or modern society.

Many prominent feminists such as Germaine Greer (1971) and Simone de Beauvoir (1953) have claimed that family ideology is used in a patriarchal society to tie women to men and marriage. Their view is that girls are socialised from infancy to become wives and mothers through play, story, toys and tradition. It is this that makes women tolerate the exploitation implicit in a traditional nuclear family.

Marianne Hester and Lorraine Radford (1996) suggested that The Children Act of 1989 (enforced 1991) reinforces traditional beliefs about family life and family values. When divorce had taken place because of male violence towards the women, this was not taken into account when making custody and access arrangements for children.

**Research issues** It is very difficult to prove conclusively that ideological messages actually do have an impact on how people think. Many people have been brought up with constant exposure to the ideology that a nuclear family is a norm for our society but are still able to resist the overwhelming pressure to form a nuclear family or to act in a conventional gender role.

## Watch out

Because feelings about families can be very strong, some candidates tend to express personal and political views when writing about this area in the exam. Be cautious and make sure that you back up anything you say with factual evidence or some illustrative material drawn from the studies.

## Think it through

Almost every family I knew echoed, 'Father, Mother, Sister, Brother'. So, naturally, I expected to know the joys of a daughter. 'Aren't you going to try for a girl?', friends asked in disbelief. I feverishly defended my decision to stop having children. 'We only ever wanted two kids. Really. I'm thrilled with my boys.' But, in the back of my mind, I wondered who I was really trying to convince.

I was the product of a genderly balanced family. Saturdays gushed with the excitement of mother–daughter shopping trips, while my brother and father roughed it up at the hockey rink. My mother glowed as my Brownie troop leader. My father shone as my brother's soccer coach. Almost every family that I knew echoed, 'Father, Mother, Sister, Brother'. So, naturally, I expected to know the joys of a daughter. I longingly strolled through department stores, running my fingers over velvet dresses and ruffled socks.

Franco, S. *The perfect family*: www.pregnancytoday.com/reference/articles

1 Explain the meaning of the term 'traditional family'.

2 Outline one characteristic of traditional families.

3 Evaluate the suggestion that traditional families rely on the exploitation of the women in them who act as carers.

# Round-up

The view that a family consists of a heterosexual couple and their children is still widely promoted and supported, even though this is a less common form of family than it once was. Those who have a strong belief in traditional family forms are often strongly religious or have conservative thinking on social issues.

# How have families changed since the nineteenth century?

Debates on family change in British society are significant to sociology because there are political and ideological issues about what family changes mean for people. There are two aspects of change:

* *Structural change*: The structure of families has undergone massive change; more family structures and forms are now acceptable. Much of the evidence for such change comes from government statistics on births, marriage and divorce.

* *Qualitative change*: This debate centres on whether relationships between people within families have changed significantly. The evidence here is much less clear cut and comes from sociologists conducting small-scale research into family life.

*The average number of children per woman of childbearing age has been below two since 1973.*

### KEY STRUCTURAL CHANGES TO FAMILIES

* Fewer children are born to women so that nowadays the average completed family size is now around 1.7 children.
* Divorce rates peaked in 1993 at 180 000 but steadied to a rate around 159 000 in 1999.
* Fewer couples are marrying and those that do often cohabit before marriage. The age of first marriage is rising steadily to 29 for men and 27 for women.
* There are more single people living alone at all ages.
* People are more likely to live away from their close relatives.
* More people are likely to live as couples after their children have left home or before they have children. According to *Social Trends 32* (2002), nearly one quarter of all households consist of couples.
* There are more reconstituted or blended families. These are families that consist of children from more than one relationship living together, perhaps after divorce and remarriage. This accounts for about 6% of all families with children where the head of household is under 60 years of age.

### KEY QUALITATIVE CHANGES IN FAMILIES

The key qualitative changes in families are a matter for debate. However, the main sociological points are as follows:

* Many people believe that relationships between husbands and wives are more equal. However, a number of sociologists (such as Sara Delamont, 2001) believe that the extent of change is over-rated.
* Relationships between parents and children may be less close than they once were, because there are more families where both parents go out to work. Some recent writers with a traditional view of family life, such as Peter Saunders, have suggested that this change is a cause of social problems such as youth crime.
* There is more tolerance of pre-marital sex and extra-marital affairs, which once would have been seen as a proof of low moral standards.
* People are more open about living in 'gay' relationships. This would have been well hidden before the 1960s because homosexuality was against the law.

How much have male and female roles in the family really changed?

## Important studies

In their book *The symmetrical family*, Young and Willmott (1973) started much of the qualitative debate when they suggested that relations between men and women in families were becoming more equal. This work is now very dated and was heavily criticised by feminists at the time.

In *Women of their time* (1998) Jane Pilcher conducted qualitative research on women from the South Wales region and discovered that families at the start of the twentieth century and between the two world wars had **gendered division of labour**, but that men would and did help with housework at times of difficulty. However, she argues, there has been little change in family relationships because while contemporary men can and do help in the home, even today they still show reluctance to take on housework tasks.

Gendered division of labour: Work is allocated on the basis of gender, so women do domestic work and men work outside the home.

FAMILIES AND HOUSEHOLDS

# How does the modern family differ from the nineteenth-century family?

Although the family is in a constant state of change, there have been some significant long-term changes to family life and values in Britain since the nineteenth century.

Extended families: Nuclear family plus grandparents, uncles, cousins, etc.; may share a home or keep in close contact.

| | Nineteenth-century family | Modern family |
|---|---|---|
| *Change in status of women* | Women have lower social and legal status. Fertility rates are high. | Women have greater legal and contraceptive rights and more independence. |
| *Change in status of children* | Birth rates and death rates are high, especially for working-class children. Many children go out to work before they are 10 years old. | There are fewer children and they are protected by legal rights. Children must attend school until at least the age of 16. |
| *Changes in role of men* | Men work long hours, but are dominant in the home. | Men have more leisure time and are expected to participate in family life. |
| *Change in family form* | Families are often **extended**, with relatives sharing homes or living close together. | Nuclear families are still the most common family form, but a wider variety of family types are accepted. There is greater geographical mobility. |
| *Change in role of family* | Family is significant for people's social lives; home life is valued. | Social and leisure needs are increasingly met by agencies outside the family. |
| *Change in family morality* | The moral code is rigid so that failure to comply can result in social shame. Much abuse and domestic violence is hidden and ignored. | Moral codes are flexible. Discussion of violence and sexual abuse is more open. There is some public awareness and support, so people are more able to resist poor domestic circumstances. |
| *Change in sexual codes* | Only heterosexuality is acceptable and sexual relations are expected to take place within marriage, and to result in children. | There is increasing separation of sexuality from marriage and more tolerance of alternative sexualities. |

## Think it through

'Cherry Norton, Social Affairs Editor of *The Independent*, argues that in the UK 'fatherhood has been transformed in the past 30 years'. Part of that transformation has been an emphasis on the importance of the father's role in children's lives. Yet the change in status of fathers... may be largely ceremonial. Certainly fewer and fewer British men are experiencing traditional fatherhood. In the 1960s, six out of ten men were living with dependent children. Today, the latest figures from the Office for National Statistics show that only 35 per cent do.

[*The passage in the book by Maushart goes on to discuss various legislative changes that are taking place in modern Britain, such as unpaid paternity leave.*]

All this is welcome, and yet the emphasis on the New Fatherhood, UK-style, has been very much on the rights of fathers rather than on the rights (let alone needs) of children. Questions of access and entitlement centre on raising Dad's claims to a level equal to Mum's claims. One survey published in 2000 by the National Childbirth Trust, for example, found that new fathers overwhelmingly wished to have more involvement in pregnancy and birth, as well as more leave to care for their babies after they were born. Prominence has also been given to research showing that 'fathers who live with young children work harder, get better jobs, are more sociable and attend church more frequently' than other men.

Maushart, S. (2002) *Wifework*: Bloomsbury, London

1 Outline the changes that have taken place in the role of fathers in modern families over the past 30 years.

2 Suggest three factors that may have contributed to changes in the role and status of fathers in the modern British family.

3 Evaluate the suggestion that the changes that have taken place in the modern British family have been exaggerated.

## Can we trust official statistics?

Sociologists cannot be certain of the accuracy of the official statistics of social patterns in the past because families tended to hide problems that were considered shameful, such as divorce, or a child outside marriage. For example, mothers might have registered a grandchild as their own in order to save a daughter the shame of bringing up an illegitimate child.

## Round-up

**Families have been undergoing structural and qualitative changes that are closely linked to moral, social and technological change in society. While there is statistical evidence that significant change is taking place, there is a debate as to the actual extent and significance of that change when it comes to the reality of people's lives.**

# What has happened to the population of Britain since World War II?

Demography: The study of population.

The study of populations is known as **'demography'**. To understand something of how families have changed in British society, it is necessary to look at the population changes that have taken place in British society since the end of World War II in 1945.

The changes that have taken place in Britain are also typical of much of Western Europe and the USA. These changes could have a serious impact on the nature and structure of our society. The three main areas of change are as follows:

- the number of children being born is dropping below that which is needed to maintain a stable population
- the average life expectancy is rising and the proportion of older people in the population is growing rapidly
- people are becoming increasingly mobile, both within countries and between borders.

*Social Trends* is published annually and details an astonishing amount of information about changes in British society in an easy-to-read format. You can also find government statistics on the website at www.statistics.gov.uk, from where it is possible to download *Social Trends* free.

Birth rate: The number of live births per thousand of the population in one year.

Death rate: The number of deaths per year per thousand of the population.

## Changes in living arrangements in later life (60+) by gender

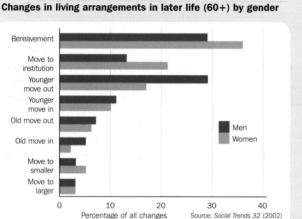

Percentage of all changes    Source: *Social Trends 32* (2002)

1 What percentage of males will experience bereavement (death of a partner) in old age?

2 Which gender is more likely to experience bereavement?

3 Suggest reasons why females are more likely to move to an institution than males.

4 Discuss ways in which our society will need to adjust in order to cope with an ageing population.

## Fertility rates (live births per thousand women of childbearing age) by age of mother at childbirth

|  | 1961 | 1971 | 1981 | 1991 | 2000 |
|---|---|---|---|---|---|
| *Under 20* | 37 | 50 | 28 | 33 | 29 |
| 20–24 | 173 | 154 | 107 | 89 | 69 |
| 25–29 | 178 | 155 | 130 | 120 | 95 |
| 30–34 | 106 | 79 | 70 | 87 | 88 |
| 35–39 | 51 | 34 | 22 | 32 | 40 |
| 40 and over | 16 | 9 | 5 | 5 | 8 |
| *All ages* | 91 | 84 | 62 | 64 | 55 |

Source: *Social Trends 32* (2002)

1 What trends can you identify in the rate of teenage pregnancies since 1961?

2 In which year were fertility rates for women at their highest?

3 In which year were fertility rates for women at their lowest?

4 In which age group were women most likely to give birth in all years?

5 In which age groups has the fertility rate of British women dropped least since 1961?

6 What trends can you identify in the patterns of fertility of British women?

## Marriages and divorces in the UK

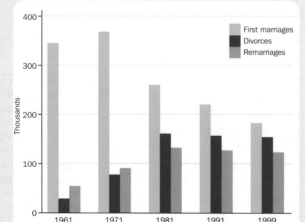

Source: *Social Trends 32*

1 What has happened to the popularity of marriage and remarriage since 1961? Identify the main trends.

2 Which decade saw the highest rise in divorce statistics?

3 Identify trends in divorce patterns since 1961 in the UK.

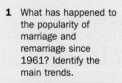 The official government-statistics website www.statistics.gov.uk is a 'must-see' for students of sociology.

## Demographic changes in British society since 1945

| | 1945 | Modern Britain |
|---|---|---|
| **Birth rates** | In the period immediately after World War II ended, birth rates rose very quickly in a period known as the 'Baby Boom'. This ended in 1953, but there were smaller birth-rate increases later, when the females born in the boom had children of their own. | Birth rates are dropping very significantly, with the average number of children born to each female falling.

The average age of the birth of the first child has risen because women are generally starting families later than their own mothers did. |
| *Teenage pregnancy rates* | These appear to be relatively low, but statistics may not be accurate because families were ashamed of pregnancy outside marriage. Some children conceived outside marriage were hidden, abandoned or adopted in secret. Rates rose in the latter part of the twentieth century but have fallen again in recent years. | Allen *et al.* (1998) point out that the rates for teenage births has fallen over the past 20 years and that these are a small proportion of total births. Many of these births are to women in stable partnerships. The statistics show that the rate of teenage births is higher in Britain than most other European countries, where the fall in teen births has been more dramatic. |
| *Changes in ethnicity* | Although Britain has always been an ethnically diverse population, the majority of these people would generally have been white-skinned Europeans. Nevertheless, there were some areas, around seaports in particular, that had large and stable mixed-race communities.

Immigration of non-white people from Commonwealth countries began on a larger scale in the late 1940s and early 1950s. | Britain is an ethnically diverse society, which has absorbed people from a variety of white and non-white communities. Non-white populations tend to be larger in major cities and in inner London. |
| *Life expectancy* | In 1945, life expectancy was lower than it is today. The old-age pension was set at 65 for men, on the assumption that it would only be needed for a year or so.

Smoking was an extremely common social habit in all classes and many people had experienced poverty in childhood that had undermined their health. For women, regular pregnancy and childbirth brought their own risks.

Many homes were poorly equipped, damp, cold and unhygienic in comparison to modern homes. | Life expectancy has increased dramatically, especially for those in the higher-income brackets who enjoy good access to health-care, quality food and leisure and who have a culture that values health and fitness.

Increased longevity, however, means that many people experience a lowered quality of life in old age because, although they may survive previously fatal conditions such as strokes, they also become vulnerable to disability, Alzheimer's disease and cancers. |
| *Child mortality rates (death rates)* | Children were at greater risk of early death through infectious diseases such as measles, mumps, polio and TB, or through congenital deformity.

According to public-health records, mortality rates for babies were high, but falling. | Children are routinely protected from childhood illness through vaccination programmes.

Death rates from certain illnesses have dropped as medical technology has improved.

There are higher survival rates for premature babies and those experiencing disability through birth accident.

According to *Social Trends 30* (2000), child death rates remain variable according to the social class, marital status and age of the mother. |

# Important studies

The best evidence for changes in the population of Britain can be drawn from government statistics, which are generally extremely accurate. All births and deaths must be recorded by law, and this information is supplemented by other data collection such as the National Census, which takes place every ten years. *Social Trends*, which is published annually by the government and is held in most public libraries and many resource centres, provides a brief summary of important information and changes. This material is widely used by sociologists.

As the amount of detailed data collected by the government has increased, our knowledge of the demography of Britain is fairly accurate. In addition, records have been collected for over 200 years, although the early material is generally not very detailed. We can see how patterns of population change have developed.

## Watch out

Be cautious about making statements about the changing population of Britain. There are a number of popular misconceptions and misunderstandings that do not reflect the true picture of life in modern Britain. When supporting examination answers with claims about changes in population, make sure that you are certain that your data is accurate. Your examiner will spot a wild guess very quickly!

# Round-up

The structure of the population of Britain is undergoing relatively rapid change. There are fewer children born, and these children are born to older mothers. Many of the mothers are not married to the fathers of their children even if the parents are in stable relationships, but this is through choice. Children are less likely to die from infectious disease than they were 50 years ago. There is an increase in the numbers of those over 65 and Britain has an ageing population. People in early retirement tend to be in better health than once would have been true for people over retirement age. The elderly old are also long-lived, but there has been an increase in the numbers of dependent old people.

# Why are birth rates falling in Britain and Western Europe?

Throughout Western Europe there is a growing tendency for women to have smaller families and to delay the birth of their first child until they are over 25 years of age. This trend has been influenced by women's changing social, economic and moral circumstances, and has been aided by changes to the technology of reproduction which now enables people to make choices that were not available to their grandparents.

**What woman wouldn't want to be a wife and mother?**

## Conceptions: by marital status and outcome (England & Wales)

| | 1987 | 1991 | 1995 | 1998 | 1999 |
|---|---|---|---|---|---|
| **Conceptions inside marriage leading to:** | | | | | |
| | % | % | % | % | % |
| Maternities | 56 | 52 | 49 | 44 | 44 |
| Lebal abortions | 5 | 4 | 4 | 4 | 4 |
| **Conceptions outside marriage leading to:** | | | | | |
| | % | % | % | % | % |
| Maternities inside marriage | 5 | 4 | 3 | 3 | 3 |
| Maternities outside marriage | 20 | 25 | 28 | 30 | 31 |
| Legal abortions | 14 | 15 | 16 | 18 | 18 |
| **All conceptions** (thousands) | 850 | 854 | 790 | 797 | 774 |

Source: *Social Trends 32* (2002)

1  What trends can you identify in the total number of women conceiving children?

2  What pattern can you identify in the number of married women conceiving children?

3  What pattern can you identify in the number of unmarried women conceiving children?

4  What are the differences between the conception and maternity choices of married and unmarried women?

**SOCIAL, LEGAL AND TECHNOLOGICAL FACTORS THAT HAVE INCREASED WOMEN'S CONTROL OF THEIR OWN FERTILITY**

- The contraceptive pill and other forms of contraception
- IVF treatment
- Hormone treatments
- Surrogate motherhood
- Fertility drugs
- The legalisation of abortion in 1967
- The social acceptance of birth outside marriage for some women.

One of the most notable advances in the health and life chances of women in the latter part of the twentieth century was their ability to control their own fertility. While contraceptive techniques have been used for generations, generally they were not very effective. The most effective form of contraception was the condom. However, this was invented to protect against venereal disease and was under the control of men, who could choose whether to use it or not. The advent of effective and safe contraception in the 1950s and 1960s had a dramatic effect on the lives of many women.

Women could take paid employment outside the home after marriage because they no longer faced the probability of regular pregnancy and childbirth. Note, however, that working-class women have always worked outside the home, often leaving children to be cared for by relatives.

Sexual activity for women was no longer linked almost exclusively to marriage. Women could be sexually active without the risk of childbirth and the consequent stigma of being an unmarried mother.

Changes in the social position of women and the expansion of higher education in the 1960s and 1970s meant that far more women entered higher education. Work became significant in many women's lives rather than being a time-filler before marriage. The increasing number of women in work and education led to many of them delaying the birth of their first child.

*Fertility rate: The number of live births per thousand women of childbearing age (defined as 15–44 years).*

*Social Trends 2002* points out that, while the 25–34-year-old age group has the highest **fertility rate**, the fertility rate for women aged between 35 and 39 has doubled over the past twenty years. The average completed family size for women today is below two children, and is falling. Fertility in Britain is lower than is needed to maintain the current size of the population.

## Falling birth rates

- It is often stated that some women choose not to have children so that they can focus on their career. However, the evidence is not so clear cut. It is certainly the case that combining paid work and parenthood is very difficult. Childless women do not have to make a choice between the two and so women who are promoted are often those without children, either through choice or accident. It is not so much that there is a choice between paid work and parenthood as that paid work is easier if you are not a parent.

- Parenthood has a low status in British society, despite the fact that it is a norm. For example, there is little support via the benefit or taxation systems for people with children in Britain compared with other European countries.

- A number of studies have shown that families with young children are likely to experience poverty, particularly if the mother is very young or the parents have low earnings from unskilled jobs. Gordon *et al.* (2000) suggest that 18% of families with one child and 40% of lone parents experience poverty.

- In our society, it is common for women to undertake education and establish careers beyond the years when their bodies are at their most fertile. If women choose to attend higher education courses and perhaps establish themselves in professional work, they may delay pregnancy. It can be difficult for some women to conceive without medical help when they are much beyond the age of 30. It is even possible that with the introduction of such initiatives as the student loan in 1999, graduates will feel the need to establish themselves financially before taking on the responsibility of parenting.

- Due to social and technological changes in the twentieth century, women are now able to exercise choice over fertility in a way that is quite new. Should contraception fail, there are aids such as the 'morning after pill' and abortion. Abortion was strictly illegal before 1967 and many women became infertile or died as a result of botched or unhygienic operations at the hands of illegal abortionists. There has been a steady but fluctuating rise in the number of abortions. However, abortion figures are not fully reliable because they may include pregnancy terminations of foreign nationals who are unable to obtain terminations in their home countries and will therefore travel to Britain for the operation. Abortion rates are highest for pregnant women aged between 16 and 34, but are relatively low for those under 16 or over 35.

### Think it through

Certainly, the average age of mothers at first birth has increased in most Western countries. As women face increasing fertility problems after the age of 30, delaying the decision to have children may result in infecundity (*infertility*). Also, delaying a decision combined with low targets of family size may combine to result in childlessness. The classic case of 'forgetting' to have children until it is too late has been facilitated (*made easier*) by the advent (*arrival*) of effective contraception but this in itself does not create childlessness. Motivations to avoid having children may be deliberate or indirect, perhaps unwitting.

Adapted from: McAllister, F. with Clarke, L. (1998)
*Choosing childlessness*, Family Policy Studies Centre, London

1. Outline and identify two ways in which changes in the role of the women is changing fertility patterns in modern society.

2. Identify and explain two reasons why many couples may wish to delay parenthood until they are past their thirtieth birthday.

## Important studies

In their study of both women and men who have chosen to remain childless (*Choosing Childlessness*, 1998), McAllister with Clarke, the researchers point out that many childless people feel that they have made a positive decision. They claim that parenting is a low-status occupation in our society; it is fraught with difficulty and insecurity and conflicts with other demands people have in their lives. Those who chose childlessness often set high standards for parenting and so felt it impossible to reconcile the strains that parenting brings with their other interests and concerns and their desire to live full and active lives.

Barlow, Duncan, Evans and Park (2001) pointed out that although one in five children was born to an unmarried couple, fathers had no legal rights over their children, even if they were providing financial support. An unmarried father may not take his child on a foreign holiday, cannot provide medical consent and, most importantly, has no legal right to custody if the mother were to die. Many are unaware of their lack of rights.

### Watch out

Remember in any discussion of this question that although it is women who conceive and bear children, men may also be involved in the decision-making process as to whether women will bear children. Allen and Bourke Dowling with Rolfe (1998) found that fathers are often influential when teenage mothers are deciding whether to continue with a pregnancy.

## Round-up

Birth rates are falling for all women. As they gain control over their bodies and their reproductive lives, many women are choosing to limit their families or to remain without children. However, the reasons for this are complex and related to the low status of parenting in our society and the high standards of care that are expected for children.

# What recent social changes have affected the family?

Some fnctionalists claimed that the nuclear family, consisting of married parents with dependent children, was to be found in every society. This family form is still common in Britain, but there are also many people who do not live in a traditional nuclear family. Pressures on families to change have come from a number of sources:

- *Economic* – the movement of women into paid work is often seen as a benefit to them because as they earn money, they now have greater power to influence how it is spent. They are no longer dependent on a male breadwinner and can choose whether to marry or to remain married.

- *Moral* – Fewer people seem to subscribe to traditional religious teaching on family and marriage. This enables them to exercise sexual and moral choices that previous generations could not have accepted.

- *Pragmatic* – Many household decisions are made on practical grounds, so that as weddings become increasingly expensive, it is a rational choice to delay marriage until more significant debts such as down-payments on houses or student loans are paid off.

- *Ideological* – For many couples, particularly in the 1970s and 1980s, objections to marriage were based on political thinking about the nature of marriage as an institution that oppresses women.

- *Legal* – laws governing family and family relationships have changed and so it is easier to divorce now than ever before. In addition, as couples choose not to exercise the legal right to marry, so separating becomes simpler as well.

- *Changes in female expectations of marriage* – women may have earned the right to work, but study after study shows that working mothers carry out significantly more of the childcare and domestic labour than men. In addition, women are often expected to be emotionally supportive and nurturing of their adult male partners. They are now able to exercise a choice not to do this.

- *Social security and benefit changes* – the Welfare State will support women and their children if a relationship fails. It is sometimes claimed that young women will become pregnant in order to gain benefits, but the research evidence for this is limited. However, women who are in relationships that collapse may still retain their children and they can survive on basic levels of income, which are provided by the State.

- *Contraception and abortion* – women in Britain from the 1970s onwards were the first to be able to control their fertility with any degree of reliability. Previously contraception was in male hands or dangerous to the woman. This has freed men and women to have sex without necessarily intending marriage, or even a relationship.

- *Changes in the structure of the population* – there are proportionally larger numbers of older people and fewer younger people in the population. This means that there are more people living as couples or in single-person households. The Office of Population Censuses and Surveys suggests that there will be an increase of 50% in the number of old people over the next 30 years, reaching a total number of 14.8 million (source: www.statistics.gov.uk). The current population of Britain is 58.8 million.

**What do the illustrations show us about changing family patterns?**

## THE POSTMODERN FAMILY?

Kidd (1999) states that, 'We cannot even say what constitutes a "family" today. The postmodern approach to the family is characterised by:

• choice   • freedom   • diversity   • ambivalence   • fluidity.

These observations mean that family relationships are "undecided" – we can only expect individualistic responses to the problems of the creation of social identity within and without the "family".'

**Children of divorced couples by age of children, England and Wales 1970–91**

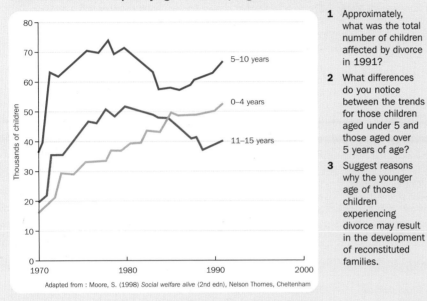

1 Approximately, what was the total number of children affected by divorce in 1991?

2 What differences do you notice between the trends for those children aged under 5 and those aged over 5 years of age?

3 Suggest reasons why the younger age of those children experiencing divorce may result in the development of reconstituted families.

Adapted from : Moore, S. (1998) *Social welfare alive* (2nd edn), Nelson Thornes, Cheltenham

Important studies

Smart, Wade and Neale (2002) interviewed 65 children who spent their time more or less equally divided between their separated parents. This arrangement where parents live separately but each retains equal share of the care of children is known as **co-parenting**. Their research is presented from the point of view of the children, but they note that co-parenting is becoming more common in Britain, particularly as a result of the 1984 Children Act, which encourages contact between children and both parents in the event of divorce or separation.

Co-parenting: Where separated or divorced parents take equal roles in caring for children, who spend some time in one household and the rest of their time in the other.

Beanpole families: Families that are very small, perhaps consisting of one or two adults and a single child, with the patten repeated through the generations.

## Round-up

The family is not a static structure but one that develops and evolves in response to changes in the social environment. It remains popular, so that even though people may divorce, they do not reject family life totally, but often go on to form further relationships. This has resulted in an elongated family structure in which many parents are older and have fewer children. They may also form a series of sexual partnerships throughout their lives.

## Think it through

### NUCLEAR FAMILY GOES INTO MELTDOWN
#### Generations learn to link up to cope with lonely lifestyle

THE nuclear family of mum, dad and 2.4 kids is splitting up. Researchers have coined a name for the emerging British household – the Beanpoles. They 'live together' and have 1.8 children.

As Britons live longer, divorce rates rise and couples have fewer children, the traditional family – married parents with two or more children – is giving way to co-habiting couples with a single child.

A new study by the London-based research group Mintel shows family groups are getting 'longer and thinner – like a **beanpole**'. While 20 years ago the average extended family comprised three 'nuclear' generations, family groups are now made up of four generations of often co-habiting couples, each with an average 1.8 children.

'The family is undergoing radical changes under the pressure of an ageing population, longer lifespans, increased female working, the tendency to marry later in life, the falling birth rate and the rising divorce rate,' the study says.

John Arlidge (2002) *The Observer*, Sunday 5 May (www.observer.co.uk/uk_news)

1 Explain the meaning of the term 'beanpole family'.

2 Suggest three reasons for the development of the beanpole family in modern British society.

3 Evaluate the suggestion that the traditional nuclear family is no longer suited to the needs of modern society.

# How are traditional family structures changing?

We will now look at what is happening to families as a result of the changes discussed in earlier sections and at the various forms of family that can be found in contemporary British society.

Membership of a family is not a static situation. As we progress through life, we are members of different households and families. We may, for instance, share homes with others while we are students, or co-habit and even have children with more than one person before settling to a marriage. We may choose to live independently as adults – an increasing life-choice for many. There is a widening complexity in our kinship networks. We become parents, aunts or uncles, grandparents or step-parents. As society has become more fluid, there are more possibilities for individuals to participate in a variety of family structures.

Clearly there are more forms of family structure in modern society than would have been acceptable in the past. One of the big changes in the late twentieth century was the normalisation of family arrangements that in the past would have been a source of stigma. For example, illegitimacy and family break-up certainly did occur in the past but people would have gone to some trouble to conceal these events. Here we look at some of the ways that family forms are changing in response to the changing mores of our society.

**Couple:** Two adults who share a sexual relationship and a home.

**Grandparenting:** As life expectancy increases and more women go out to work, the role of grandparent is becoming more significant. For example, in many families, grandparents provide childcare for their grandchildren.

## Modern family and household forms

| | |
|---|---|
| *Blended family* | This is a family that contains children from more than one relationship or marriage within it. |
| *Lone-parent family* | This is a family that consists of one adult member and a child or children. It can be formed as a result of divorce, separation or widowhood or through choice. |
| **Couple** | Two adults who share a sexual relationship and a home. In the past, this situation occurred after children had left the home, but it is now popular with people before they settle down to children and, perhaps, a marriage. Some couples actively choose childlessness. |
| *Empty-nest family* | Parents with adult children who have left home. As life expectancy increases, a larger number of people are surviving to experience a life after their children have moved on. Sometimes this move may be permanent, but it can also be short-term, while the children are at college or experiencing work or training. |
| **Grandparenting** | Increasingly, older people may take on the care of younger family members, perhaps in the case of family break-up or to allow younger adults to work for a living. |
| *Fostering* | Children whose families are no longer capable of providing care are often placed with parent substitutes who are paid small amounts to care for these children. In the past, such children would have been placed in institutions known as orphanages. |
| *Cross-cultural family* | This is an increasingly common form, in which families are formed between people of different ethnicities and cultures. |
| *Adoption* | Parents legally accept another person's child as being their own. In the past, this was not uncommon and illegitimate children were adopted. Some adoptees, but by no means all, are from families with a history of neglect, violence or abuse and some may be older or have special needs of some kind. |
| *Singledom* | This is the state of living alone. Once this was more common among older people, but many younger people now live alone through choice. It may even be the choice of established couples who choose to have a close relationship while living in separate homes. |

### Household type, 16–25 year-olds (%)

| | 1982 | 1987 | 1992 |
|---|---|---|---|
| Parental | 61 | 58 | 58 |
| Kin | 2 | 2 | 2 |
| Peer and others | 5 | 5 | 7 |
| One-person | 4 | 6 | 6 |
| Lone-parent | 1 | 3 | 3 |
| Partners | 14 | 14 | 14 |
| Parents and child(ren) | 14 | 13 | 10 |
| All (= 100%) | 2925 | 2704 | 2248 |

Source: *Sociology Review*

1 What trend can you identify in the percentage of young people who lived in the parental home between 1982 and 1992?

2 What trend can you identify in the percentage of young people who have formed their own families?

3 What proportion of young people in 1992 were lone parents?

4 In your view, how significant are the changes that you can see in the table to the sociology of family structure?

**People in employment with a second job: by gender, Spring 2000**

| | People with a second job (thousands) | | | As a percentage of all in employment | | |
|---|---|---|---|---|---|---|
| | *Males* | *Females* | *All persons* | *Males* | *Females* | *All persons* |
| United Kingdom | 513 | 696 | 1209 | 3.3 | 5.6 | 4.4 |
| North East | 13 | 28 | 41 | 2.1 | 5.8 | 3.8 |
| North West | 50 | 68 | 118 | 2.9 | 4.9 | 3.8 |
| Yorkshire and the Humber | 45 | 54 | 99 | 3.5 | 5.2 | 4.3 |
| East Midlands | 32 | 52 | 84 | 2.8 | 5.7 | 4.1 |
| West Midlands | 46 | 67 | 113 | 3.4 | 6.1 | 4.6 |
| East | 47 | 68 | 115 | 3.2 | 5.7 | 4.3 |
| London | 66 | 70 | 135 | 3.5 | 4.6 | 4.0 |
| South East | 76 | 101 | 178 | 3.4 | 5.5 | 4.3 |
| South West | 66 | 90 | 155 | 5.0 | 8.3 | 6.5 |
| England | 441 | 597 | 1039 | 3.4 | 5.7 | 4.4 |
| Wales | 17 | 38 | 55 | 2.5 | 6.8 | 4.4 |
| Scotland | 36 | 50 | 86 | 2.9 | 4.7 | 3.7 |
| Northern Ireland | 19 | 10 | 29 | 4.9 | 3.5 | 4.3 |

Source: *Labour Force Survey*, Office for National Statistics (2000)

1 Which area of Britain has the highest proportion of people with second jobs?

2 Which area of Britain has the lowest proportion of people with second jobs?

3 What gender differences do you note between the numbers of people with second jobs?

4 Which area of Britain goes against the general trend?

5 Suggest what significance the information in this table might have for family life in modern Britain.

## Think it through

### GRANDPARENTS 'JUGGLE CAREER AND CARING'
People in 50s and 60s feel pressure to work on

GROWING pressure on people in their 50s and 60s is set to divert grandparents from helping their working daughters and sons with childcare, according to a report today from the Joseph Rowntree Foundation.

It found a shortage of young people in the population – confirmed by the national census on Monday – would make employers do their utmost to retain older staff.

This would shrink the numbers of retired people who were able to care for their grandchildren or frail older relatives, said researchers from the Institute of Education in London.

...Almost as many men as women said they provided care, but women's caregiving was more intensive. More than a third of those providing care were doing so for fewer than five hours a week. But a quarter of women caregivers and an eighth of men were providing 20 or more hours of informal care a week.

John Carvel, Social Affairs Editor (2002), *The Guardian*, 2 October

1 Explain why employers might wish to retain older employees in the future.

2 Using the stimulus evidence, explain three family pressures that exist on people between the ages of 50 and 60.

3 What changes in family form do you consider to be most significant in British society up to now? Support your views with evidence.

## Research issues

Research into family variation might seem to you to be a sensible area for research. However, there are ethical issues related to studying family structure in cases where people may be asked to reveal information that they would rather conceal. Examples might be where an adoption has taken place or perhaps a father is in prison for a long sentence. People whose families are in the process of breaking up, or whose family break-up was recent, will feel very vulnerable to close questioning.

## Important studies

In a study for the Joseph Rowntree Foundation, Judy Dunn and Kirby Deater-Deckard (2001) discovered that children had found relationships with their grandparents to be very supportive and significant in the weeks following family break-up. Over one quarter of their sample of 460 children had not had the family break-up explained to them.

In another study for the Joseph Rowntree Foundation, Broad, Hayes and Rushforth (2001) discovered that children preferred to be cared for by extended family members in the case of family break-up or abuse. This was preferred for a variety of reasons, including the sense of being loved, safe and secure. They also valued being within their own ethnic background. They disliked the lack of freedom and the poverty associated with living with older people.

## Round-up

Family structures are becoming more variable, although the most common family type remains the nuclear family. However, when the type is studied closely it becomes apparent that there are variant forms of nuclear family developing in our society, such as the beanpole family and the blended family. For some children, particularly in cases of family break-up, natural grandparents take the place of biological parents and create variant forms of the traditional nuclear family.

# What alternatives are there to the family?

**Commune:** A number of families and single adults sharing accommodation and living expenses, usually for ideological and social reasons.

Throughout history there have been attempts by various groups to set up alternatives to conventional family structures. These range from the convents and monasteries of the Middle Ages to the **communes** that became fashionable in the 1970s but which have existed at all times in history. Challenges to traditional family structures are not new, but are probably more tolerated now than they once were. However, the strain of challenging social conventions may be difficult for individuals, who are then forced to develop new forms of relationship in the absence of a traditional model.

Gay families/couples: These are same-sex individuals who choose to live in a partnership.

The communal living movement was very strong in America in the nineteenth century, where a number of such groups, including the Oneida Community, were established. Some had a religious philosophy underlying their practice, whereas others were political. Many of these groups were utopian; their members thought they were going to establish the perfect society. In the 1970s, there was a second flowering of the utopian commune movement, which was associated with 'counter-culture'. Those who rejected capitalist life-styles and adopted hippy ideals set up communes in many rural areas of the USA. Some of these communes were short-lived; others still survive to the present day. There are two basic types of communal living:

- free communes in which individuality is encouraged and rules are developed as they go along – these communes tend to have frequent changes of members and not to last for very long

- structured communes, which share a set of rules based on an underlying philosophy – there may be shared economic arrangements structure and a formal leadership system (typical of religious groupings).

**Kibbutz:** A form of communal living that developed among Jewish families in what is now known as Israel before World War II. It involved groups of families sharing childcare, work and domestic duties, and was often based on farming.

One of the best-known communal living experiments was the Israeli **kibbutz**. This was not designed to replace families but to help people survive in difficult conditions. It began during the early part of this century when the land that is now Israel was called Palestine and was governed first by the Turks and later by the British. Jewish people escaping ghetto life in Europe migrated to what they considered to be their Holy Land. In Palestine, the conditions were very difficult. The land was a desert and people banded together to farm. Men and women worked desperately hard and as equals. When children were born, it was simpler to ask one or two people to look after them all so that the remaining women were free to work. People shared all other jobs such as cooking and waiting on table. Some kibbutzim survive to the present day, but only a limited number of Israelis choose to live in them. Many kibbutzim have evolved over time to a more family-orientated life-style.

The ladies of Llangollen were an established, same-sex couple who lived together for 50 years at the turn of the eighteenth century and the start of the nineteenth century. They are generally described as 'close friends', despite their choice of male clothing and refusal to accept marriage to male partners

http://www.thefarm.org/lifestyle/cmnl.html *This is an illustrated essay written by someone who experienced a childhood in a hippy commune. It examines the ethos and ideals of the commune as a way of life.*

## Gay couples

In the current social and political structure, it is more acceptable for homosexual couples to share their lives openly, although there is still lively debate about their being able to adopt children. Many **gay** people today openly live in couples or as families. However, the extent to which this is socially tolerated remains in question. Andrew Yip (1999) points out that the stigma of being part of a same-sex couple may mean that the partners cannot expect the same degree of social support from family and friends as heterosexual couples. In addition, as Dunscombe and Marsden (1993) have pointed out, in traditional families, the female is often a subservient partner who takes primary responsibility for childcare and domestic tasks. This traditional pattern may be disrupted in same-sex relationships where such roles are negotiated.

> **"** *In many cases, both lesbian and gay couples have children by previous relationships or have adopted children. Thus, apart from their sexual orientation they may not wish to significantly challenge the norms of the nuclear family .* **"**
>
> Dallos and Sapsford, 1997

## Postmodern families

More and more people delay forming their own families; some may choose to remain single or childless. This has led some sociologists (Stacey, for example) to argue that there is such a thing as a 'postmodern family'. This, she suggests, is because families and gender no longer follow strict patterns of social expectations (Stacey, 1990). People who reject traditional patterns of social life have to renegotiate family arrangements and relationships to suit their own personal needs.

EAST LONDON LADIES looking for a Dad as well as Sperm. Two happily committed girls who have been together for four years are looking to have a family. Would you like the opportunity to be part of our family? Sperm donation and co-parenting wanted.

Adapted from advertisement on www.gayfamilyoptions.org/

Bruno Bettelheim (1969), a psychoanalyst, studied the children of the Israeli kibbutz system in a study that became very influential in the 1970s. In it he claimed that they were particularly well adjusted socially but that their relationships were shallow because they bonded with the peer group among whom they were raised as intensely as with their parents. This work remains controversial, not the least because Bettelheim was accused of abusive behaviour, after his death, by the then grown children with whom he had worked. Nevertheless, his conclusion was that living a communal life does not emotionally damage children.

A Gay Pride march

## Think it through

Over the whole of Scandinavia, as in other European countries, some groups are forming residential communes based on the notion of community spirit. Such groups are normally composed of intellectuals and are often created by architects... These communes are normally composed of separate private units, with large scale communal amenities. The individual units are houses or flats of normal size composed of small private rooms with more spacious dining room and kitchen, utility room, games room and sauna... The people who live in these communes think that they can thus benefit from the combination of family and community life, which it is impossible to attain in normal residential conditions... Women feel that it is easier to organise shared household tasks within a large group than with a single man. If everyone has agreed to take part in the housework, the cooking, the washing up and child care, men cannot get out of it as easily as in a normal family.

Burguire, A., Klapisch-Zuber, C., Segalen, M. and Zonabend, F. (1996) *A history of the family* (Vol. 2), Blackwell, Oxford, pp. 500–1

1  Explain the meaning of the term 'residential commune'.

2  Suggest three different reasons why people may choose a residential commune over a more traditional family arrangement.

3  Evaluate the suggestion that within a traditional household it is difficult for females to organise shared household tasks with males.

# Round-up

**People have made conscious attempts over the years to establish community lives that challenge traditional family structures. Those that seem to have survived best are those where there is a philosophy and shared understanding of what communal life should be like. There is increasing tolerance of family structures that are based on alternative sexuality. If a structural approach to family – such as that used by the functionalists – is adopted, then these arrangements are not family. They see family relationships in terms of organisation, blood or marriage ties. If one defines family in terms of emotion, duty and kinship, then these relationships are, in fact, family.**

# How culturally diverse are British families and households?

Attitudes towards families vary widely in the many cultural groups that make up modern British society. Immigrant groups that have come to live in Britain since 1945 have brought many cultural traditions with them. Minority ethnic groups have to adjust their thinking to cope with a new and sometimes threatening culture. However, terms such as 'African-Caribbean' or 'Asian' mask a huge diversity of cultural traditions, forms, religions and languages.

Indigenous British society also includes a variety of ethnicities, including the Scots, Irish and Welsh, all with their own cultural values. Researchers who assume that middle-class English culture is the same as British culture have often overlooked these groups. Similarly, the family life of the wealthier classes in Britain may not reflect family life among the poorer elements of society. For instance, there is the tradition amongst upper-class British people of sending children away to a boarding school, sometimes from as young as 5 years of age. Other classes and cultures might view this arrangement with horror, despite the fact it can confer considerable educational and social advantage on the children concerned.

'Yes, a family – heterosexual couple, monogamous shared possessions, spend social time together...'

## AFRICAN-CARIBBEAN FAMILIES IN BRITAIN

In some parts of the Caribbean, society is matriarchal (based around women), a possible legacy of slavery. Other Caribbean islands have male-dominated cultures. African-Caribbean immigrants in the 1950s and later tended to carry their cultural views into Britain and reproduce their social patterns in their new country. Generally, however, Caribbean families appear to have differing approaches to family relationships depending on their attitudes, religious and political belief and their island or culture of origin. This has resulted in a very high rate of single parenthood among those of African-Caribbean ancestry. Traditionally, child-rearing is seen as a collective family responsibility, which does not necessarily end for extended relatives even after divorce ends a marriage. Berrington (1996) points out that in many African-Caribbean families males and females are in steady partnerships, care jointly for children but are in a 'visiting union', which means that they do not share a household. Mirza (1992) suggests that males are good partners, respectful of female career ambitions and supportive of their children.

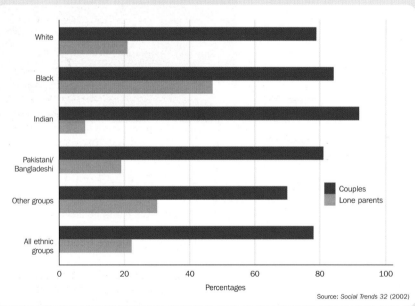

**Families with dependent children: by ethnic group (Great Britain)**

Legend: Couples / Lone parents

Percentages (x-axis: 0, 20, 40, 60, 80, 100)

Ethnic groups: White, Black, Indian, Pakistani/ Bangladeshi, Other groups, All ethnic groups

Source: *Social Trends 32* (2002)

1  Which family type is most frequent in all ethnic groups, couples or lone parents?

2  Which ethnic group had the largest percentage of lone parents?

3  Which ethnic group had the smallest percentage of lone parents?

4  What social and economic differences may exist in the category 'black', as used in the graph?

5  What social differences may exist in the category 'couple', as used in the graph?

I'm a British born Chinese person, but my parents are from Vietnam and Hong Kong. My mother was adopted into a British family, so I've got a strong British background. My grandparents are from Yorkshire. But my dad came from Vietnam. He originally studied in France but he ended up in England, he trained to be a dentist here. My parents met over here and I was born here.

Chinese family is central to Chinese culture. It's very important to have a tight extended family. I make an effort to see my parents every week and I speak to them quite regularly. An important aspect of the Chinese community is food. We love our food. It's not only a delicious feast, it's a way of meeting up with families and friends. At Chinese New Year, in Hong Kong it's a really big celebration.

Now I am older I am really proud of my Chinese identity. I think it's important that we establish not only the Chinese part of our identity but the British Chinese identity. I have my Chinese side and my English side. I feel happy that I've got two different cultures that I can glean the best bits off really.

Sarah Yeh, 28. Adapted from text on
http://www.bbc.co.uk/radio1/onelife/personal/race/audio_chinese.shtml

1 Explain two ways in which Chinese culture is similar to traditional British culture.

2 Explain the ways in which family is central to Chinese culture.

3 Evaluate the suggestion that there is a single 'British' tradition of family life.

In *Living in rural Wales* (1993), Jones points out that for Welsh speakers, cultural notions of the family and the continued existence of the Welsh language are inextricably linked. The Welsh language includes a set of values that are based on concepts of family life, hearth and home and emphasises knowledge of the Bible and local family traditions.

Mirza (1992) studied young African-Caribbean women in two London schools in the 1980s. She found that young black women were dedicated to the idea of careers in adulthood. Their own mothers worked, often as nurses or social workers, and they expected the same from life. Many black girls rejected the concept of marriage, but still expected jobs and a family. They also expected their partners to allow them to work. Mirza portrays black males and black families as being committed to equality, with males supporting female ambition.

## ETHNIC CHINESE FAMILIES IN BRITAIN

Chan and Chan (1997) suggest that the concept of family is very important in Chinese culture. Chinese couples may marry as a result of a parental arrangement, but couples also exercise personal choice of partner. It is expected that all members of the family will work to support the family economically, so males and females work together in the family business. In China, importance is placed on family honour and tradition so the family consists of parents, grandparents, uncles and aunts. Older people are perceived as having wisdom and are generally treated in a respectful manner, so Chinese children in Britain are expected to respect and obey their elders. Chinese people within Britain are often located in areas where there are few other such families. According to Smith (1991) the ethnic Chinese form nuclear families in Britain but are isolated within society. They attempt to retain social connections with family members in other areas of Britain or in the home areas, but this is difficult, especially if they are working long hours. Elderly Chinese people who have limited English and few English social connections may come to feel isolated and useless.

## ANGLO-PAKISTANI AND BANGLADESHI FAMILIES

These are generally Muslim families and so there is a strong loyalty to the principles of Islam. Families are patriarchal in structure and it is expected that females will remain domestic. However, this tradition is also being challenged by a new generation of British Asian women who are less content to live within the home. Nevertheless, male children have more freedom in the home than female children (Halstead, 1994). Marriage is seen as a union between two families, and so weddings may be arranged, sometimes within the extended family.

Beishon et al. (1998) point out that females are expected to live in the family home of the husband, and to show respect to the husband's family. In Britain, fewer families are extended or share a household, though this once would have been common. Children are an important part of family life.

## Coursework advice

If you are fortunate enough to embrace two cultures by being both British and a member of a minority ethnic group, this would be a very interesting area to study for coursework. You could investigate attitudes to family, to gender socialisation of children or to kinship. Someone who does not understand the cultural traditions of a different ethnic group should avoid this topic.

# Round-up

People from minority ethnic cultures that have become part of British society adapt to British cultural traditions, but retain features of their own family and cultural backgrounds when they form families. These vary considerably from culture to culture and also within cultures, so it can be dangerous to generalise too strongly. Nevertheless, sociologists have identified patterns that seem typical of certain ethnic groups.

✳ In an arranged marriage, partners consent to the union. In a forced marriage, one party does not agree but the wedding still takes place. Forced marriage is illegal in Britain.

# Are conjugal roles in families changing?

Just as many women began to query their traditional female roles so, too, some men in the arts and media began to challenge traditional masculinity in the 1970s

The question for sociologists is whether the challenge to male roles in the 1970s was just fashion or whether it represented a real shift in social and domestic power

Until the 1970s there was little public querying of the roles and responsibilities of men and women within the family, except perhaps by individuals such as the French feminist, Simone de Beauvoir. In families that were studied or described by mainstream writers, the roles of men and women were seen as separate. Men lived public lives based on work and social or sporting clubs where they associated with other men. Women generally lived private lives, associated with home and children. Clearly, this is an over-simplification of reality because many working-class women did in fact have paid work outside the home, but frequently their jobs reflected their domestic roles, so most were carers, cooks and cleaners.

Academic interest was sparked by a famous, but later criticised, study in 1973 made by Young and Willmot, who produced their influential book *The symmetrical family* (Young and Willmot, 1973). Young and Willmot studied young families in a suburb in London and were among the first to notice a changing pattern in conjugal relationships. They discovered that some men were helping their wives in the home. The level and quality of the support was not high, but Young and Willmot saw it as evidence of a new equality in **conjugal roles**. They developed a theory of family that suggested men and women were becoming equal in the home.

**Symmetrical family:** A family in which men and women have some degree of equality.

**Conjugal roles:** The roles played by adult males and females within a family; may be 'joint' or 'segregated'.

This view was supported by a public fashion for unisex, where clothing and hairstyles were not gendered. Pop stars such as David Bowie and the rock group Queen challenged gender specific roles with glamorous feminine styles.

This gave rise to the suggestion of **new masculinities**, that was more of a journalistic fiction than a properly researched sociological phenomenon. **New men** were believed to challenge traditional male roles and take an interest in domestic life and the home. Men undoubtedly did begin to do more in the home and many took on caring roles, but whether this was a challenge to masculinity or was simply a practical response to changing female work patterns remains a matter for debate. Wilkinson used the term 'genderquake' to describe the radical changes that she perceived as occuring between the gender roles within society. Most research in this area found that men did not in fact take on much of the **domestic labour**. Employed women were doing what was known as the '**dual shift**', working by day, and doing cleaning, cooking and childcare in the evening.

**New masculinities:** This is the change in traditional male roles whereby men are enabled to get in touch with their caring and domestic side.

**Domestic labour:** The work of the household, usually known as housework.

**New men:** A man who challenges traditional male gender roles and is willing to take on domestic and other traditionally female roles.

**Dual shift:** The work that women do in the home after they have completed paid work outside the home.

## Think it through

The author is describing a report by HMSO, the government publishers, Social focus on men (2001).

'This, the first study to focus on men's experiences of work, home, leisure and society, looks in depth at attitudes and habits. While there are encouraging signs of change – more men than ever before leave fatherhood till their mature thirties, they take better care of their health and fewer of them are the main breadwinner in their household – the report also reveals some depressingly familiar statistics. For example, despite the effects of 30 years of equality, men still outnumber women in top jobs, outstrip them in pay and fail to fully share domestic responsibilities (they play with their children for 45 minutes a night – half that of their female partners, most of whom also work).

'However, it's how men spend their leisure time that is perhaps the most interesting. They spend an average of three hours a day watching TV (favourites include football and soaps such as *EastEnders*) and listening to the radio and spend more than £10 a week on TV, video audio equipment and computers – double that of women. For reading material, the newspaper of choice is still *The Sun* (almost one-third of under 25s read it) and men are less likely than women to read a book.'

Sheppard, S. (2001) 'New Man: exploding the myth', in *National Statistics Horizons, Issue 19*, Autumn, HMSO, London

1 Explain two ways in which male roles within the household have changed.

2 Explain two ways in which male roles within the family have seen little change.

3 Evaluate the suggestion that male and female roles within the family have undergone very little change over the past 50 years.

*Go to www.statistics.gov.uk and have a look at the Bookshelf area of the National Statistics Website under Social and Welfare to see if you can find details of the Social focus on men report.*

# Important studies

Radical feminists Delphy and Leonard (1992) claimed that where a family has a male head of household, despite the relative earnings or wealth of the family, it is he who takes a dominant role. Women do not just take on domestic and childcare duties; they also fulfil a sexual and emotional role. They must support the male in his work, arrange entertainment, and flatter their husbands to keep them happy. Males, however, have more leisure, more freedom, and the best of the food and material goods. If there are two cars in the family, it is he who gets the biggest.

Beishon, Modood and Virdee (1998) discovered that amongst all minority ethnic groups, females tended to take on more responsibility for domestic labour than men. White men showed themselves to be willing to take on housework, and white households were more likely to pay for help with chores. Many men in Pakistani and Bangladeshi families felt it was a woman's duty to care for home and family, and so some were unwilling to allow their wives to work in paid employment unless it was necessary for family income.

*Barclays Bank conducted research in 1999 and found that 82% of their customers between the ages of 30 and 40, with incomes over £30 000 per year, employed domestic services rather than waste time on DIY or chores like washing or ironing. Mintel, the market research company, has identified a staggering growth in domestic services. Between 1988 and 1999 there was a 185% increase in domestic services.*

Ward, T. (2000) 'The new reserve army of domestic labour' in *Sociology Review*, Vol. 10(1), September.

* 'In 1999 the most common reason for women to be granted divorces in England and Wales was the unreasonable behaviour of the husbands'. *Social Trends 32* (2002), p. 44.

* Given that most cleaners are women, perhaps there is a class dimension to the question of adult conjugal roles. Are middle-class women relying on working-class women to take on traditional female tasks such as domestic labour?

# Round-up

There have been apparent changes in the roles of men and women within the family. It is not unusual to see males undertaking domestic roles. At the same time, females are more likely to participate in paid work outside the home. Whether these changes are due to fundamental shifts in male and female relationships within the family or whether they are a response to changes in the economics of family life remain a matter for discussion. Feminists feel that women still undertake more than their fair share of domestic responsibility.

# Are single parents a problem for society?

> ❝❝ *The lone-parent family is not in itself a problem but the term has, in a similar way to step-families, become embedded in pathology. There is a sense that both mother and child are somehow losing because they can't achieve the ideals of a nuclear family.* ❞❞
>
> Dallos and Sapsford (1997)

> ❝❝ *It is better for children to be born into a two-parent family, with both father and mother...* ❞❞
>
> Warnock Report (1984)

> ❝❝ *As men are more likely to remarry fairly soon after divorce, and as most custodial parents are mothers, the single-parent household typically consists of a custodial mother and children. For many younger women the single-parent household phase of the process is a relatively temporary, though exceedingly stressful phase, as they are more likely to remarry or find a new partner [than older women are].* ❞❞
>
> Robinson (1991)

Single parents are not a new phenomenon. There have always been single parents; it is the cause of single parenthood that has changed over the years. In the nineteenth and first half of the twentieth century, some women continued to bear children late in life and adult life expectancies were relatively short. This meant that single parents had usually experienced the death of their marriage partner.

In modern Britain, single parenthood has no single cause. People may become single parents through widowhood, separation, desertion, divorce or because they have chosen to have a child without being in a partnership. The table on the right suggests that lone mothers head 20% of all families with dependent children.

During the late 1970s, single mothers became a political debating point.

- It was widely held by politicians and some of the right-wing daily newspapers that young women were becoming single parents in order to jump housing queues for council property. In 1993, the American commentator Charles Murray actually went so far as to claim that 'the single most important social problem of our time' is illegitimacy. David Marsland has suggested that single mothers no longer need to rely on men because they survive on benefits, so they have developed a dependency culture.

- There is evidence to link single parenthood with poverty, high crime rates and delinquency. Many politicians argued that the cause of crime was the lack of male role-models in boys' lives, whereas feminists tended to argue that other causal factors, such as poverty, create both crime and single parenthood.

**Families with dependent children headed by lone parents (GB) %**

|  | 1971 | 1981 | 1991 | 1999 | 2001 |
|---|---|---|---|---|---|
| **Lone mothers** | | | | | |
| Single | 1 | 2 | 6 | 8 | 9 |
| Widowed | 2 | 2 | 1 | 1 | 1 |
| Divorced | 2 | 4 | 6 | 6 | 6 |
| Separated | 12 | 2 | 4 | 4 | 4 |
| All lone mothers | 7 | 11 | 18 | 20 | 20 |
| Lone fathers | 1 | 2 | 1 | 2 | 2 |
| **All lone parents** | 8 | 13 | 19 | 22 | 22 |

Source: *Social Trends 32* (2002)

✱ **The New Right** is a political philosophy associated with conservatism in politics and which reasserts traditional Christian family values. This view had some influence in the 1970s and 1980s but less now.

 *A variety of sites offer holidays and services to one-parent families, which is an indication of the growing size of the market. Gingerbread* **www.gingerbread.org.uk**, *a political pressure group, serves the interests of single-parent families and their children. Also* **www.oneparentfamilies.org.uk** *offers help and advice to single parents.*

## POSSIBLE CAUSES FOR THE STATISTICAL LINK BETWEEN SINGLE PARENTHOOD AND PERCEIVED SOCIAL PROBLEMS

- Many single parents experience poverty as most of them are female, and female average earnings tend to be lower than male average earnings.

- There may have been dysfunctional adult relationships and quarrelling before the separation, which created disturbed vulnerable children.

- Family abuse and violence may have occurred before the family breakdown.

- Many families that separate come from lower social classes and there is a known link between social class, school underachievement and criminal behaviours.

- In some African-Caribbean cultures, there is a tradition of single parenthood, with mothers actively choosing to raise children without a father. There is also a known link between ethnicity, school underachievement and criminal behaviours among males. However, it is difficult to claim that anti-social behaviour is purely the result of single parenthood when African-Caribbeans may also have been adversely affeced by racism.

Are unmarried mothers a problem for society?

## ECONOMIC ARGUMENTS USED IN THE LONE-PARENT DEBATE

In 2002, published government statistics showed that:

- social-security and benefit payments cost taxpayers £115 billion
- education cost £54 billion
- health and social services cost £65 billion.

Those three large government departments spend over half of the total public spending of £418 billion of this country, a fall since 1997 when they accounted for two-thirds of public spending.

A common media stereotype of the 1980s and 1990s depicted selfish young women having children and costing taxpayers money through benefit payments. However, Allen, Bourke Dowling with Rolfe (1998) found that most teenage mothers they interviewed had become pregnant by accident, but that they had been under pressure from their partners to keep the child. Many of these partners subsequently severed the relationships and had little contact with the baby they had fathered.

### Who is poor in modern Britain?

| | Total number (million) | Proportion poor (%) | Number in poverty (million) |
|---|---|---|---|
| Adult women | 22.2 | 24 | 5.3 |
| Children | 13.0 | 35 | 4.5 |
| Adult men | 21.1 | 20 | 4.2 |
| Elderly | 9.8 | 31 | 3.0 |
| Lone-parent family | 4.3 | 63 | 2.9 |
| Unemployed | 4.6 | 78 | 2.3 |
| All | 2.9 | 25 | 14.1 |

Source: *Sociology Review* (Sept 2000)

This table shows that there is a very high proportion of lone-parent families who experience poverty. What other patterns relevant to the study of the family and households can you see from studying this table?

### Childhood poverty

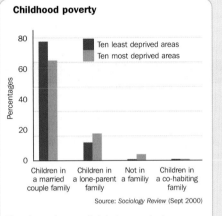

Source: *Sociology Review* (Sept 2000)

The chart shows a link between single parenthood and poverty, but does single parenthood cause poverty and a culture of welfare dependency, as the New Right suggest?

### Who do children talk to?

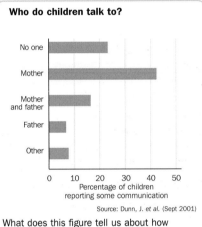

Source: Dunn, J. *et al.* (Sept 2001)

What does this figure tell us about how children communicate with each parent?

## Think it through

### Child Support Agency

*Our Vision*
- To deliver an excellent child support service to help reduce child poverty.

*Our Mission*
- Putting children first by ensuring parents meet their maintenance responsibilities.

*Our Values*
To continuously improve by:
- Giving an excellent service to every customer.
- Involving, investing in and dealing fairly with our people.
- Enhancing our performance by working effectively without our partners and resources.

*Our Aims*
Here are our main aims:
- To make accurate maintenance assessments, ensure payments are regular, and to take action to enforce paments where necessary.
- To provide a fair and efficient service that is easy for people to get access to.
- To provide clear, accurate and up-to-date information about the child maintenance system.
- To establish and maintain effective working relationships with the courts, advice agencies, customer representative groups and other organisations who are interested in our work.
- To help the Department for Work and Pensions to evaluate and develop child support policy and to make sure that we can respond effectively to change.
- To use our resources efficiently and effectively.

We also:
- trace and contact non-resident parents
- sort out paternity disputes when a man denies he is a child's father
- collect and pass on maintenance payments, taking action to make the non-resident parent pay if necessary
- deal with applications for departures from the formal assessment formula
- where appropriate, prepare and present appeals to be heard by the Independent Child Support Appeal Tribunal Service
- work with the Benefits Agency in cases where clients receive social security benefits to ensure correct payments and protect against fraud.

Child Support Agency, www.csa.gov.uk

1 What is the stated aim of the Child Support Agency?

2 How does the CSA expect to meet its aim?

3 Which government agencies work with the CSA?

4 Evaluate the suggestion that males who refuse to support their children create problems for society.

## Round-up

It is difficult to prove the idea that lone parents are a problem for society as a result of their single-parent status. Much debate has been clouded by ideological views of the nuclear family as being the best form of family. In addition, there are claims that single parents are somehow inadequate because their children may experience school failure and engage in criminal activity. There are economic issues for the government as well, because providing money to support lone parents through benefits is expensive.

# What are the patterns of divorce in Britain?

## Marriage

A marriage is a legal contract between two people. A divorce is the legal termination of such a contract. Marriages can also be 'annulled'(cancelled), but for this to happen it has to be proved that the marriage was not actually legal when it took place and that therefore the partners are not bound by a legal contract of marriage. The traditional Christian view of marriage suggests that divorce is not morally acceptable. Many Christian churches still refuse to allow couples a religious ceremony if one or both of them has been previously divorced. Until the second part of the twentieth century, many people saw a divorce as a matter of social shame and stigma. However, there has been a massive shift in norms and values in the past 50 years so that divorce, while still seen as a personal misfortune, is no longer regarded as a source of disgrace or dishonour.

**Marriages and divorces**

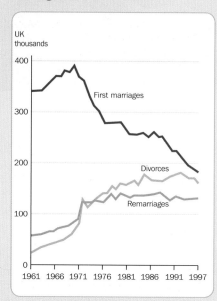

Source: *Social Trends 30*, p. 37

This graph shows that there have been significant changes in patterns of marriage, divorce and remarriage in Britain over the past 40 years. The task of the sociologist is to identify these patterns of change and to suggest reasons for them.

| Changes in divorce legislation – a historical overview | |
| --- | --- |
| Before 1857 | Divorce was only allowed by Act of Parliament and was thereby restricted to the wealthy and powerful. |
| 1857 Matrimonial Causes Act | Divorce was allowed in a Court of Law in England and Wales. Men had to prove adultery to obtain divorce, but women had to prove cruelty or desertion as well as adultery. Expensive legal procedures. |
| 1923 Divorce Reform Act | This allowed wives to divorce husbands for adultery alone. |
| 1937 Divorce Reform Act | Desertion, cruelty and insanity were added to adultery as legal grounds for divorce. |
| 1949 Legal Aid and Advice Act | Legal aid was made available for divorce proceedings. |
| 1969 Divorce Reform Act | 'Irretrievable breakdown' of marriage became the sole grounds for divorce. Evidence can be adultery, desertion, unreasonable behaviour, or separation (two years when both want divorce, five years if one does not). |
| 1984 Matrimonial and Family Proceedings Act | Divorce possible after one year of marriage rather than three. |
| 1996 Family Law Act | Divorce allowed even when there is no evidence that marriage has broken down. 'Cooling off', mediation and conciliation meetings encouraged. Not fully implemented. |

## Divorce

### Long-term trends

The overall trend in the twentieth century was for the number of divorces per thousand marriages to increase. There are several possible reasons for this.

- *Changes in divorce law* – divorce-law reform has generally made divorce more accessible to larger numbers of people.

- **Secularisation** *of marriage* – fewer people feel bound by traditional Christian teaching with regard to divorce.

- *Changes in the economic status of women* – women no longer require marriage as a means of economic support; other sources of income are now available to them through work or the welfare benefits system.

- *Changes in womens' expectations of marriage* – abusive relationships may have been tolerated in the past because people had fewer options; today, people know that they do not have to stay in situations that they find unbearable.

**Watch out**

It is tempting to see increasing divorce rates as evidence that marriages are not as successful as they were in the past, but this is not an acceptable argument for an examination answer. We know little about the quality of married couples' relationships in the past, because divorce was not a very easy option if a marriage failed. Your exam answers should therefore focus on the social reasons why divorce is taking place rather than the personal reasons.

 The term 'secularisation' is used to describe the gradual loss of formal religious belief from society.

## Recent trends

Throughout the 1990s, the Office for National Statistics has reported a decrease both in the number of divorces and in the divorce rate. They suggest that this is because there has been a decrease in the number of first marriages, which are significantly more likely than remarriages to end in divorce.

## Cohabitation

Norms and values are changing and more unmarried couples are living together (cohabiting). As a result of this, divorce statistics have become less valid as a measure of the number of relationships that break down, because cohabiting couples do not have to seek a divorce.

### Decrees absolute (divorces), England and Wales

| Year | Divorces (thousands) |
| --- | --- |
| 1993 (peak) | 165 018 |
| 1999 | 144 556 |
| 2000 | 141 135 |

Source: adapted from *Population Trends 109* (2002)

## Think it through

Research over 25 years suggests that the vast majority of children whose parents divorce suffer no long-term damage. E. Mavis Hetherington, professor emeritus at the University of Virginia, is touring America this weekend with this analysis from her best-selling book *For Better or Worse: Divorce Reconsidered*.

Ask an adult why they are disturbed and they often attribute their state, criminality or ill-health to divorced parents. But, by tracking 2500 people in 1400 families from childhood, Hetherington has been able to analyse not just outcomes but exact causes. Her data includes not only statistical information but tens of thousands of hours of 'secret' videotape of families at dinner, relaxing or fighting their ways through trauma and rows.

Hetherington concludes that almost four out of five children of divorce function well, with little long-term damage. Within two years, the vast majority are beginning to 'function reasonably well'. Perhaps just as important, 70 per cent of divorced parents are happier after the divorce than they were before.

Adapted from: Vulliamy, E. and Summerskill, B. (2002) 'D-I-V-O-R-C-E', *The Observer*, Sunday 27 January

1 Outline the main findings of Hetherington's research.

2 Suggest two reasons why some people regard divorce as evidence of a breakdown in society.

3 Outline and evaluate the view that divorce statistics no longer reflect the number of broken or unsatisfactory relationships in British society.

 http://www.fnf.org.uk/ *Families Need Fathers is a voluntary self-help society providing advice and support on children's issues from a masculine perspective.*
http://www.womensaid.org.uk/ *Women's Aid is a national charity that promotes the protection of women and children experiencing domestic violence. It takes a woman's perspective.*
http://www.adviceguide.org.uk *The Citizens Advice Bureau offer excellent fact sheets providing legal information about issues related to family, marriage and divorce, from the legal perspective.*

## DIVORCE IN THE UK

- The average duration of a marriage is approximately 10 years.
- Just over half of all divorcing couples have dependent children under 16 years of age.
- The average age of divorce is between 25 and 29 years, but is rising. This is probably because the age of first marriage is also rising.
- Couples from the lower socio-economic groups are more likely to divorce than those in higher groups.
- Couples who marry when the bride is under 20 are more likely to divorce.
- Cohabiting couples are more likely to split up than married couples.

### Grounds for divorce in 1997

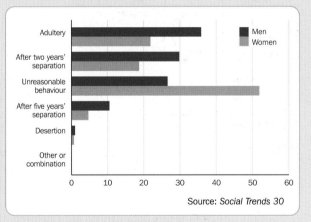

Source: *Social Trends 30*

What are the differences between male and female grounds for divorce?

# Round-up

**Long-term trends show that there has been a steady increase in the number of divorces. There are a number of reasons for this pattern, which relate to changing norms and values in society as well as changes in the law. Recently, the number of divorces has fallen. We know relatively little about what prompts marriage breakdown. As fewer couples choose to marry, divorce statistics are becoming a less reliable measure of the quality of relationships or the number of 'broken families'.**

# How are parent–child relationships changing in British society?

## Researching childhood

Legally, a 'child' is anyone under the age of 18. Another term for anyone under the age of 18 is 'minor'.

The term 'child' may also denote the social relationship of son or a daughter. Adults may still be children to their living parents and owe them special duties and responsibilities.

The relationship between a parent and a child is one of the most intimate areas of family life. It lies at the very core of what makes people a family, and yet it is a curiously under-researched area of social relationship. The difficulty is that the best sociological methods for understanding the meanings that people attach to family life are qualitative: observations, focus groups and unstructured interviews – and these all involve some intrusion into what is a very private area of social life. Also, the parent–child relationship involves strong emotions. Adults may not be reliable informants because they may misremember or misrepresent the events of their childhood. Children are often unable to rationalise or fully explain their emotions. Finally, it is extremely difficult to generalise from the very small samples that qualitative studies normally use.

The most frequently quoted study of childhood is the much-contested, socio-historical study by Philip Aries (1962). In his study, Aries claims that childhood as a separate status did not exist in Europe until relatively recently. This book is now over 40 years old but has not yet been replaced by a modern theory of childhood and childrearing. In Britain, the study of childhood is often related to pathological (damaged) families and those that are seen as unusual or abnormal. This means that the children studied are not typical of all children, but have experienced stress and family disruption. Other studies look at single aspects of childhood; for instance, Iona and Peter Opie investigated the playground games and culture of childhood in a series of texts and studies in the 1960s and 1970s (e.g. Opie and Opie, 1969).

### Changing childhood

There are clear changes in parent–child relationships:

- The parent–child relationship is extending beyond what would have been expected 60 years ago, when working-class children began work at 14 and contributed to family income. The raising of the school-leaving age and the significance of education and training means that many people are economically dependent on their parents beyond formal adulthood at 18 years old.

- Increasingly, as life expectancies are extending, adult children may find themselves caring for their own ageing parents – a burden that typically falls on daughters, who may themselves be working or taking responsibility for their children and grandchildren.

- Where both parents are employed, they may find it difficult to spend time with their children. Where neither parent is employed, or the family income is low, parents will have little money to spend on their children.

- Parental fears over child safety mean that many children spend more time supervised and indoors than would have been the case before road traffic was heavy and the well-publicised cases of child abduction have led parents to be concerned about 'stranger danger'.

- Children are now more exposed to the media than was the case before the advent of television, video and computer technology. It is possible that, for some children, parents are a less significant agent of socialisation than once would have been the case. This is a view put forward by the feminist, Beatrix Campbell (1993), who suggests that boys in single-parent families are learning a model of aggressive masculinity drawn from action movies.

Parents may be money-rich but time-poor, or time-rich and money-poor.

It is easy to assume that the parent–child relationship applies only to people under the age of 18. Remember that in many families, 'children' may be pensioners in their sixties or seventies who are providing care for older, living dependent parents.

harry venning

www.jrf.org.uk, the website of the Joseph Rowntree Foundation, contains useful information related to a variety of social issues. Use the search engine to research parents and children.

# Important studies

Philippe Aries (1962) claimed that childhood is a social construction that has developed relatively recently in Western society. Children were once perceived as being small adults; they dressed as adults did and often worked with adults on farms and in factories. Childhood as a 'special' period of life was an invention of the Victorian middle class who displayed sentimentality in their attitudes towards their own children. Nevertheless, working-class children were still employed as servants, in factories and mines. While the evidence Aries used has been criticised as being limited, the general thesis has been accepted as a sound one.

In the 1950s and 1960s, John and Elizabeth Newson (1968) interviewed large samples of parents and found evidence of differences between the social classes in child-rearing practice. Similar findings were made by Davie et al. in a famous longitudinal study, From birth to seven (1972). Both studies were concerned with social class; however, these studies found evidence that middle-class parents had different values (and used different techniques in the socialisation of their offspring) to those of working-class parents. For instance, the Newsons suggested they tended to be more verbal in their relationships with their children, talking through issues such as behaviour and attitudes.

Gillies et al. (2001), in their studies of teenage children, suggested that while many families experience difficulties when children go through adolescence, most of their study samples felt that family relationships underwent positive changes focused on companionship and responsibility as the children grew to adulthood and family relationships took account of the growing maturity of the children.

## Think it through

### CHILDREN'S SPEAKING SKILLS IN DECLINE

Some would blame the parents, others the Teletubbies. Either way, children arriving at nursery school have apparently shown a marked deterioration in their speaking and listening skills in the past five years.

Three out of four headteachers who responded to a survey, run jointly by the National Literacy Trust and the National Association of Head Teachers said they were concerned about the lack of language ability among three-year-olds. The headteachers pinned most of the blame for the decline on the time

children spent watching TV and video games. They said this detracted from the time children spent talking to their parents, interacting with them and learning to engage in imaginative play.

Neil McClelland, director of the trust, said: 'There is a concern here that children are coming into early-years classes less able to listen to each other and speak and we feel that is an issue we must tackle.'

'I don't want to give the impression that all TV and video games are bad but I do want parents to communicate

with their children more instead of just putting them in front of the TV and leaving them there.'

He urged parents to buy spin-off books from children's TV programmes and read them to their children if they had shown an interest in the show. He added: 'The right to be talked to and listened to should be the right of every toddler. Most brain development occurs between birth and the age of two so babies and toddlers need a quality linguistic environment just as much as they need nourishing food.'

Source: Garner, R., Education Editor (2002), 'Children's speaking skills in decline', The Guardian, 3 August

1 Explain two reasons why many headteachers feel that children's linguistic skills are in decline.

2 Explain two ways in which parents can support their children in the development of linguistic skills.

3 Describe and discuss how children's status within the family has changed over the past 50 years.

> **"** Parental identities based on being needed and wanted can be a source of purpose and satisfaction. So teenagers' growing independence can herald an 'identity crisis' for parents. **"**
>
> Langford, W., Lewis, C., Solomon, Y. and Warin, J. (2001) Family understandings: Closeness, authority and independence in families with teenagers, Joseph Rowntree Foundation and Family Policy Studies Institute, London, p. 26

# Round-up

Parent–child relationships are under-researched in Britain, despite being at the core of family structure. There are practical and ethical reasons for this shortage of knowledge. Nevertheless, the changes that have taken place in family structure and the economic life of people in Britain have clearly had an impact on nature and quality of family life, both for children at the start of their lives and for adult children who must care for parents at the end of their lives.

# What impact does an ageing population have on family relationships?

Concepts such as 'ageing' and 'elderly' are social constructions. This means that they are not fixed by biology but are defined by social customs and practice. Just as there is no clear point at which childhood ends, so there is no defining age at which one becomes old.

## An ageing population

- More people in the UK are living longer. In 1901, 1.7 million people were over the age of 65. By 2001, males over 65 and females over 60 totalled 10.8 million, from a total UK population of 58.8 million.

- The proportion of people aged over 60 is growing, from 16% in 1951 to 21% in 2001.

- Those over retirement age are sometimes divided into two groups. Those at the younger end of old age may well be fit, healthy and actively pursuing hobbies and activities. The 'elderly old' (often defined as those over 85) are more likely to be unwell or disabled. They may have become dependent on the State or on relatives to support them.

- There are more 'elderly old'. In 1984, 6.3% of the population was aged 75 and over; by 1999 this figure had risen to 7.3%. In 2001, 1.9% of the population was aged 85 and over (that's 1.1 million people), compared to 0.4% (0.2 million) in 1951.

- This increase in the proportion of older people means that in 2001, for the first time, there were more people aged over 60 in the UK (21%) than there were children under 16 (20% – a fall from 24% in 1951).

Many of the elderly come from minority ethnic backgrounds. Their expectations of old age may be different from those of the wider population. They may have specific needs that are not being met by the general provision made by social services.

## Ageing and the family

Old age need not be a social problem. Many older people continue with work, education and leisure activities and are able to support their children through services such as child-minding and baby-sitting. Many devote time to socially valued activities such as voluntary work for charities and in education. Friendship groups and reunion societies are popular with those in the 'Third Age'. They have time, money and liberty to spend on holidays and consumer goods. Many older people have realistic expectations of healthy and valuable family lives in their retirement.

Retirement is often called the 'Third Age', as in 'the University of the Third Age'.

However, there are serious social implications arising from the increase in the number and proportion of older people in the British population. Almost every study conducted on poverty has suggested that the retired population is vulnerable to poverty. In addition, the elderly old are more liable to experience ill-health and disability than the younger old. Dementia affects approximately 20% of people over 85 years of age. (Dementias, of which Alzheimer's is probably the best known, are physical diseases that can damage a person's ability to learn and destroy short-term memory. These are very disabling conditions.)

This gives rise to concerns for families.

- Care for the elderly can be expensive, with fees for some nursing homes being well over £1000 a month. Those elderly people who have assets over £16 000 must pay for their own care. If they have property such as a house that they wish to pass on to their children, they may have to sell it in order to pay for private care.

- The elderly old may not have the same access to friendship groups and networks that younger people are able to arrange for themselves. As a result, some of the elderly may experience social exclusion and isolation. This is a particular concern for those who do not have family members living nearby.

- Many of those who care for the elderly are themselves no longer young. In 1995, 27% of carers who devoted over 20 hours a week to caring were themselves over 65 years old. Marriage partners may care for a sick husband or wife but, with increasing age, older people may be cared for by their own children who are themselves past retirement age.

- Older people are not spread evenly throughout the country and there are high concentrations in certain parts of the country. Eversley (1984) points out that the south coast of England is a 'geriatric ward' because it is attractive as a retirement area. The 2001 Census shows that Worthing is the local authority with the largest proportion of elderly old, at 4.6%. Family members may not live close enough to elderly relatives to give active support.

- The burden of caring often falls to women. In 1990, the Equal Opportunities Commission pointed out that 66% of carers are female, though men can be supportive and can also be the main carer. Coote *et al*. (1990) estimate that 25% of middle-aged women are supporting a dependent adult with no financial support from the government. Caring may reduce a person or a family to poverty, particularly if they are relying on state benefits and pensions to survive. As families are smaller and the elderly are living for longer, some children will be caring for demented or sick parents over long periods of time, when they themselves have retired from full-time work.

There is no defining the age at which one becomes old

www.ace.org.uk, the website of Age Concern, contains a remarkable amount of helpful information.

## Think it through

Any changes to the supply of unpaid care could have important effects on the demand for paid care and thus the cost to individuals or the State. By unpaid care we mean care and support from family, relatives and friends, which, in terms of hours (and perhaps in terms of monetary value), far exceeds what the state and individuals provide by way of paid-for care. It is sometimes assumed that Government can influence the supply of unpaid care by taking certain measures to ensure that families and relatives care for their older people. However, in a free society a Government can do little... to influence the way in which families or relatives decide whether to care for their older members...

There are about 5.7 million people providing some hours of informal care, most of whom will be caring for older people. Most carers spend no more than about 4 hours a week providing unpaid care, but about 800 000 people provide unpaid care for 50 hours a week or more. More women than men provide informal care. People aged between 45 and 64 comprise the single largest group of unpaid carers. The largest group providing unpaid care is those providing help to their parents or their parents-in-law...

...There is genuine concern about the effects on the supply of unpaid care because of changes in family structure brought about by falls in birth rates, higher divorce rates, re-marriage, greater family mobility and less living together of families across generations.

*Adapted from: Sutherland, Professor Sir Stewart, Chairman (March 1999)*
*With respect to old age: Long-term care – Rights and responsibilities –*
*A Report by the Royal Commission on Long Term Care, HMSO, London*

1 Outline the typical social characteristics of a family carer of an elderly person.

2 Suggest three ways in which family members who care for the elderly are supporting the State through their actions.

3 Evaluate the suggestion that, as family structures change, the State will have to take on a greater role in the care of the elderly sick and disabled.

## Watch out

When writing about older people, be careful to avoid stereotyping them all as infirm and dependent. While many elderly people are on low incomes, and a substantial minority needs to be cared for, the majority are healthier and wealthier than ever before.

# Round-up

For many people in Britain, retirement can be a positive and active experience, when they can give support and help to their adult children and grandchildren. However, the very old may become vulnerable to sickness and ill health. As the population of Britain ages and the proportion of older people in the population expands, the burden of their care increasingly falls on families, often women who are themselves also working and no longer young. As families change, many of the elderly infirm may not have younger family members to care for them in their old age.

# What about violent or abusive families?

Families are not always a safe haven

Families can sometimes be difficult and dangerous places.

- People who die violently are most likely to die at the hands of someone that they know.

- Selbourne (1993) points out that the largest category of murder victims in most years is children under the age of 5 years, at the hands of a family member. The figure has remained static at about 80 children a year since 1985.

- Women's Aid groups estimate that a woman dies every three days at the hands of a partner.

In the past, much domestic violence and abuse would have been accepted or ignored, primarily because women and children had very little power, socially, legally or financially. The situation has changed radically for women, who are now in a position to make choices, although many victims still remain silent for many years. It is now more common to speak in public of domestic violence and it has become a soap-opera storyline. However, the focus on women as the victims of domestic violence masks the true picture of abuse and violence, which is more complex.

There is a variety of forms of abuse within families.

- Sexual abuse is sexual activity that occurs between close family members, particularly between adults and children.

- Neglect is when a person's physical needs for food, cleanliness or warmth are ignored.

- Physical abuse is also known as domestic violence and refers to actual physical harm, which one family member may inflict on another.

- Emotional abuse is more difficult to define, but refers to how family members may seek to dominate others through constant ridicule, shaming, rejection, or terrorising.

Feminists suggest that it is men who commit domestic violence and abuse because they are able to exert power over weaker women and children. In reality, the picture is more complex than this. There is evidence that some older people suffering from dementia are subject to violence, neglect and abuse by their relatives. Women can be violent and abusive towards men and towards their children. The sociological debates are clouded by emotionalism and fear.

## WHAT IS ABUSE AND WHAT IS VIOLENCE?

'Abuse' is a term that is difficult to operationalise. However, a working definition is that it is behaviour that satisfies the person doing it, but upsets, hurts and offends the person to whom it is done.

'Domestic violence is physical, psychological, sexual or financial violence that takes place within an intimate or family-type relationship and forms a pattern of coercive and controlling behaviour. Crime statistics and research both show that domestic violence is gender specific – usually the perpetrator of a pattern of repeated assaults is a man.'

www.womensaid.org.uk

In everyday terms, 'violence' tends to mean physical violence. However, women's groups define violence more broadly, using it to include behaviours that others might call abuse.

This debate about the use of words reflects wider disagreements and conflicts in this area of sociology.

Of all crimes reported to the British Crime Survey 2000, more than 1 in 20 were classified as domestic violence. (Source: Women's Aid website)

According to a WHO report, among women aged 15–44 years gender violence accounts for more death and disability than cancer, malaria, traffic injuries or war put together. (Source: website of the International Planned Parenthood Federation www.ippf.org/resource/gbv)

Coursework advice Despite the fascination that many have with questions of violence and abuse, first-hand research of those who have experienced violence and abuse is not an appropriate area for coursework. There are far too many ethical issues for a novice sociologist to handle and this is an area best left to those with experience and expertise in the study of family relationships. However, a review of secondary data, both qualitative and quantitative, might form the basis of a coursework project.

# Important studies

Hester and Radford (1996), in their studies of domestic violence and the law, suggested that not only did traditional patterns of male dominance in families still exist but that The Children Act of 1989 (enforced 1991) reinforces traditional beliefs about family life and family values. When divorce had taken place because of male violence towards the woman, this was not taken into account when making custody and access arrangements for children. Males were therefore able to continue abusing and controlling their ex-wives and partners beyond the end of the marriage.

Lockhurst (1999), in his studies of male survivors of domestic violence, suggests that, because males are traditionally seen as controlling and aggressive, the problem of woman-on-man violence is underestimated, under-researched and underfunded. He claims that feminists have dominated the research so that only women are seen as victims of domestic violence.

## Research issues

It is difficult to operationalise the concept of domestic violence. For example, most people in England accept the smacking of children for disciplinary reasons, but some European countries (e.g. Norway) ban this altogether and regard some English behaviour towards children as cruel and abusive. There are also qualitative differences in what may count as violent abuse. A severe beating is easy to classify as violence; however, is a slap always evidence of violence? Emotional abuse is even more difficult to define and has been claimed by men as a defence in trials when they have killed their wives.

## Think it through

### BRITISH ASIAN MARRIAGES SCARRED BY RISING ABUSE

The first national symposium on domestic violence in minority communities was told this week that growing numbers of third and fourth-generation British Indians and Pakistanis were sliding into depression or attempting suicide to escape their daily torment.

The suicide rate among British Asian women who suffer domestic abuse is two to three times greater than for non-Asian victims and there is growing depression and isolation. Attempts to escape the abuse, which in some cases included genital mutilation and assaults from the extended family, had seen women being traced and murdered by their families.

Research by Blackburn with Darwen Council, where about 19 per cent of the 137 000-strong population is from an ethnic minority, revealed the extent of the problem. Ghazala Sulaman-Butt, a policy officer, interviewed about 100 Asian women, many of whom were severely depressed and isolated after enduring psychological, physical and sexual violence. None was prepared to speak out for fear of bringing shame to the family izaat, or honour, which renders broken marriages taboo. Mrs Sulaman-Butt said: 'Domestic abuse is a feature of every community and is fast escalating within the Asian communities... culture and tradition plays a major part in the survivor's decision to tolerate the abuse.

'Such is the power of izaat that women have committed suicide or attempted suicide rather than leave an abusive relationship.'

1 Explain and discuss the term 'domestic violence'.

2 Suggest why some people find it difficult to believe that males can be the victims of domestic violence.

3 Evaluate the view that domestic violence is a female problem.

Source: Akbar, A. (2002) 'British Asian marriages scarred by rising abuse', *The Independent*, 12 October

## Round-up

'Violence' and 'abuse' are difficult terms to define, but their existence within some families means that the family is not always a safe haven for its members. The privacy and intimacy of family life can be a source of danger to the vulnerable and weak, who may experience abuse, but be powerless to protect themselves. Sociological studies of domestic violence have usually been carried out by women. However, to view only women and children as the victims of abuse is to underestimate the complexity of domestic violence and abuse.

# How do government policies affect families?

B ritain, unlike some other European countries, has no Minister for the Family, but the law has always influenced family life, both directly and indirectly.

## Direct influences

- Laws determine whom we may marry, the age we may marry, how many people we may marry, and how a marriage can be ended. A marriage certificate is evidence of a formal contract between two people, which can be ended only by law. This legislation is based on Christian morality.
- Laws affect a family's income, both through benefits such as Child Benefit and through taxation such as the allowances for married couples and for children. Laws determine the public services available for families and children, such as childcare, health and social services and community care.
- Laws influence behaviour within families, including the nature of the relationship between husband and wife (e.g. marital rape is now illegal), sexual behaviour, abortion, and the protection of children against violence and neglect.
- Recent laws have made parents responsible for the criminal actions of their children.
- **Custody** laws in the event of separation and divorce enable some parents to maintain contact, or ensure that they make financial provision for their children.
- Adoption and fostering laws and regulations govern the right of adults to take parental responsibility for a child who is not biologically their own.

Custody: Rules that govern the rights of a parent or other carer with regard to a child.

## Indirect influences

Laws aimed primarily at other areas of social life may also affect families. In fact, it is hard to think of any area of policy that doesn't affect the family in some way.

- *Housing*, e.g. government policy on the balance between private- and public-sector housing will particularly affect low-income families.
- *Education*, e.g. types of school provided affect parental choice in selecting schools.
- *Health*, e.g. laws will affect the right to obtain *in-vitro* fertilisation or to use reproductive technology.
- *Transport*, e.g. the provision of public transport will affect job opportunities and, therefore, family incomes.
- *Employment*, e.g. people are affected by rules about maternity leave, or the hours that young people can work.

## What is 'family policy'?

New Right: A political philosophy that emphasises traditional moral and social values, particularly with regard to the family.

While governments of all parties claim to value the family, the Conservative government policies of the 1980s and 1990s were influenced by **New Right** political beliefs, which attach great importance to the family. The resulting policies have

Alan and Judith Kilshaw paid £8 200 to adopt twin babies from the USA, via the internet. However, the children were returned to the USA as a result of legal action by another couple, who had also paid money to the birth mother. To what extent should the government intervene to control and legislate for such activity?

- Changes in the law over the past 150 years reflect changing perceptions of families and family life. Women and children are no longer seen as the property of the man, but as independent people with rights within the family. Women can control their own financial affairs.

- Non-married partners have similar but not the same rights and responsibilities as those of married partners.

- Legislation has extended into what were previously seen as areas of private life where government had no business to intervene.

Nearly 35 000 children were placed on local child protection registers in March 1995. This amounts to 0.35% of all children under 18 years of age. The Government protects these children, in theory, from abuse by neglect, violence, emotional damage and sexual exploitation via the efforts of social services departments. (Alcock, P., Erskine, A. and May, M. (1998) *The student's companion to social policy*, Blackwell, Oxford)

been continued – albeit in a much-modified form – by the post-1997 Labour governments, which continue to attach importance to the family but have taken a rather more flexible approach to policy-making.

New Right thinking affected Conservative government legislation in various ways.

- A belief in traditional family values led to legislation that emphasised parental responsibilities. For example, the Child Support Agency was set up in 1991 to encourage parents to provide financial support for children in the event of marriage break-up. This also had an impact on criminal laws, which made parents responsible if their children were implicated in delinquent behaviours.

- Government agencies were given power to intervene in situations where children are endangered or in need of protection. For instance, there are regulations governing the role of schools in the case of children who are 'cared for' by social services. Sometimes these rules are affected by ideologies of family that may be considered partiarchal or Christian in ethos.

- There was concern about the role of the biological family. The New Right had a genuine desire to see the rights of birth parents extended, so The Children Act of 1989 gives fathers the right of access in the case of relationship breakdown between parents. This has been controversial – fathers who physically and emotionally abuse mothers still have the right of access to their children. Adopted children have had the right to access archive material in order to contact birth parents since 1975. Biological parents may soon have the right to access records related to children they gave up for adoption.

- There has been a growing concern with the rights of children, which is not just an element of New Right thinking, but part of a growing global concern enshrined in the United Nations Convention on the Rights of the Child, adopted in 1989. This has meant that institutions such as schools and local authorities are encouraged to set up youth forums and student councils. Children are now consulted on their wishes by social service departments responsible for their welfare.

## Think it through

### ADOPTION BOOST FOR GAY COUPLES

THE GOVERNMENT TODAY promised MPs a free vote in the Commons about whether to allow unmarried and gay couples to adopt children.

Although single people and unmarried couples, including homosexuals, are now regularly approved to adopt, only one partner can be registered as the child's legal guardian, leaving the other with no legal rights as a parent.

[The Health Secretary] Alan Milburn told MPs during Commons question time: 'The government's objective is to increase the number of children who have the opportunity, through adoption, to grow up as part of a loving, stable and permanent family.'

If the measures were passed by MPs in a free vote it would be up to the courts and adoption agencies to decide who would be suitable to adopt, he explained.

Adapted from: *The Guardian*, 7 May 2002
(http://society.guardian.co.uk/adoption/story)

1 Outline the proposed changes in the law governing the adoption of children by gay and unmarried couples.

2 Suggest two reasons why some people regard these changes in the law as necessary.

3 Outline and evaluate the view that governments can have a significant impact on the family lives of people in Britain.

### THE LAW DOES NOT SUPPORT ALL KINDS OF FAMILY RELATIONSHIPS

There are areas where the law appears to fail certain kinds of families. For instance, the extended family is often disregarded by legislation. There has been some debate about the rights of grandparents to maintain contact in the event of family breakdown or adoption of their grandchildren away from the family. The issues are serious enough for interest and pressure groups to develop in this area. The Children Act allows eligible relatives to apply for access orders, but in practice, this does not always happen. Tax incentives and pension laws seem to benefit people who choose to remain single. Feminists also point out that legislation seems to assume that women are the primary carers for children by offering them maternity leave, but not encouraging fathers to spend time with young children.

## Round-up

**Government policies can affect families in two ways. There are direct laws (affecting family structure) and indirect legislation (relating to education, social services, benefits and the economy), which also has an impact on family life and relationships. Political and ideological beliefs about the nature of the family underlie much government legislation and there is often an assumption that men are breadwinners and women are carers, which does not reflect the reality of the lives of many people in modern Britain.**

www.ncb.org.uk, the National Children's Bureau website, includes a list of recent legislation that impacts upon the child in British society.

# Do families have a future?

FAMILIES AND HOUSEHOLDS

**One of the oldest communes in Britain is the Findhorn community in Scotland, founded in 1962 (www.findhorn.org).**

In the 1970s there was a serious debate both in sociology and in the media, which suggested that the family as a social institution was dying. Rising divorce rates, changing sexual morality and increasing single parenthood through choice suggested that people were looking for alternative lifestyles that did not include traditional family life. A number of young professional people in European countries set up communes of various kinds and there was a fascination with the Jewish **kibbutz** system of communal family living.

Criticisms of the traditional family came from a number of directions.

**Feminism:** A theoretical perspective adopted mostly by women, which sees females as being oppressed by a patriarchal society.

- **Feminists** saw the family as a social institution that trapped women into a culture run by and for the benefit of men. There was political pressure to recognise that women and their children experienced unacceptable violence in the home. Radical feminists advocated lesbian lifestyles as being a political choice freeing women from the oppression of men, rather than as a response to a felt sexuality. Liberal feminists pointed out that women in marriage were likely to experience depression and had higher suicide rates than unmarried women.

- Marxists saw traditional families as reflecting the capitalist structures of society. Men viewed their wives as property. Children would inherit the wealth accumulated during lifetimes of work. In addition, the family reinforced false social values that produced a conformist workforce in order to labour in factories.

- Radical psychiatrists such as Laing (1960) and Cooper (1970) argued that family life literally made people mad. They saw **schizophrenia** as a rational response to the unnatural pressures of life in a nuclear family.

**Schizophrenia does not mean 'split personality'. Look this word up in a psychology textbook to find out its real meaning.**

During the 1980s New Right thinkers argued that the family as we know it could die out and believed that this was a serious threat to individuals and society. Charles Murray (1993), Peter Saunders (1995) and David Marsland (1989), in common with many conservative politicians, saw the family as under threat from the same changing moral values that made single parenthood acceptable in some sectors of society. Single mothers were associated with a range of social problems, such as criminal behaviour in young men, social irresponsibility that made it acceptable to receive benefits without attempting to work, and the failure of children to thrive educationally and socially.

Many people believe in a 'golden age' when things were better in the past than they are today. There is a widely held belief that families were happier in the past because there was little or no divorce and families seemed to stay together. In reality, the picture may be more complex because people who had family problems would have hidden the evidence for fear of family shame. We have little real evidence from the past to estimate how many people lived in loveless and unhappy family homes but had to stick together because they had little or no choice in the matter.

**www.princes-trust.org.uk** *gives access to The Prince's Trust fact-sheets, covering a variety of issues relating to young people and social change and well supported by statistical evidence.* **www.barnardos.org.uk/future_citizens/index.html** *is a good site, with interesting questions and stimulating materials to get you thinking about families.*

| No | Yes |
|---|---|
| Family structures are disappearing; many people choose not to marry. | Family structures are merely changing. People may not have legal marriages, but they still form stable and recognisable partnerships. |
| An increasing number of children are born outside married relationships. | The majority of children are born to married couples, but many cohabiting couples marry after their children are born. |
| Divorce rates are high; this suggests that people marry too quickly and then don't work at their relationship. | It is difficult to know how many marriages in the past were unhappy; divorce was not an option for those couples. In addition, many divorcees remarry – it is not marriage as such, but the partner who was unsatisfactory. |
| Increasing numbers of women and children report violence and abuse. | In the past, abuse within families was not taken seriously and people were unaware of the scale of the problem. People nowadays have higher expectations of family relationships. They no longer accept abuse. |
| The State has taken over many of the traditional family roles such as care of children's education and health. | Many people still take on the burden of care for family members; the government is effectively subsidised in the role of care by extended family members who support the sick and disabled in their own homes. |
| Women are finding the traditional domestic and caring role unsatisfying so they are returning to work in large numbers. | Males are adapting to the changing economics of family life. Many are taking on domestic burdens and childcare as part of their contribution to the life of the family. |
| More people are in non-traditional families, e.g. those headed by gay couples. | These people may have a different sexuality, but they still choose to form relationships that are recognisable as families. Some people go on to develop these relationships by having (or adopting) children. |
| Changes in women's working patterns have eroded their desire to have children. | Birth rates are indeed falling. However, it is not clear whether this is due to the fact of female work or to the low status of parenting and the lack of support for parents from employers. |
| Many children are now raised in families that do not fit a traditional pattern and experience the break-up of their families while they are still young. | There is evidence to suggest that a loving family relationship in some form is a good way to raise children; many young offenders and troubled young people come from unstable home backgrounds or have been in care. |

## Think it through

### GOVERNMENT PROPOSES CLASSES IN NON-TRADITIONAL FAMILY LIFE

SCHOOLCHILDREN should be taught about divorce, 're-partnering' and homosexual relationships in new 'parenthood education' lessons, according to government guidelines published today.

The final draft of the new guidelines, which emphasises the importance of 'stable relationships' but acknowledges that there is 'more variety about partnerships and family form', were leaked yesterday. The guidelines encourage teachers to share with pupils their own experience of parenting and relationships to 'bring to life' their lessons.

Tory MPs today expressed concern at the changes. 'We don't want to teach children that divorce or breaking up are normal or good,' said Julian Brazier, President of the Conservative family campaign. 'Our first duty is to teach children that parenting should fall within marriage.'

The new parenting curriculum will be taught alongside sex-education classes and include a section on '21st century parenting' – such as the concept of 're-partnering', when a parent establishes a new relationship after the break-up of a marriage or former relationship.

Although the education secretary, David Blunkett, is thought to have wanted more emphasis on traditional marriage, other education experts involved in compiling the guidelines were anxious to avoid making children who come from single-parent homes or have unmarried parents feel 'second class'.

Taylor, R. (2000) 'Classes in non-traditional family life proposed by government', *The Guardian*, Friday 12 May,

1 Describe the proposed changes on parenthood education.

2 What key family values do both Tory MPs and David Blunkett feel should be taught to children in school?

3 Outline and evaluate the suggestion that changes to family structure in modern Britain imply dissatisfaction with traditional family life.

## Watch out

From reading the newspapers and watching soap operas on television, you would definitely start to think that family life is on the way out. Take care to balance this view with evidence from properly conducted sociological research.

## Round-up

Writers in the 1960s and 1970s tended to regard changes in family patterns as a good thing, so that predictions of the death of the nuclear family were welcomed as being liberating. Later, more right-wing writers viewed the same changes as being pathological and dangerous for society. While there are changes in family structure that are well documented and clear from official statistics, the family (in terms of emotional complexity and personal satisfaction) probably remains much as it always has been for most people.

# Families and households: summative review

This image shows an idealised image of what a family should be. But what is the reality of the recent family history behind a picture showing people at a happy time in their lives? It is the job of the sociologist to recognise the difference between image and reality and to attempt to see beneath the surface in order to investigate how families really operate.

For most people, the family is their important social grouping and it is therefore not surprising that it is an area of such concern to sociologists and politicians. It is from our family that we will learn our norms, values and mores. It is with our families that we expect to experience the major rituals of our lives: births, marriages and deaths. In essence, the family is the first place where we will learn our own culture because it is within the family that we are socialised from the selfishness of childhood into the socially aware and responsive adults that we become.

Functionalists explain the role of families in our lives when they point out that families perform a number of tasks:

- the socialisation of children
- providing support and stability for adult personalities
- providing sexual control
- providing a sense of identity
- meeting the physical and emotional needs of individuals.

The debate about the nature of the family focuses on family change and family structure because there are those who insist (for ideological, legal, religious or moral reasons) that some family forms are better than others. In Britain, the mainstream ideology of the family is based on the view that a family should consist of a heterosexual couple and their children (the nuclear family). This view is based on Christian teaching, which emphasises marriage for the whole of adult life and with the purpose of procreating children. This type of family is sometimes called 'the cereal packet norm', in recognition that this form of family is the type targeted by advertisers of domestic products. Other cultures have a variety of different experiences of family organisation and structure, but in Britain these are not always accorded the same status and support as the nuclear family. Plural marriage of one partner to more than one spouse is punishable with a prison sentence in the UK, though acceptable, if not desirable to Muslims.

## Is the family under threat?

Those with a strong emotional or ideological attachment to the idea of the nuclear family have argued that nuclear families were always typical of Britain, and that we should be concerned about the falling number of families that conform to the traditional pattern. There are strong arguments to counter this view – we know very little about families in the past. However, we do know that the Victorian ideology of the happy nuclear family hid the reality of a society that accepted child abuse and prostitution, wife battering, high levels of child mortality, illegitimacy, drug abuse in the home, the prevalence of mistresses and adultery, and a situation in which women and children had very little power over the activities and actions of men.

Looking at modern families, there appears to be greater tolerance of a variety of family forms. Divorce, cohabitation and single motherhood are accepted as normal life events, whereas these life situations would have been regarded as unusual fifty or sixty years ago. Those on the New Right argue that this represents a moral decline and that family life is under threat, whereas others see this as the sign of a changing society and regard it is being of no especial significance in terms of the popularity of the family.

## Changes to family life since 1945

These are many and varied and can be summarised as follows.

- There are fewer children born nowadays.
- Many people are remaining voluntarily childless.
- Children are financially and emotionally dependent on their parents for longer.
- More people cohabit.
- There has been an increase in divorce, though in recent years this trend has gone into reverse.
- There has been an increase in blended families, i.e. where there are children from more than one relationship.
- There has been an increase in single parenthood so it is possible for a woman now to choose whether or not to have children alone.
- The average age of motherhood has increased.
- Marriage occurs later in life.
- Men and women tend to be more flexible in their allocation of domestic roles.
- Women are more likely to participate in the paid workforce
- There has been a highly significant fall in adult mortality so that people are now living into extreme old age.
- For those in early retirement and with sufficient income, older age can be very positive in terms of supporting their children, their own older parents and enjoying leisure.
- For those in later old age there are attendant problems, possibly with health or disability issues.

## Reasons for changes to family life

There are many reasons why changes have taken place in family life, but most fall within one of the following categories.

- *Ideological and political change*
  - Many men genuinely believe in equality for women and children so they have modified their attitudes and behaviour towards their wives and daughters.
  - Many women have been affected by the ideas of gender equality promoted by feminists throughout the century.
  - The government has tried to make men more responsible for their children via the Child Support Agency.

- *Pragmatic change*
  - Men have very little choice but to help in the home if their wives and partners are working long hours.
  - House prices have risen so that two salaries are needed to pay a mortgage on a home.

- *Legislative change*
  - Divorce is easier to obtain than it once was.
  - Homosexuality has been decriminalised.

- *Moral and social change*
  - Fewer people feel the need to be bound by Christian religious teaching on family and marriage.
  - Divorce has become more widely acceptable and family forms have undergone structural change as a result.

- *Medical and technical change*
  - Contraception is more easily obtainable.
  - People live longer and in better health.
  - People can use medical technology to have children beyond the natural age of conception or as a result of donation of sperm and eggs.

## Moral panics and the family

Many people consider that the family is in moral danger and this has provoked media debates on a number of issues. Over the past twenty years, there has been discussion of a variety of topics that would never previously have been mentioned in any public forum because family life was hitherto considered private and there were also taboos about discussing sexuality. A very dark side to family life has been revealed, though not all moral panics are equally grounded in factual basis. Some areas of concern have been:

- *child abuse within the family* – there is now greater awareness of very sad cases where children have experienced cruelty and murder at the hands of their carers.
- *domestic violence* – both females and males have been murdered at the hands of their partners.
- *single mothers* – young single mothers have been especially targeted by press reports as irresponsible, choosing to have children at the expense of taxpayers.

Irrespective of the validity or otherwise of the moral panic about these subjects, the public perception is such that governments have been forced into creating laws in order to show that they are acting on public concerns. Some of the panics have therefore led to major policy decisions and changes.

## The future of the family

It can be dangerous to try to predict what the future will bring. However, simply from looking at current trends, one can see a number of patterns emerge that may impact on family life in the future.

- The proportion of older people in the population will grow as fewer children are born and death rates fall.
- While most older people will enjoy good health for much of their retirement, the number of dependent elderly will increase.
- The average age of first-time mothers will become steadily older; many women will remain childless either by choice or because they have no option.
- Marriage rates will continue to fall, whereas cohabitation will increase.
- People still tend to form families, but fewer of these families will conform to the traditional 'cereal packet' norm as other types of family structure become more widely acceptable.

# Families and households: self-assessment questions

1   Identify the three different forms of family structure that are studied by sociologists.

2   Complete each of the following sentences using the appropriate word from the list (i–iii).

  a  The term used to describe leaving paid employment as a result of age or ill-health is known as _____.

  b  The term used to describe the period of retirement when people are still relatively healthy and can enjoy leisure pursuits is known as _____.

  c  The term used to describe extreme old age, sometimes accompanied by ill-health or disability is known as

     _____.

  i   The third age
  ii  Elderly old
  iii Retirement

3   Suggest two ways in which older people can support their families.

4   Match the term with its correct meaning.

  a  Marriage to multiple partners at the same time
  b  Marriage to a single partner at a time
  c  Marriage to more than a single partner, but only one at a time

  i   Monogamy
  ii  Serial monogamy
  iii Polygamy

5   Which of the following explanations comes closest to explaining the term 'New Right'?

  a  Having new ideas about the nature of the family.
  b  A political philosophy that emphasises traditional moral and social values particularly with regard to the family.
  c  Voting for the Conservative party in elections.

6   What is the meaning of the word 'household'?

7   Suggest two different ways in which the concept of family can be operationalised.

8   What is the difference between a horizontal and a vertical extended family?

9   What is the average completed family size in Britain?

  a  3.5 children
  b  2.4 children
  c  1.7 children

10  Decide whether each of the following statements is true or false.

  a  The average age of marriage in Britain is falling.
  b  More divorce is taking place each year.
  c  There are now more blended families in Britain than there were 20 years ago.

11  What proportion of British households are lone-parent families?

  a  35%
  b  15%
  c  6%

12  Suggest three factors that have contributed to family change in Britain.

13  Match each of the following terms with its meaning.

  a  Parents with adult children who have left home.
  b  Older people who take on the care of younger family members.
  c  Children who are placed with parent substitutes who are paid small amounts to care for these children.
  d  Families formed between people of different ethnicities and cultures.

  i   Grandparenting
  ii  Cross-cultural families
  iii Empty-nest families
  iv  Fostering

14 Describe two different forms of communal living.

15 The system of communal living established in Israel is known as:

a Kaddish

b Kosher

c Kibbutz

16 Which of the following meanings comes closest to explaining the term 'arranged marriage'?

a The marriage is viewed as a contract between two consenting adults, but it is negotiated between families.

b Two adults who have never met before are married because their families insist.

c People are forced into marriage with a stranger against their will.

17 What is the term used by feminists to describe the control of society and the family by men?

18 What sociological term would you use to describe each of the following?

a A family where men and women have agreed some degree of equality in the home.

b The tasks that are traditionally associated with adult male and female roles within a family.

c Men who challenged traditional gender roles for males and who were willing to work in the house and take on domestic challenges.

19 Which of the partners in a marriage is more likely to initiate a divorce?

20 What are the causes of single parenthood?

21 Which French historian claimed that childhood is a modern social construction?

a Philippe Pisces

b Philippe Aries

c Philippe Libra

22 Which of these statements about divorce are true and which are false?

a The average duration of a marriage is approximately 5 years.

b Just over half of all divorcing couples have dependent children under 16 years of age.

c The average age of divorce is between 35 and 39, but is falling.

d Couples from the wealthier socio-economic groups are more likely to divorce than those in lower groups.

23 Is cohabitation an alternative to marriage?

24 Suggest four reasons why divorce statistics tended to rise throughout the twentieth century.

# Families and households: a timeline

Engels, basing his analysis on Marxism claims families are concerned with ownership and control of women and children. Capitalism is reproduced within family (1880s)

Beginnings of welfare support, improving public-health measures increase life-expectancy for children so families increase in size from start of century

Anthropologists look at family forms in other cultures

1900 1 2 3 4 5 6 7 8 9 1910 1 2 3 4 5 6 7 8 9 1920 1 2 3 4 5 6 7 8 9 1930 1 2 3 4 5 6 7 8 9 1940 1 2 3 4 5 6 7 8 9

Development of reliable contraception (the Pill). Growing acceptance of ideas of feminism

Legislation to support family, e.g. Child Support Agency. Changing technology of reproduction so that IVF child is born

Labour support for traditional view of family results in legislation that forces parents to take responsibility for children: parental imprisonment for truancy, legislation related to anti-social children

American studies into family see nuclear family as being 'normal' family. British studies look at nuclear and extended families in working-class areas. Acceptance among mainstream sociology of subordinate/domestic role of women

Feminists begin to look at the socialisation of girls into subordinate family roles; challenges to traditional notions of family from a variety of different groups

Concern with changing status of boys and crisis of masculinity. Fear that boys in single-parent families have no acceptable male role-model

1950 1 2 3 4 5 6 7 8 9 1960 1 2 3 4 5 6 7 8 9 1970 1 2 3 4 5 6 7 8 9 1980 1 2 3 4 5 6 7 8 9 1990 1 2 3 4 5 6 7 8 9 2000 1 2 3

Post-war divorce rates increase dramatically due to legal aid being introduced. Baby boom – large number of children born

Focus on changing conjugal roles, acknowledging beginnings of male willingness to take on domestic roles. Beginnings of feminism as a popular concern

Liberalisation of variety of laws affecting social rights: abortion, divorce and homosexuality. A variety of gender-equality laws make employment more attractive to women. Challenges by feminists to accepted family practice such as domestic violence

Moral panics about single parenthood, reaction from New Right, which sees family as under threat from changing moral values

Women now accepted in workplace; birth-rates fall among educated women. Increasing life-expectancy means that average age of population is growing older

Growth in policy-oriented research and research into family organisation to see what makes a 'successful' family

# Section 3  Education

# Education: a mindmap

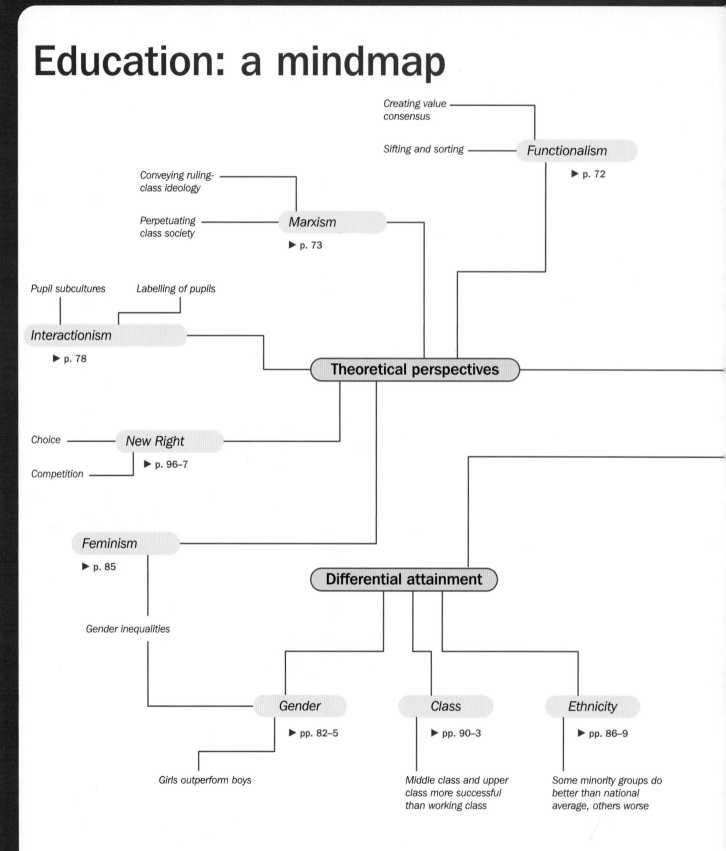

Creating value consensus

Sifting and sorting

*Functionalism*

▶ p. 72

Conveying ruling-class ideology

Perpetuating class society

*Marxism*

▶ p. 73

Pupil subcultures    Labelling of pupils

*Interactionism*

▶ p. 78

Choice    *New Right*    Competition

▶ p. 96–7

**Theoretical perspectives**

*Feminism*

▶ p. 85

Gender inequalities

**Differential attainment**

*Gender*

▶ pp. 82–5

Girls outperform boys

*Class*

▶ pp. 90–3

Middle class and upper class more successful than working class

*Ethnicity*

▶ pp. 86–9

Some minority groups do better than national average, others worse

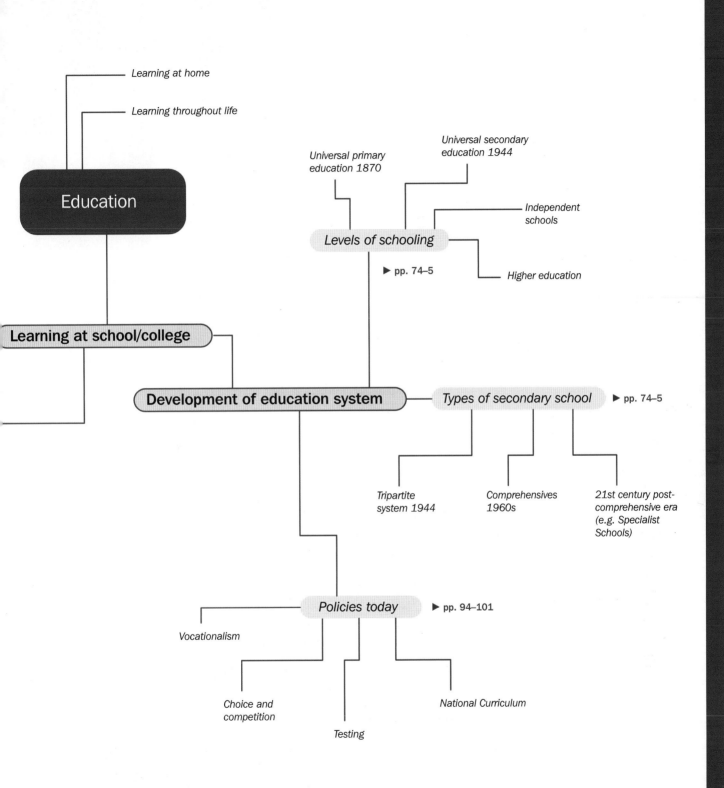

Learning at home

Learning throughout life

Education

Universal primary
education 1870

Universal secondary
education 1944

Independent
schools

*Levels of schooling*

▶ pp. 74–5

Higher education

**Learning at school/college**

**Development of education system**

*Types of secondary school* ▶ pp. 74–5

Tripartite
system 1944

Comprehensives
1960s

21st century post-
comprehensive era
(e.g. Specialist
Schools)

*Policies today* ▶ pp. 94–101

Vocationalism

Choice and
competition

Testing

National Curriculum

# What is education?

The term 'education' refers to a wide range of experiences through which we acquire knowledge, skills and values in everyday life. Education happens throughout our lives. It takes place in many different settings. Some of these are formal, such as schools, colleges and universities. Most of this section will be concerned with education in formal settings, especially schools.

## Socialisation

Some would argue that the most important education does not actually take place in formal settings. The knowledge, skills and values that are most essential are learned in early childhood, within the home and usually from parents. This process of '**primary socialisation**' is essential to equip everyone with what they need in order to become a fully functioning human being. Studies of feral children – children brought up in the wild, sometimes by animals, and with little if any human contact – suggest that children who miss out on primary socialisation can never learn to become members of a society. They will, for example, struggle to communicate in human language, and may reject some basic aspects of culture, such as wearing clothes and eating cooked food.

In many cultures in the past, there was little or no formal education. People had to learn what they needed to know from parents or others in their community without attending schools. This still applies in some developing countries, where some children do not even attend primary school. They will have learned much from observing what goes on around them and being part of it; they may have learned valuable work skills, or even to read and write. The desire to learn is a universal part of human nature, and learning will happen even where there are no teachers.

### Agencies of socialisation

Although primary socialisation takes place in childhood, the process of socialisation continues throughout life. Children are soon socialised into the norms and values of their school and their peer group. They also learn from other agencies of socialisation, such as the mass media and religious institutions. Schools are one specialised type of institution charged with providing formal education for children, but the mass media provide educational programmes and publications, and religious institutions often provide formal education (such as Sunday Schools), both for children and adults.

Until fairly recently, it was possible to say that the age of 5 years provided a neat boundary between primary socialisation within the family and secondary socialisation when the child began formal education. However, this boundary is no longer clear, because now many children are cared for and taught for some of the time by childminders, playgroups, nurseries, and so on. Many parents also teach pre-school children some skills in a fairly formal way.

### Social control

The agencies of socialisation can also be seen as agents of social control. Whereas the word 'socialisation' suggests that it is a helpful and positive process, enabling people to fully participate in their culture, the idea of social control draws attention to the ways in which the process may be negative. Those who have power in a society may control the rest of the population through schools, the media, religious institutions, and so on. This view is taken by Marxists, who are concerned with how the ruling class maintains its power by persuading the working class to accept ideas and value that are against their interests, and by feminists, who are concerned with the ways in which men exercise power over women. The ideas and values taught through the agencies of social control will be aspects of an '**ideology**'.

Who do we learn from?

One of the most famous stories about feral children is that of Amala and Kamala, the 'wolf children' of Midnapore. But how accurate are the accounts of their lives? Are they fact or fiction? (Maclean, 1979)

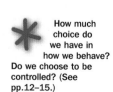

How much choice do we have in how we behave? Do we choose to be controlled? (See pp.12–15.)

EDUCATION

### Education in different cultures

But you, who are wise, must know that different nations have different conceptions of things and you will therefore not take it amiss, if our ideas of this kind of education happen not to be the same as yours. We have had some experience of it. Several of our young people were formerly brought up at the colleges of the Northern Provinces: they were instructed in all your sciences; but, when they came back to us, they were bad runners, ignorant of every means of living in the woods... neither fit for hunters, warriors nor counsellors, they were totally good for nothing.

We are, however, not the less oblig'd by your kind offer, tho' we decline accepting it; and, to show our grateful sense of it, if the Gentlemen of Virginia will send us a dozen of their sons, we will take care of their education, instruct them in all we know, and make men of them.

*Response of the Indians of the Six Nations to a suggestion that they send boys to an American college, Pennsylvania, 1744.*

1 Explain the differences between education as conceived by the Indians of the Six Nations and as conceived by the white settlers in Virginia.

2 Give examples of the kinds of things that would be taught to boys in the two cultures.

3 What might the different experiences of education for girls in these two cultures have been?

 *The parent of every child of compulsory school age shall cause him to receive efficient full-time education suitable:*
*a) to his age ability and aptitude, and*
*b) to any special educational needs he may have,*
*either by regular attendance in school or otherwise.*

*The 1996 Education Act, Section 7*

## Home education

The law does not say that all children must go to school, but rather that all children must be educated.

The 1996 Education Act supports this by saying that it should be a general principle that children are educated in accordance with the wishes of their parents.

According to the Home Education website, about 85 000 school-age children do not attend school; they are taught by private tutors or by their parents. Parents do not need to seek permission to educate their children at home; they do not have to explain their decision or have any special qualifications or equipment. They can follow the National Curriculum, in whole or in part, or can choose not to follow it at all. Local education authorities have a duty to ensure that an education is being provided and that it is suitable. Many parents who choose home schooling belong to networks that put them in touch with others who have chosen home schooling.

## Important studies

Ivan Illich (1973) was a strong critic of schooling. In his book *Deschooling society*, he argues that the most valuable learning takes place outside schools, and that rather than making it possible for people to learn, schools (through the hidden curriculum) perpetuate an unjust social order. Schools get in the way of learning, and he advocates making learning possible, for people who want it, as and when they need it. Compulsory schooling should be ended, and resources for learning made available to those who want to learn at any time in their lives.

### Watch out

When you are reading exam questions, always be careful to check whether they are asking about 'education', 'socialisation', or 'schooling'. They are not the same thing and you must make it clear to the examiner that you know the difference.

## Round-up

Education happens throughout life and in many settings. Some education is informal, but the main parts of your study of the sociology of education will be concerned with the formal education that takes place in schools and other institutions such as colleges and universities. Education is part of the processes of socialisation and social control.

 *The Home Education website is at* www.home-education.org.uk
*Education Otherwise is an organisation supporting home schooling (and taking its name from the final word in the clause of the Act quoted above.) Its website is* www.education-otherwise.org

# What are the functions of schooling?

Education in schools can be seen as having at least two important effects for society.

1 Education transmits cultural values.
2 Education contributes to social stratification.

Sociologists do not agree, however, about how to interpret these effects. This disagreement is between:

- the functionalists, who see education in schools as helping the stability and functioning of society
- conflict theorists, such as Marxists, who see education in schools as justifying and perpetuating inequality.

Is society meritocratic...

...or do some start with an advantage based on their social background?

## Functionalism

**Function:** A term used by functionalists to describe the way in which a social institution contributes to the survival and well-being of a society.

Functionalist sociologists see education as contributing in several ways to the continued stability of society – that is, education has several **functions**.

- Schools pass on the culture of a society from one generation to the next.
- Schools continue the process of socialisation that begins in the family; therefore, they act as agencies of socialisation.
- Because children are socialised into a shared set of values, education can help them feel they belong to a particular society and that they have shared interests with other members of that society. The shared values may be based on a religion, but do not have to be. They may include, for example, respect for authority, a sense of fair play or feelings of patriotism towards one's country. This can be particularly important in societies that are ethnically diverse.

A second contribution schools make to the smooth running of society is through 'sifting and sorting' people into different occupational roles. Those who do well in the education system are rewarded by being able to reach occupations that have high pay and high status. In effect, schools identify students' skills and abilities, selecting the more able for more challenging and advanced studies and guiding others towards courses and work more suited to their abilities. This has been described as a '**meritocracy**'. Social background is not seen as important. Because of the teaching of a shared value system, it is accepted as fair by most people; those who are successful are seen as deserving their success, and those who miss out blame themselves rather than the system. This system allows plenty of **social mobility**; people from working-class backgrounds can be upwardly mobile if they merit this.

**Meritocracy:** A system in which the rewards go to those who have talent and ability and who work for the rewards.

**Social mobility:** Movement up and down between social classes – for example, from working class to middle class.

> ### THE FUNCTIONS OF EDUCATION ACCORDING TO FUNCTIONALISTS
>
> - The transmission of norms and values to the next generation.
> - The sharing of culture, creating a sense of identity within a community or society.
> - The allocation of people to different roles within society.

> ### THE FUNCTIONS OF EDUCATION ACCORDING TO MARXISTS
>
> - The ruling class uses education to transmit its ideology to the rest of the population.
> - This ideology persuades the working class to accept its position.
> - The ruling class is then able to maintain its power and privilege and perpetuate the class structure.

## Marxism

A very different approach comes from the Marxist perspective. Marxists would look at the ways in which schools instil a common value system, and would see this as the imposition of a set of ideas that suit the ruling class – an ideology. From this point of view, education seems like indoctrination. Children are taught a set of values that will make them 'good' workers for the capitalist system. Much of this is done through the 'hidden curriculum'. This concept is not used only by Marxists, but it has particular relevance here. For example, in schools, children learn to be punctual and to do as they are told by those in authority. This is preparation for the world of work. (The hidden curriculum is explained in greater detail on page 77.)

Marxists see school as being closely linked to work. Through the hidden curriculum, most children are taught not to have high expectations of work or of life, and to expect to be bored a lot of the time. The hidden curriculum in a top public school is very different; here children may be taught to expect to have a high-status occupation in which they will have to exercise authority over others. But the allocation to occupations is seen by Marxists as unfair, not meritocratic. In most cases, class background shapes the level of educational attainment and thus future occupation. Middle- and upper-class parents can provide advantages for their children: independent schooling, private tutors, access to books and other resources, and so on. If the pursuit of occupations is a race, then those from working-class backgrounds start with a handicap. There is therefore very little social mobility.

### How relevant is this debate today?

This debate has been going on for many years – but it remains important and relevant. You can use the two approaches here to help you make sense of some recent developments in education. For example, has the abolition of grants for students made it less likely that students from working-class backgrounds will enter higher education? How would this fit in with the idea that the education system is a meritocracy? The discussion here has been mainly about class; can you apply the ideas to gender and ethnicity as well?

## Social mobility

How much social mobility is there? Several large-scale social surveys have tackled this question by comparing people's class background (measured, for example, by father's occupation) with their current class position. The evidence tends to show that most people in middle-class occupations are from middle-class backgrounds, and that upward mobility from the working class to the middle class is not widespread. This seems at first sight to prove that Britain is not a meritocracy, because class background seems to be an important factor. It can be argued, however, that the success of middle-class children is due to their higher ability. This is a controversial argument, which many sociologists would reject.

# Important studies

Bowles and Gintis (1976) presented arguments about the effects of education and how the education system transmits ideology. Education makes society seem fair and just. It legitimises inequality. It reduces class conflict by persuading the working class that, because they have failed in the education system, it is fair that they have to accept low-paid work. Among the myths that contribute to this are:
- that success in education is based on merit
- that education is the way to be successful in the world of work.

Hidden curriculum: The ways in which pupils learn values and attitudes other than through the formal curriculum of timetabled lessons.

**Research issues** The obvious problem with social mobility research is that it will always be behind the times. You have to wait until the children of each generation have achieved their highest position in the social-class system before you can measure how mobile they have been – and by then things will have changed again. And should the mobility of women be measured separately from that of men?

# Round-up

There are two main approaches to the sociological study of the role education plays in society – the functionalist and the Marxist. Functionalists stress the ways in which education in schools contributes to the smooth running of society through teaching shared values and allocating people to appropriate occupational roles. Marxists see the same processes as the instilling of an ideology and the blocking of opportunities for most of those from working-class backgrounds.

## Think it through

1 Identify and explain one function of education illustrated in this photograph.

2 How might the evidence in this photograph be interpreted by (a) a functionalist sociologist, and (b) a Marxist sociologist?

# What different types of schools are there?

## Private schools

In the UK private schools are also known as 'independent' schools. They are financed by the fees that parents pay for their children to attend. The top private schools, those which belong to the Headmasters' Conference (HMC), are also, confusingly, known as 'public schools'. There are more than 2000 registered private schools and the number of schools and pupils attending them has been growing slowly but steadily in recent years. There are about 600 000 pupils aged 5–16 in private schools – about 7.5% of the total school population.

Private schools are outside the state sector of education. They do not have to follow government education policies; for example, they do not have to follow the National Curriculum or enter their pupils for SATs (standardised assessment tests). They are, however, subject to some government rules and regulations, including inspections.

The HMC, comprising 233 top private schools, was formed in 1871 to protect these schools from government interference. Many members of Britain's élite are former pupils of these schools. HMC schools have traditionally produced many top politicians, civil servants, officers of the armed forces, business people, and so on. This has helped make the independent school sector a powerful lobby that has been able to withstand attempts to reform or abolish it. For many years schools that admitted girls could not join the HMC, but now most of the schools are **co-educational**, at least in the sixth form.

**\*** You might try searching the internet for references to the HMC in newspapers, to find out what it does and what its policies are.

Co-educational: A school attended by both boys and girls.

### ARGUMENTS IN FAVOUR OF PRIVATE SCHOOLS

- *Choice* – The existence of private schools makes it possible for parents to have greater choice. The wide range of private schools, including 'progressive' schools such as Summerhill, further extends this choice. Private schools also often offer different subjects, such as Latin, which has almost disappeared from state schools.
- *Success* – Many (though not all) private schools are academically successful, achieving good exam results. Some parents see them as providing better education than the state sector. This is usually attributed to factors such as smaller class sizes, better discipline, more work and a more academic ethos than exists in the state sector.

### ARGUMENTS AGAINST PRIVATE SCHOOLS

- The existence of private schools creates a two-tier system; private schools for those who can afford them and state schools for those who can't. Parents who can afford to are, in effect, buying advantages for their children, which undermines attempts to make Britain more meritocratic.
- It is unfair that some pupils receive a better education because their parents can afford it, not because they deserve or need it.
- Private schools do not usually have mainly local pupils, so they are not part of a community in the way state schools are expected to be.
- Public schools have produced an élite that is conservative and has held back change.

## The state sector

State schools, also called maintained schools, are paid for by the Local Education Authority (LEA). No fees are payable.

There are three stages of education:

- *Primary* – ages 5–11, key stages 1 and 2
- *Secondary* – ages 11–16, key stages 3 and 4
- *Further* – above the age of 16 (the term 'further education' is normally used in colleges rather than schools).

Higher education refers to university-level education, which students enter at age 18 or over.

Many secondary schools have a sixth form, taking students aged 16–19. In some areas there are sixth-form colleges, often taking students from a number of small secondary schools that would not have sufficient numbers to have their own sixth forms. There are also further education colleges, offering a wide range of full-time and part-time courses in both academic and vocational areas and at all levels, from basic skills to postgraduate.

In most areas, there are primary and secondary schools. In other areas, however, there are middle schools teaching pupils who have attended a first school and who will move on to an upper school. Almost all children starting primary or first school have had some education, in a nursery or other pre-school institution.

## The education system since World War II

After World War II, a new national system of education was created. There were three types of secondary school, and so this system is referred to as the 'tripartite system'. It comprised:

- *Grammar schools* – for 'academic' children, selected by a test at the age of 11 (the '11 plus'). Grammar schools taught the classics, maths, science and other demanding subjects for the GCE O-level (ordinary level) examinations.
- *Technical schools* – these specialised in technical education, helping pupils to prepare for manual occupations.
- *Secondary modern schools* – these were for the majority, offering a basic education with few opportunities to take exams, although later CSE examinations were introduced, seen as a lower level than O level.

These three types of schools existed alongside independent schools. They continue to exist today in some areas (for example, parts of Kent and Buckinghamshire) where local authorities managed in the 1960s and 1970s not to follow government directives to introduce comprehensive schools. Comprehensive schools are those that take all pupils, regardless of ability, from their **catchment area**. Their adoption as the norm for secondary education from the 1960s onwards reflected a big change in thinking about education. The earlier tripartite system was based on the assumption that different kinds of children had different educational needs, which could only be met by providing different kinds of schools. Underpinning the comprehensive system, on the other hand, was a belief that all children should be given the same opportunities to succeed.

The comprehensive system has now evolved into three types of maintained schools:

- *Community schools*
- *Foundation schools* – many of these were previously grant-maintained schools – that is, they had opted out of local authority control and were maintained directly by central government
- *Voluntary schools* – usually church schools, although there are a few linked to other faiths, such as Judaism and Sikhism.

Many maintained secondary schools (of all types) have become specialist schools in a subject area such as technology, sports or languages. Under the New Labour government, some are also 'beacon' schools, which spread their good practice to other schools in their areas. Most maintained schools are comprehensive but some select part of their intake.

This growing variety reflects the educational policies of different governments. The variety of schools is partly caused by a long-running debate over the desirability or otherwise of selection. The comprehensive school, which was intended to be the 'normal' secondary school, has been criticised and undermined by reforms.

Parents are now faced with a wide choice of schools at every level of education, and the choice becomes wider the further the distance children can travel. At age 11, starting secondary school, for example, the choice might be between a single-sex Church of England school, a co-educational sports college and a co-educational comprehensive or, for some, a private school.

## Think it through

Of course I wouldn't want my own children to go to a bog-standard comprehensive.

1 Examine some of the reasons why some parents choose independent schools for their children.

2 In what ways do independent schools affect how meritocratic the school system is?

3 Why have governments not reformed or abolished independent schools?

WWW The website for the Department for Education and Skills, **www.dfes.gov.uk**, has a mass of information about how schools are funded and organised. However, it may be easier to search the website of your own local education authority.

 The changes in how schools are organised and classified are so frequent that it is often hard to keep up with them! Do you know which kind of school you attend? Has it changed recently?

## Coursework advice
It might be interesting to make a study of the different kinds of school in your area, to see whether there is any link to the social class of the people in the catchment area. Perhaps you could look for a link between particular schools and the price of houses nearby.

Catchment area: The area around a school. Children living in a school's catchment area are normally given priority when places are allocated.

Beacon schools are to become 'advanced' schools by 2005.

## Watch out

In a sociology exam, you are unlikely to be asked simply to describe all the different types of school. However, when you refer to different types of school in an answer, be careful to use the right names.

# Round-up

The variety of schools and educational institutions that exists today is a result of different policies followed by different governments. Far from there being a uniform national system, educational provision varies enormously between different areas, so that parents choosing schools for their children can face a bewildering range of options. Schools can also be classified by whether they are co-educational or single-sex and whether they select some or all of their pupils.

# What happens in schools?

The hidden curriculum?

**M**any of the factors that influence education are outside the school, while others are within the school. The two sets of factors interact, often in very complex ways. This section looks at some of the processes, values and interactions within schools and at what importance they might have. Sociologists who investigate these factors are often working at the micro level, looking at what happens within one school, and are adopting an **interactionist** approach. The research methods used are often **ethnographic**.

**Ethnography:** The use of direct observation, sometimes combined with other methods, to help the researcher to understand the point of view of those being studied.

## The formal curriculum

Perhaps the most obvious answer to the question 'What happens in schools?' is that pupils learn through lessons that are taught as part of the curriculum. England and Wales have a National Curriculum, which sets out what subjects should be taught. Those that are seen as essential – English, Maths and Science – are taught to all pupils throughout their compulsory education; for other subjects, schools (and, as they get older, pupils) have some choice. Sociology, despite its relevance to pupils' lives and futures, is not seen as essential and most pupils do not even have the chance to study it until they have finished their compulsory education.

Underlying the open, formal curriculum is the assumption that it is possible to divide knowledge into subject disciplines. Knowledge is compartmentalised, taught in chunks labelled 'history', 'science', and so on. These divisions are social constructions – that is, they are not natural but are the result of decisions made by people about how to divide up knowledge. This method of teaching can prevent pupils from understanding the many ways in which different areas of knowledge are connected and overlap. Interesting and important areas of knowledge often fall into the gaps between subjects and are therefore neglected in schools.

**'Citizenship'** has recently been introduced as part of the compulsory formal curriculum in schools. Why do you think this is? Are there other subjects or areas of knowledge that you think should be added to the formal curriculum?

## Teachers

The formal curriculum is taught by teachers – professionals who have qualified to teach, usually through a one-year postgraduate certificate or through a four-year degree in education.

The majority of teachers are female, but the majority of head teachers and other senior staff are male. These differences become more noticeable in infant and primary schools, where there are very small numbers of male teachers but about half of all head teachers are men.

There are relatively few teachers who are African-Caribbean, Asian or from other minority ethnic backgrounds.

## Think it through

1 What aspects of the hidden curriculum are present in this photograph?

2 In what ways can the organisation of a classroom strengthen the power and authority of teachers?

## The hidden curriculum

Many sociologists take the view that the informal or unofficial learning that happens in schools is important, perhaps even more important than the formal curriculum. They refer to this as the '**hidden curriculum**'. This is a rather misleading term because it does not really refer to a curriculum but rather to the effects of the ways in which schools and teaching and learning are organised. This term has been used in many different ways.

Some of the aspects of school life that have been seen as part of the hidden curriculum are:

- the organisation of schools as hierarchies, with teachers and others having power over pupils
- the organisation of the school day, with lessons and breaks at set times, a daily routine, and insistence on punctuality
- school rules, such as prescribing a uniform, how to address teachers and rules about what is and is not allowed
- the physical layout of the school and the provision of facilities for pupils
- the ways in which pupils are allocated to different teaching groups
- the seating arrangements in classrooms
- the ways teachers behave towards pupils and the expectations they have of them.

Taken together, all of these aspects shape the education of pupils, and contribute towards some pupils doing well and others not. They also give powerful messages to pupils about how much they are valued and respected.

The term 'hidden curriculum' has been used extensively by Marxist sociologists. They have used it to emphasise the ways in which schools prepare working-class pupils for the world of work:

- by having a hierarchy of authority – pupils have to learn to do as they are told
- by insisting on punctuality
- by lowering expectations – pupils learn not to expect to find fulfilment or pleasure in their work.

The hidden curriculum of a public school can be seen as preparing pupils for adult life in very different ways. Pupils may learn:

- that they are seen as special and that much is expected of them
- that they are expected to see themselves as better than those who go to other schools
- that they should expect others to accept their authority
- that they should expect to enter professions or other work that is highly valued and rewarded.

The term 'hidden curriculum' has also been used by feminists, who have drawn attention to the ways in which schools transmit messages about sex and gender roles to pupils.

## Pupil/teacher relationships

Pupils within schools have very little power, and much of what happens to them is beyond their control. The most basic point here is that school is compulsory; pupils do not have the freedom to choose not to go to school or to leave when they wish. So, pupils' lives are ordered for them by authorities who claim to act in the best interests of pupils, but in this case not always with their agreement!

Teachers act as agents of social control. They have to enforce school rules even when they personally disagree with them. While in school, pupils have to do as teachers tell them or risk punishment. Teachers have much more power, at least in their interactions with pupils; for example, they have the power to impose punishments. The interactions are, however, far from one-sided; pupils, especially in a group or class, are able to engage in bargaining with teachers. For example, teachers may be willing to engage in a trade-off – 'Behave yourselves till the bell and I won't set any homework today.'

## Important studies

In an important study, Jackson (1968) saw the hidden curriculum as three (unofficial) Rs – rules, routines and regulations. Children had to learn these in order to survive in the classroom. They also had to develop strategies for coping in the classroom, and these strategies got in the way of learning the official curriculum.

Hidden curriculum: The ways in which pupils learn in schools other than through the formal curriculum.

### Research issues

The hidden curriculum is a difficult concept to operationalise. It cannot be directly observed so, in order to investigate it, decisions have to be made about what will be taken as evidence of its existence. Researchers who want to prove the existence of an aspect of the hidden curriculum need to be careful not to define it in such a way that they are certain to find evidence of it.

### Coursework advice

The hidden curriculum of your school or college would make a fascinating area for you to study. But take care! You may find that you are seen as challenging the authorities, rather than conducting objective social research.

## Round-up

As well as learning what they are taught in the formal curriculum, pupils also learn through the hidden curriculum. There are many different aspects to the hidden curriculum, and writers from different perspectives put different emphases on them. Within schools, teachers act as agents of control; however, pupils are not entirely powerless.

# What subcultures exist within schools?

Subculture: A group sharing values and ways of behaving that make them different from the rest of society.

Moral panic: Exaggerated social reaction to a group or issue, amplified by the media with consequent demands for action.

## Studying anti-school subcultures

Silent subversion?

Delamont (2000) has pointed out that most of the research on **subcultures** in schools has focused on working-class boys who are strongly anti-school. There has been a **moral panic** about the underachievement of working-class boys in schools since the early 1990s. However, sociologists were recording the same phenomenon much earlier. One of the first was David Hargreaves' account (1967) of boys in a secondary modern school; the best known is probably *Learning to labour* by Paul Willis in 1977. While using ethnographic research, Willis was influenced by Marxism in seeing the lads (the term the boys he studied used for themselves) in the context of class conflict and seeing schools as a means by which the working class is kept in its place.

These studies, based on ethnographic research, describe boys who:

- hate school
- truant
- avoid work
- cheat when they have to do some work
- are insolent and aggressive towards teachers
- despise boys who work hard at school
- are dismissive of girls
- are often openly racist and sexist
- are involved in delinquency and sometimes serious crime outside school.

The values of these subcultures were the opposite of the school's values, so they can be described as 'anti-school subcultures'. They provided the boys involved with an alternative source of status. The boys were seen as failures by the school, but could gain prestige in the eyes of their mates by making trouble.

Although these subcultures of white, working-class boys have attracted considerable attention, other researchers have found very different subcultures among African-Caribbean and Asian boys, for example, and among girls. There are also subcultures that are not anti-school, and may even be in favour of school.

## Subcultures today

Since the 1980s, research on groups of pupils within schools has tended to move away from the concept of subculture, which implies a consciously adopted and followed set of values. Instead, researchers describe the variety of ways in which pupils can respond to the school situation. For the majority, this involves resistance to some aspects of school, negotiation of some aspects and acceptance of many. In different situations, pupils – sometimes the same pupils – may keep in with teachers, grudgingly conform or be defiant.

There is a range of possible explanations for the values and behaviour of groups of pupils. These include:

- factors beyond school, such as relative deprivation and marginalisation
- the ways in which ideas about masculinity and femininity have changed
- changes in the economy and labour market
- ways in which success in school is seen as feminine
- sexism and racism within schools.

Another change since the classic studies by Willis and Hargreaves is that racism and sexism are now openly challenged, both within schools and within the wider society. The type of boys described in those studies will now be more aware of these issues, and openly racist and sexist comments may now be restricted to fewer situations.

 Sociologists tend to study the unusual or abnormal, but it is just as difficult – and sometimes more interesting – to try to explain 'normal' behaviour.

# Important studies

How do girls who are placed in low streams and are labelled as failures by the school react to this? Hey (1997) offers some answers: some girls truant but their behaviour is less confrontational and seen as less of a problem than the more visible bad behaviour of boys. The focus of Hey's research in two London comprehensive schools was not subcultures as such, but the social networks that girls form in schools. Like the male sociologists studying boys, she used ethnographic methods, spending her time doing what the girls did (including truanting!). She found that cliques tended to form among girls from the same class background, the cliques being based on a core of best friends, with other girls moving in and out of favour. Working-class girls reacted to their powerless situation in school by using their attractiveness to manipulate boys and male teachers. They resisted school by various methods that were less visible and less confrontational than those used by boys.

Sewell's work (1997) has some continuity with the earlier studies of Hargreaves and Willis, in that it identifies a group of boys with strong anti-school values. The African-Caribbean boys he studied were so confrontational that they smoked cannabis on school premises and could be violent towards other pupils and staff. They were very aggressively masculine. Sewell sees their behaviour partly as a response to racism in schools and to racist teachers. As well as this group, Sewell identified three other responses to the school adopted by African-Caribbean students, so the 'rebels' should not be taken as 'normal' or as typical of African-Caribbean boys. Yet they did attract by far the most attention, both from the school in terms of discipline and from Sewell as the sociologist.

Mac an Ghaill (1988) describes a group of young women from African-Caribbean and Asian backgrounds in an inner-city sixth-form college who called themselves the Black Sisters. They were strongly critical of the college, the schools they had been to, how streaming had discriminated against them, how their abilities had been underestimated and how they had been forced to follow an ethnocentric curriculum. Yet they had decided that gaining qualifications was in their best interests, so they got on with it and did well, through determination and through supporting each other. Teachers expect bright pupils to be conformist. They aren't always: these girls were anti-school but pro-education.

## Think it through

### Description of an Asian anti-school boys group

'The Warriors were seen as the best organized and toughest group and so were respected and feared... they wish to project a tough image that challenges the stereotype of the 'passive Asian'... They claimed that when they first came to Kilby school, they were all conformists. During the third year, attitudes and orientations toward the school began to crystallize. The Warriors group came together as they found boys with a similar response. Their shared view of the school was that of a system of hostile authority and meaningless work demands.'

Mac an Ghaill, M. (1988) *Young, gifted and black: Student–teacher relations in the schooling of black youth*, Open University Press, Milton Keynes

1 What factors can lead to the emergence of anti-school subcultures and groups?

2 Why have groups of working-class boys attracted more attention than girls and middle-class boys?

3 In what ways might black or Asian anti-school groups be different from white ones?

4 Why do you think the boys who became warriors stopped being 'conformists' when they did?

## Research issues

Ethnographic research involves trying to see the world as it appears to those being studied, and these studies of the anti-school subcultures of working-class boys succeed in this, arguably too well. The boys tend to come across as heroes; it is clear that Willis (1977) is broadly on their side. The boys are glamourised as working-class anti-heroes striking back against a system that has failed them. Delamont points out an interesting paradox here: that the sociologists who studied these boys would themselves have been the hard-working, high-achieving boys approved by their schools and despised by the Lads of their day.

## Coursework advice

Studying a group in your school or college, perhaps through participant observation (see pp. 122–3) sounds interesting but it is much more difficult than it sounds. The risk is that you simply describe how the group spends its time – and that is not sociology You will have to use sociological theories and concepts in devising the project and in analysing your findings.

# Round-up

There is a long-standing tradition of research (usually ethnographic) in secondary schools that has identified working-class boys as being a problem and as behaving aggressively in schools. Such research often tends to take the side of such anti-school subcultures. However, only a small minority of pupils belong to such subcultures. Other groups, for whom the term 'subculture' may be less appropriate, resist or conform to school values to different extents. Perhaps the most under-researched are those who do not rebel or cause problems for the school – the majority.

# How do processes in schools affect individuals' achievements?

## Labelling

Interactionism: A perspective within sociology that focuses on small-scale social interaction rather than on structures and institutions.

'**Labelling**' is a term used widely within sociology but its origins are in the **interactionist** perspective. It refers to the way in which we all classify people we meet into types. This is a normal part of social life and interaction. Within schools, the idea of labelling is particularly applied to how teachers interact with pupils, because it is argued that this can affect educational attainment.

Hargreaves (1967) found, through observing what happened in secondary schools, that teachers made initial judgements about pupils based on their behaviour, ability and potential. This involved classifying the pupils into certain types. Over time, confirmed by further observation, these first impressions became labels. Teachers then had what they believed to be knowledge about a pupil, based on everything from manners to quality of work to what other teachers said about them. Teachers used this knowledge to explain behaviour and attainment. This could work in both positive and negative ways.

Labelling: The process in which individuals or groups are thought of by teachers, or other agents of social control, in terms of types or stereotypes, usually negative.

 Becker suggested that there was an 'ideal pupil' from the teacher's point of view. Describe what you think an ideal pupil would be like in your school or college. Would the pupils' 'ideal pupil' be the same?

## Self-fulfilling prophecy

Teachers' expectations, based on labels and communicated to the pupil through behaviour and spoken and written comments, can lead to a **self-fulfilling prophecy**. This means that when the pupil accepts the label as being true, it becomes part of how they see themselves (their self-concept). This will then affect their behaviour.

Self-fulfilling prophecy: A predicted outcome that helps to bring about that outcome.

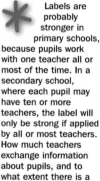 Together, labelling and the self-fulfilling prophecy are the key concepts in the labelling theory approach in the sociology of education and of deviance.

On the other hand, labelling can lead to a self-negating prophecy. Although the teacher is in a position of authority, and seen as having expert knowledge, the pupil may contest the label. This is easier to do if support is available, from parents, peers or perhaps other teachers. The pupil who is told they can't do maths may redouble their efforts to prove that they really can and that the label is wrong. Labels can be negotiated, even rejected.

Labels are probably stronger in primary schools, because pupils work with one teacher all or most of the time. In a secondary school, where each pupil may have ten or more teachers, the label will only be strong if applied by all or most teachers. How much teachers exchange information about pupils, and to what extent there is a 'staffroom culture', may also be important here.

The labelling approach tends to lead the sociologist into being on the side of the person labelled. However, we need to consider what it was in the first place that led to the label being applied. The pupils who have reputations as troublemakers are unlikely to be innocent victims of labelling – they probably did cause trouble at some point!

# Streaming, banding and setting

## Mixed ability classes and streaming

The ways in which schools group pupils for teaching can affect how well they do and can involve labelling and the self-fulfilling prophecy. The main methods of grouping are set out below:

- *Mixed ability* – pupils of all abilities are taught together.
- *Streaming* – pupils are grouped by ability and are with the same pupils for all or most of their subjects, so that there will be a 'top stream' of the academically most able and a 'bottom stream' of those seen as low achievers.
- *Banding* – pupils are placed in large groups covering a fairly wide range of ability, which are then divided into teaching groups.
- *Setting* – pupils are placed in different ability groups for different subjects, so that, for example, a pupil might be in a top set in maths but a mixed ability set in English.

In primary schools and the first years of secondary school, mixed-ability classes, with pupils of all abilities, are common. Even in mixed-ability classes, there may be ability groupings for particular activities. Banding and setting are often used later in secondary education and especially in the GCSE years, when grouping by ability can help teachers prepare their classes for a particular tier.

Streaming, banding and setting are supposed to be based on ability. However, there is considerable evidence that other factors also affect decisions about groupings. For example, 'bright' pupils whose behaviour is seen as a problem may not be allocated to the top sets because it is thought that they will disrupt the learning of other pupils. This has been said to particularly affect African–Caribbean boys.

## Class, gender and ethnicity

Stereotyping, labelling and the school procedures for grouping are all related to class, gender and ethnicity. The experiences of boys and girls from different classes and ethnic backgrounds are explored on pp. 82–93. For example, on pp. 90–1, you can read about recent research looking at how the re-introduction of streaming and setting in some schools has affected working-class boys.

## Think it through

The following is a summary of Connolly's (1998) findings from studying 5- and 6-year-olds in a primary school.

> Because the 'Bad Boys' (a group of four Black boys) played together they were seen as a group of black boys. When teachers, with the best intentions, drew attention to their behaviour, it reinforced the image their white peers had of them as 'bad'. This created a situation where the boys were likely to be verbally and physically attacked and drawn into fights and situations, which confirmed their reputations. This shaped the boys' sense of who they were and the reactions of their peers to them. On the other hand, Wesley, a black boy who played in a group that because it was otherwise white was seen as a group of 'boys' (seen in gender but not racial terms), was able to avoid being pulled into the processes that so affected the Bad Boys.

1 Explain the information about the 'Bad Boys' in this summary using the concepts of labelling and the self-fulfilling prophecy.

2 Explain the information about Wesley using the concepts of labelling and the self-negating prophecy.

3 In what ways might the labelling process be different for girls?

*Paul Connolly has his own website, which includes a section on the sociology of education:* www.paulconnolly.net

## Important studies

Rosenthal and Jacobson (1968) studied the idea of self-fulfilling prophecy in schools and claimed to show that children whom teachers were told would be high achievers did well because of teacher expectations. However, their research was ethically dubious; the researchers gave false information to teachers and the education of some children may thereby have been affected.

## Coursework advice

The staffroom is a mystery to those who, like students, are not allowed in it, and the television series 'Teachers' should not be taken as an accurate account of what actually happens in it. But is there a 'staffroom culture' in your school or college, and if so how would you describe it? Interview your teachers to try to find out. This would make an unusual and interesting coursework project.

## Research issues

Much of the evidence about the processes described in this section is based on ethnographic research. Ethnographic research is small scale, often based on small numbers of pupils or classes within a school, not even on a whole school. We need to be wary about generalising from such findings.

## Round-up

The processes of stereotyping, labelling and the self-fulfilling prophecy as described and researched by interactionist sociologists are present in schools. The internal school processes of streaming and setting can be based on labelling, can affect pupils' self-image and can produce self-fulfilling prophecies.

# How is schooling different for girls and boys?

## Provision of schooling

In the past, education was almost always for boys; the education of girls was restricted in many ways. The early public schools were for boys only; the first public schools for girls, such as Cheltenham Ladies College, were founded in the mid-nineteenth century.

Following the Education Act of 1870, most girls and boys went to mixed elementary schools, but most secondary schools were single sex until the 1960s. In the tripartite system of secondary education for all established by the 1944 Education Act, there were fewer places for girls in grammar schools, and girls needed higher scores in the eleven plus test to get into a grammar school.

In the past, there were also very few places for women at universities. Read more about this on page 103.

Even today, how many girls have the opportunity to learn skills that have traditionally been associated with boys?

Read more about this on page 103.

## The curriculum

Before the National Curriculum, girls, especially those at secondary school, tended to study the subjects that would prepare them for their future roles as housewives and mothers. Subjects such as science were thought to be too demanding or irrelevant for them.

With the introduction of the National Curriculum, girls became entitled to equal access to all subjects. Until then, for example, many girls had dropped science subjects (especially physics and chemistry) as soon as they were able to. Girls now have to study science up to the age of 16. This has been seen as an important step towards equality, but it has not solved the problem, because relatively few girls continue to study sciences post-16.

The National Curriculum also made it possible for boys to learn some subjects, from which they had until then been excluded.

## Organisation

The ways in which mixed schools are organised can reinforce to pupils the importance and significance of gender roles. For example, it may be taken for granted that registers are separated into boys and girls; seating plans may be based on gender; PE and games may be segregated. Courses for student teachers now make them more aware of such issues.

 **Some school subjects can be seen as clearly 'gendered' – that is, they are 'boys' subjects (physics, technology) or girls' subjects (dance, child development). How would you classify sociology?**

**Despite the provisions of the National Curriculum, only 2303 of the 40 699 candidates for GCSE Home Economics in 2002 were boys.**

## Staffing

Teaching, always a female-dominated profession, has in recent years become even more female dominated. In the 1960s, 25% of primary-school teachers were male; this has fallen to about 16%. Reasons for this include the following:

- Teachers' pay has not kept pace with that of other professions.
- Men have to be more concerned than in the past about possible allegations of sexual abuse.
- More teachers are on temporary contracts or working part-time.

The senior levels in teaching and in education are however still male dominated. In 2002, for the first time in many years, the number of men training as primary teachers went up.

The result is that boys have few role models among teachers, and these are likely to be senior staff. While girls have more role models, in many schools female teachers are noticeably missing from certain subject areas, especially science and technology.

**Sexism:** Discrimination against people because of their sex; most sexism has been against women.

**Crisis of masculinity:** A term describing how the traditional ways of being a man (such as being a breadwinner) are increasingly difficult.

### Coursework advice
**Are textbooks (especially reading schemes) less sexist than they used to be? Carry out a comparative study.**

EDUCATION

### In the classroom

Teachers give boys and girls different kinds of attention (Spender, 1983). Girls are praised for appearance, good behaviour and neatness of work, but these qualities are valued less highly than what is seen as individuality or creativity in boys.

Girls tend to be more conformist in school. While this may be approved of by teachers, it can also be taken as evidence of limited or average ability. Boys are more likely to take risks in their work; poor work is taken as evidence of laziness, not lack of ability, and occasional success or effort as evidence of being a 'bright spark'. This contributes to the self-perception of boys and girls; boys tend to overestimate their abilities, girls to underestimate theirs.

### Learning resources

Traditional textbooks, some of which are still used in schools, often contain **sexist** materials and images in which:

- the woman's role is trivialised, e.g. a science textbook may show boys carrying out experiments while girls watch or are not present
- examples used may be more likely to appeal to boys than to girls
- the achievements of women and the importance of gender issues may be played down.

Newer textbooks and other resources consciously take account of gender issues and promote equality, avoiding the sexism of earlier books.

The use of resources such as science equipment may be dominated by boys. Teachers do not always challenge the physical domination of spaces by aggressive boys.

### Boys and masculinity

Most of the discussion above has been concerned with the ways in which the gendering of schooling can adversely affect girls. Since the early 1990s, there has also been a concern with the supposed underachievement of boys. Boys are in fact doing better than they did in the past, in terms of exam results, but this improvement has not been as fast as that for girls, and boys are behind girls in most subjects up to the age of 19.

Masculinity used to be accepted without question but, from the early 1990s onwards, it has become an area for concern, because of changes in wider society – especially the decline in traditionally male working-class jobs. Boys no longer had jobs waiting for them at a factory when they left school; they faced unemployment and problems in taking on the traditional male role of breadwinner for a family.

Faced by this '**crisis of masculinity**', some boys have retreated into a traditional aggressively masculine culture. School and academic work are despised because they are associated with feminine qualities. Boys' peer groups enforce a masculine code of behaviour, intimidating girls and boys who cannot or will not fit in.

At the same time, working hard in school has come to be seen as 'feminine', so that boys distance themselves from it to avoid being negatively labelled by their peers. Of course, this doesn't apply to all boys; class and ethnicity are also factors.

The influence of masculine values is much reduced after compulsory education. This partly explains the reduced gap between the achievement of boys and girls at A level and beyond. Many boys go on to achieve high qualifications and move into high-status, highly paid occupations.

# Important studies

Many boys who conform to the expected 'popular masculinity' in school would like to break away from the conformity it imposes on them. It is not seen as 'cool' to work hard in school and it is difficult for boys to win esteem from their peers if they are seen to want to improve their minds. But the boys that Frost, Phoenix and Pattman interviewed (2002) were able to analyse their situation and the hierarchies they had to negotiate with impressive intelligence. They sought ways to get the qualifications they needed, while avoiding the labels of 'boffin' or 'geek'.

Spender (1983) investigated the amount of time teachers give to boys and girls. She tried in her own teaching to divide her time equally, but when she analysed tape-recordings of her lessons found that she was giving more time to boys (58% to 42%). Boys got more attention because they attracted it, through disruptive behaviour if necessary; girls had been socialised into being passive and obedient so could be trusted to get on with work while the teacher watched the boys closely. The girls Spender talked to thought that it was natural that girls should be more quiet and passive.

## Think it through

Research carried out in Coventry showed that one of the main reasons why boys do not do as well as girls in English is because of their attitudes to the subject and to reading. Boys saw English as a 'feminine' subject that was 'alien' to their way of thinking and working; they felt 'uncomfortable' while in science they felt 'safe'.

1 What factors might contribute to the ways boys respond differently, and then achieve differently, in science and in English?

2 How could schools try to raise the achievement of boys in English?

3 Would your ideas in your answer to Question 2 affect the achievement of girls, and would this be unfair?'

Mitsos, E. and Browne, K. (1998) 'Gender differences in education', *Sociology Review*, vol.8 (1), Sept.

# Round-up

**Boys and girls have always had a different experience of schooling. As a result of research and campaigning, there has been a movement towards greater equality of provision (for example, the National Curriculum) and treatment.**

# How can we explain differential achievement between boys and girls?

## Evidence of differential achievement

Girls do better than boys throughout the education system. Here, very briefly, is some of the most striking evidence.

- In 2000, the proportion of girls achieving 5 GCSEs at grade C and above was 53%, compared with 43% for boys.
- Girls now also get a higher proportion of passes at A level, and more grade As, than boys.
- Women are now the majority of undergraduates in British universities, comprising 55% of the total (Denscombe, 2002). In 2000, women achieved more first class-honours degrees than men for the first time.

Evidence of differential achievement?

Figures like these have led to great concern in the media over the past few years about the underachievement of boys. It has been said that boys are 'failing' and that there is a 'crisis'. In fact, boys' achievements have risen year by year, so that boys are doing better than they used to. Girls' achievements have risen faster, so that they have caught up with boys, even in some subjects traditionally considered male, such as maths and science.

However, on closer examination, the picture is even more complex. For example, working-class and black girls do not do as well as middle-class boys. Significant numbers of working-class girls leave education without any qualifications. The subjects taken disproportionately by boys at higher levels (such as ICT, engineering and physics) are also highly valued by society and tend to lead to highly paid occupations. The concern over boys' achievements can therefore be seen as an over-reaction.

When girls were under-achieving in maths and science in the past, there was not the public concern there has been over boys' underachievement. Why was this?

There is also evidence that boys now feel that it is 'uncool' to be seen to work hard and do well at school. Boys who are capable of doing well may feel pressured to behave in ways that ensure they avoid the negative label of 'boffin' being applied by their peers.

One possible reason why boys turn away from reading at an early age is the material used to teach them how to read. Reading is taught mainly through story books; boys tend to prefer factual books.

## Important studies

Murphy and Elwood (1998) argue that children arrive in school with gendered interests and behaviour, based on early socialisation; for example, boys tend to play more with construction toys than girls. In school, boys and girls draw on their previous experiences to make choices that then influence their future achievement. At the same time, schools reinforce the gendered choices children are making, because different subject areas require different styles of response. For example, boys tend to do well in science subjects because the factual and analytical approach favours them; girls are less likely to have acquired and practised this to the same level.

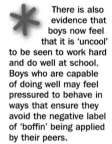

Gender socialisation continues throughout childhood and adolescence.

Primary socialisation within the family means that children arrive in school already aware of gender (and not just sex) differences

*The latest figures on educational achievement in maintained schools can be found in the statistics section of the Department for Education and Skills website:* **www.dfes.gov.uk**

# Reasons for differential achievement

In trying to explain why there are differences between boys and girls, we need to look at a range of factors: genetic (biological) factors, the home and family, the wider social context, and also processes internal to schools.

## Genetic difference?

Scientific researchers claim to have found some sex differences between males and females that would influence achievement at school – for example, it has been claimed that differences in brain structure mean that girls do better on verbal tests and boys on spatial ones. Sociologists would argue, however, that if there are real differences in scores in such tests, these are unlikely to be solely due to natural, innate differences. Boys and girls have different experiences in and out of school, which may affect the results.

## Home and family

Some writers have argued that how well boys and girls do in school is to some extent decided before their formal education even starts.

Socialisation into gender roles starts very early in childhood. Boys and girls play with different toys, do different activities around the home and often see their mothers and fathers playing different roles. Boys and girls may be born with a predisposition to particular kinds of play and activity, but socialisation then exaggerates the difference. Early play in the home may encourage boys to be more interested in scientific and technical subjects and discourage girls from these.

Early socialisation has been said to lead to girls having lower self-esteem than boys, being less confident in their ability to achieve. This is because girls are said to have less control over their lives. When they do well, they may see it as the result of luck, whereas boys are more likely to believe they have worked for and deserved success.

Primary socialisation within the family means that children arrive in school already aware of gender (and not just sex) differences.

## Wider social factors

The improved achievements of girls in schools in recent years are undoubtedly related to wider social changes. Feminism had considerable success in improving the rights of women and in encouraging greater self-confidence and ambition. There are now more role models of successful women available to girls. It needs to be remembered, however, that not everything has changed dramatically: women go out to work more than in the past, but still do most of the housework and childcare, while men continue to occupy most of the positions of power in society.

## What happens in school

The ways in which schools may influence boys and girls differently, both through the way they are structured and through everyday interactions, has been discussed on pp. 82–3.

### Reading

One of the factors behind the lower achievement of boys is probably that boys tend to be less interested in reading. From about the age of eight, many boys see reading as primarily a girls' activity, too passive and 'boring'. This may be influenced by what they see happening in the home and at school: in our society females tend to read more than males. They therefore fail to acquire the most vital skill for success in school as fast as girls.

## Think it through

**GCSE achievement by gender**

|  | Boys | Girls |
| --- | --- | --- |
| Percentages entered for 5 or more GCSEs | 89.5 | 93.1 |
| Percentages achieving 5 or more grades A* to C | 43.4 | 54.4 |
| Percentages achieving 5 or more grades A to G | 86.8 | 91.0 |
| Average GCSE points score | 36.1 | 41.8 |

From: GCSE/GNVQ Examination Results of young people in England, 2001–02, Early Statistics, taken from www.dfes.gov.uk 23 November 2002

1 What conclusions about differential attainment by gender can be drawn from these figures?

2 What reasons have been put forward by sociologists to account for these differences?

## Watch out

In any research in this area, it is essential to take into account variables other than sex. While girls' achievement has been rising overall, significant numbers of mainly working-class girls are still 'failing', leaving school with few qualifications, if any. Equally, many boys do extremely well. It is not only gender that is involved, but also social and economic background, and, of course, individual differences too. Gender is an important factor, but it is inextricably linked with other factors.

## Round-up

Girls do better than boys at all stages of compulsory education, at A level and at university. The gap is narrow in subjects traditionally thought of as boys' subjects, such as science and technology. However, the achievement of boys has been improving – that is, boys today are doing better than boys did in the past. The level of concern over the supposed underachievement of boys can be seen as an over-reaction. There are a number of possible reasons for the greater success of girls. These can be grouped under the headings of genetic differences, home and family, wider social factors and processes within schools.

# How do schools transmit ethnic and national identities?

Schools have always played a part in the transmission of a sense of national identity to a new generation. In many countries, national identity is reinforced daily; there may be a national flag flying above the school, or even in every classroom; assemblies may include the singing of a national anthem, and books and lessons may concentrate on the achievements of the nation.

In the past, the banning of the Welsh language in schools in Wales, with humiliating punishments for those caught speaking Welsh, was an attempt to force a sense of British (and English-speaking) identity on young Welsh people. Today, schools in Wales can teach through the medium of the Welsh language and a different national identity – a Welsh one – is being fostered.

In recent years in Britain, however, the main focus of debate has been the relationship between schools and the experience of children from Britain's minority ethnic groups. Pupils from such groups have had mixed success in British schools.

*What is the experience of children from Britain's ethnic minorities?*

## Important studies

Reay and Mirza (2000) found 60 supplementary schools in London, open on Saturdays or Sundays, with an average of 30–40 pupils. Most were run by women working as volunteers. They teach basic skills but also often black history and culture. By creating a black space and valuing blackness, such schools can provide a sense of identity and belonging, as suggested by this quotation:

*'When I came back with him from Saturday school Akin was jumping all over the place and saying, "Mum, why can't I go to this school five days a week?" He loved it, he was really excited. He said I know all about so and so and about so and so, all these people from black history. He was fascinated and up to now if he's going to do black history he's really excited'.*

Reay and Mirza (2000) p. 533

OFSTED's report on the education of minority ethnic group pupils, and reports on many other aspects of education, can be found at www.ofsted.gov.uk

## Racism in schools

### Institutional racism

In 1999 the Office for Standards in Education (OFSTED) said that many of Britain's schools were institutionally racist; that is, some of the ways in which schools were organised and did their teaching had the unintended effect of putting minority ethnic pupils at a disadvantage.

Several sociological studies had earlier found evidence of **institutional racism** in British schools. Racism seems to take the following main forms:

- *Discrimination in allocation to sets* – Research at 'Jayleigh' comprehensive school found that allocation of pupils to sets and streams was not based solely on ability (Commission for Racial Equality, 1992). This discriminated against Asian pupils; they needed higher marks to get into top sets and were entered for fewer GCSEs.

- *Different treatment by teachers* – African-Caribbean boys were more likely to be seen as troublemakers than other pupils and to be punished. This is a form of labelling, resulting in the self-fulfilling prophecy (see pp. 80). The rate of exclusions of African-Caribbean boys is much higher than for any other group of pupils.

### Ethnocentrism

'**Ethnocentrism**' in education refers to the ways in which what happens in schools can seem to be irrelevant to, or to ignore, pupils from minority ethnic groups. For example, particular subjects may have a narrow, white, British focus. In 1999, OFSTED drew attention to the use of out-of-date materials that could be potentially offensive and, by reflecting old colonial values, could perpetuate racial stereotyping (OFSTED, 1999). Some aspects of the National Curriculum could be said to be ethnocentric, such as the requirement to learn British history.

**Institutional racism:** This occurs when the way in which an organisation or institution operates has racist outcomes, regardless of the intentions of individuals within it.

**In what other ways might a school, or any other organisation, be institutionally racist?**

**Ethnocentrism:** Looking at an issue from one particular cultural point of view.

**Multicultural education:** Education that teaches all children about the cultures of some of the minority groups.

**Research issues** Research in this field
needs to take into account the great diversity of ethnic
groups within Britain. For example, studies rarely
consider white minorities or traveller children. While the
term 'Asian' is usually sub-divided into Indian, Pakistani
and Bangladeshi, these terms conceal the range of
ethnicities represented: of languages, religions, class
or caste backgrounds and areas of origin. Similarly, the
label 'African-Caribbean' conceals the differences
between different islands of origin in the Caribbean. It
is also used to mean 'black', when Britain's black
population contains many people of African origin.

## Watch out

Everyone belongs to an ethnic group, so be careful not to
use the term 'ethnic' to refer only to minorities or to African-
Caribbean or Asian people.

These processes are exacerbated by the fact that many,
though far from all, schools with high proportions of pupils
from minority groups are in working-class areas, often in inner
cities, and may be short of educational resources and find it
hard to recruit and retain good teachers.

## School policies

### Multicultural education

In 1985 the Swann Report (DES, 1985), which found evidence
of underachievement by African-Caribbean children in
particular, recommended that schools actively promote the
idea of Britain as a multicultural society. However, it opposed
the ideas of separate schools for minorities and bilingual
teaching. **Multicultural education** in practice meant that the
content of lessons was revised to take into account minority
groups. For example, English literature lessons might include a
poem from the Caribbean or an Indian story; in music children
might learn about and get a chance to play steel drums.
Special assemblies were held to celebrate festivals in religions
other than Christianity.

Multicultural education was well intentioned, but was open to
criticism for being a form of tokenism. It acknowledged the
presence of pupils from minority groups and attempted to
include them. However, it failed to recognise that pupils from
minority groups faced racism both in and out of school. It was
also usually seen as something that only need concern schools
that had pupils from minority groups. Despite this, there was
some opposition from parents who believed that only the
white majority culture should be recognised.

### Anti-racist education

This later phase attempted to tackle racism within schools by
acknowledging that it existed, and seeking to educate children
in ways that would get rid of it. Many schools developed written
anti-racist policies and punished racist behaviour more severely.

Concern about racism in schools and the experience of pupils
from minority groups continues to be a major interest of
educational researchers.

## Think it through

Children coped with different kinds of incidents in different
ways. Those children who had arrived in Britain recently often
did not understand what was being said to them. Other Asian
children, Bangladeshi, Pakistani and Indian, who happened to
be within earshot would painfully explain to them, they told
me, the meaning of derogatory words like 'Paki', 'curry', 'wog'
and 'scum'... Racist name-calling was not talked about
openly by the teachers and not recognized for what it was.
Verbal abuse was not seen as a discipline problem generally;
if no physical attack occurred it was something the children
had to learn to cope with on their own.

Bhatti, G. (1999) *Asian children at home
and at school*, Routledge, London, pp. 173–4

1  What problems are there for teachers and schools in trying
to combat racism against pupils from minority ethnic
groups?

2  Does your school or college have a written anti-racist
policy? If so, what does it include? Would it help the
children in the item above?

3  If your school or college does not have an anti-racist policy,
this may be because it has very few pupils from minority
groups. Do you think such schools should have a policy?
Justify your answer.

# Round-up

Britain's minority ethnic groups come from a wide range of
cultural, linguistic and religious backgrounds. Their experiences
in school are equally varied. There is evidence, however, of
institutional racism within schools, and of racist behaviour
within schools both by teachers and pupils. The response of
schools and government policies to racism has moved beyond
multicultural education to a stronger anti-racist position.

# How can we explain differential achievement between ethnic groups?

## Evidence of differential achievement

- Just under 50% of white pupils achieve five or more GCSEs at grades A to C. The figure is about 10% higher for British Indian pupils, but lower for other minority ethnic groups; for Pakistani and Bangladeshi pupils it is under 30%.
- As well as Indian pupils, Chinese and other Asian pupils also achieve above the national average.
- Although they are still behind the national average, the proportion of African-Caribbean pupils gaining five or more GCSEs at C and above went up 6% between 1996 and 1998, and the proportion of Bangladeshi pupils doing so went up 8%.
- Members of ethnic minorities are more likely than members of the white majority to stay in education after age 16; 71% compared to 58% are in full-time education (Denscombe, 2002, p. 18).
- Those who were not in full-time education were twice as likely to be unemployed as their white counterparts.

## Reasons for differential achievement

Ethnicity cannot be separated from other factors that influence attainment. We need to look at how ethnicity interacts with class and gender.

### Class

Immigrants to Britain from the West Indies in the 1950s and 1960s were mainly recruited for working-class occupations such as driving underground trains and buses. There were few West Indian immigrants who were professionals. Upward mobility of the next generation was held back by prejudice and discrimination, and the result was a high proportion of African-Caribbean pupils from working-class backgrounds. The situation of Asian families is more complex. Asian immigrants to Britain included professionals and business people from India and people of Indian origin from East Africa, but many Pakistani and Bangladeshi immigrants were from rural and poor backgrounds.

Some of the differences in educational attainment between different ethnic groups can therefore be explained by differences in class background (see pp. 92–3).

### Gender

Boys and girls respond differently both to the tensions between home and school and to experiences within school. They may also have different aspirations (see p. 85). Girls from Muslim backgrounds are less likely to go into higher education than other groups.

### *Genetic difference?*

One possible explanation for differential attainment is that different ethnic or racial groups have different levels of ability. This view now has little support. Intelligence has usually been measured by Intelligence Quotient (IQ) tests, but the validity of these tests has been challenged, partly on the grounds that they are biased in favour of children from white, middle-class backgrounds. The Swann Report (Department for Education and Science, 1985) found that after social and economic factors were controlled, there were no significant differences in IQ scores between racial groups.

Indian, Chinese and Asian pupils tend to achieve above the national educational average

## Important studies

Bhatti (1999) followed 50 working-class Bangladeshi and Pakistani teenagers who initially spoke little English. Both boys and girls reported many instances of racist behaviour by teachers (there were no Asian teachers), including ignoring them in class, not helping them and not believing them when they complained about the behaviour of white children. They felt that teachers had low expectations of them and that they often seemed to be 'invisible'; their achievements, their culture and festivals went unremarked. Some teachers even made little effort to pronounce names properly.

## Home-based factors: cultural difference

Differences in aspects of culture such as language, religion, dress and aspirations can affect attainment.

- *Language* – pupils need standard English to succeed in the British education system. In the past, language difficulties applied with first-generation immigrants, and today this may be a problem for recently arrived refugees.
- *Religion* – for pupils from some minority groups, strong religious values in the home and community provide a source of encouragement, emphasising the importance of a good education.
- *Dress and appearance* – the appearance of some pupils from minority groups may reinforce images held by teachers, whether positive or negative. For example, the visible signs of adherence to Rastafarianism may suggest to teachers a rebellious attitude and potential trouble.
- *Aspirations* – the home and community backgrounds of many pupils from minority groups offer strong support and encouragement for educational success. For many parents and grandparents, migration to Britain offered a better education and a greater chance of success for their families.

### Cultural deprivation

The theory of cultural deprivation, which has been applied to people in poverty generally, has also been applied specifically to minority ethnic groups. In particular, it has been claimed, mainly by the New Right, that the high proportion of lone-parent Caribbean families fail to provide a home environment conducive to learning. However, many African-Caribbean parents value education very highly.

### School-based factors

The ways in which schools may affect the achievement of different ethnic groups was considered on pp. 86–7.

### Wider social factors

The attainment of minority ethnic groups in schools needs to be considered in the context of a society where equality of opportunity has not been achieved. The results of discrimination against minorities are apparent in employment, housing and health. Differential educational attainment is characteristic of a society that has not yet eliminated racism.

African-Caribbean boys are often seen as being a source of 'trouble' in schools, and they account for a high percentage of exclusions from school. Some of the research on racism in schools focuses on what happens in schools – setting, different treatment by teachers and so on – which implicitly assumes that schools are creating the problem. An alternative view is that African-Caribbean boys may already be well aware of the racism of the wider society. Their poor behaviour may be real and the result of their perception of their prospects in a racist society, rather than being generated by the school itself. From this point of view, schools can only have limited success in tackling the problem – its origins and its solutions lie beyond the school.

## Tackling underachievement: beyond state schooling

Making state schools more equal is one way of addressing the problem of underachievement among minority ethnic groups. The minorities themselves are looking for their own ways forward. There is often a strong belief in and desire for improving their children's lives through education. Black British people often have a passionate belief in and desire for education, and where racism or other factors hold their children back, supplementary schools have been set up.

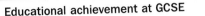

# Think it through

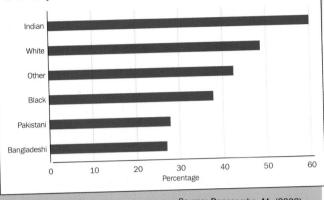

**Educational achievement at GCSE**
% of 16-year-olds achieving 5 or more A–Cs at GCSE

Source: Denscombe, M. (2002)
*Sociology update*, Olympus Press, Leicester

**1** What factors might explain why children from Indian backgrounds are more successful than white children?

**2** What factors might explain why Pakistani and Bangladeshi children are less successful?

## Coursework advice

There are many kinds of supplementary schooling, not all provided by or for minorities. They include music schools and church Sunday Schools. Are there any in your area? Who organises and runs them?

## Research issues

Ethnicity is only one factor that influences educational attainment. It is interrelated with others, such as class and gender and it is difficult to assess the relative importance of these factors.

# Round-up

The differential attainment of minority ethnic groups can be explained by a range of factors, including home, family and cultural background as well as school-based processes. In a society where there is racism, it is not surprising that some minority groups struggle; in this context, the achievement of some groups and some individuals then appears a remarkable story of success against the odds.

# How do schools transmit social-class identities?

## History of schooling of different social classes

### Before 1944

Before 1870, school education was largely the preserve of the rich and powerful. A minority of children from lower classes received a short, basic education in church and charity schools.

From the 1870 Education Act until World War II, the type of school children went to and the education they received still depended mainly on their class background (see p. 94). Upper-class children attended public, fee-paying, schools, which aimed to develop the qualities of leadership and character seen as necessary for the future leaders of society. Middle-class children attended grammar schools, which copied the style of public schools but were less prestigious and charged lower fees. Working-class children attended elementary schools, which taught basic literacy and numeracy, obedience, punctuality, and the value of hard work. England and Wales had an educational system that offered a basic schooling to all and a more privileged education to some.

Mirroring roles

### 1944 and after

The system of universal secondary education brought in by the 1944 Act reflected these class divisions. Although its aim was to create equality of opportunity, it assumed that different types of children required different education, and the ideas of difference built into this assumption were largely based on social-class differences. Upper-class families could still buy a privileged education in public schools for their children. Grammar schools took far more middle-class children than working-class children; the latter tended to go to secondary modern and technical schools.

From the 1960s, the comprehensive system attempted to remove these class divisions. However, because comprehensives were based on local catchment areas, which were often overwhelmingly one social class, the hoped for mixing of social classes within schools did not always happen. The old class differences can still be discerned in the educational system today, particularly in the fact that independent schools still exist for those who are able to pay the fees.

Correspondence theory: The view that what happens in schools mirrors (corresponds to) what will happen at work, with different classes having different experiences.

## What happens in schools

Schools are essentially middle-class institutions. Most teachers are from middle-class backgrounds, and those who are not have successfully negotiated the education system to become middle class themselves.

### MARXISM

Marxist sociologists have been particularly interested in the relationship between education and class. Schooling is seen as a way in which the ruling class maintains its power through conveying an ideology justifying the capitalist system. Schooling ensures that most working-class children fail, but it persuades them that the system that fails them is fair, so that they do not protest against it. Working-class children then have to take working-class jobs, which are lower paid and have lower status. This is known as **correspondence theory**.

Marxist theory is explained on p. 73, and you can find out more about the factors that lead to the failure of working-class children on pp. 92–3.

The processes described by interactionists (see p. 76) can be applied specifically to social-class differences in schools:

- *Labelling* – working-class pupils are less likely than middle-class pupils to meet teachers' expectations of the ideal pupil, and more likely to be labelled negatively.

- *Self-fulfilling prophecy* – a negative label, such as not being bright or being a troublemaker, can become a self-fulfilling prophecy, which is then likely to affect how well the labelled pupil does in school.

- *Setting and streaming* – the labelling of working-class pupils can lead to them being more likely to be put in lower streams or sets. This can increase their sense of alienation from the school and from education. They may also be less likely to be entered for higher tier examinations at GCSE, thus limiting the grades they might achieve.

- *Course choice* – at age 16, working-class children are more likely than middle-class children to choose vocational courses rather than to follow the traditionally middle-class route to A levels, leading on to higher education.

The government would like vocational courses to have the same status as academic courses, but this has not yet been achieved. Read more about this on pp. 100–01.

Watch out for media reports of 'failing' schools. Are these schools in working-class areas with working-class intakes?

### Can schools make a difference?

Schools with high working-class intakes are often in deprived areas. They may have a reputation for poor behaviour or lack of success, as measured by league tables. They may have difficulty retaining and recruiting staff because of difficult working conditions, high levels of stress and low staff morale. Despite this, many schools do produce results that are better than expected when the social-class background of pupils is taken into account (Macbeath and Mortimore, 2001). However, even the better schools seem unable entirely to remove the influence of social-class background on educational attainment.

## Think it through

Evidence from more recent studies suggests that the reform of schooling from the late 1980s to the mid-1990s, at a time when traditional male working-class jobs in the heavy manufacturing industries were in decline, exacerbated rather than reduced school resistance. By increasing emphasis on performance and on competition within and between schools and by raising the stakes in terms of compliance to a school culture that was class orientated, schools were more rather than less likely to be viewed as hostile institutions... The reintroduction of streaming and the promotion of setting by school subjects for many such boys would confirm their failure to succeed...

From: Arnot, M., David, M. and Weiner, G. (1999)
*Closing the gender gap*, Polity Press, Cambridge, p. 43

1 How have reforms in schooling attempted to reduce class divisions?

2 How has the impact of these varied for boys and for girls?

Research issues There are difficulties with operationalising the concept of 'class'. A person's class is usually set from the occupation of the main wage-earner in the family but this is far from straightforward. Researchers don't always have access to the necessary information on each pupil's background, and, in any case, occupation is a fairly crude measure of class.

## Important studies

In 1986, Abraham carried out an ethnographic study of a comprehensive school (published in 1995), which he called Greenfield and which had a wide range of intake by both ability and social class. He studied both class and gender, and the interactions between them. Among the main findings related to class were the following:

- Working-class pupils were more likely to be in lower sets.
- Lower sets were more unruly in their behaviour; pupils in lower sets were more likely to be sent out of lessons or reported for bad behaviour.
- Pupils in lower sets were more likely to opt for practical subjects, often on teachers' advice.
- Lower sets were not given the opportunity to study some topics.

Abraham's research confirmed the theory that schools play a major part in perpetuating class inequalities, though, of course, his study was of only one school. It also suggests that reducing setting, while it might lower a school's overall results, would be an effective way of reducing class differences in education.

Abraham's research was carried out before the National Curriculum was introduced. How might this, and other changes, have affected what happens in Greenfield?

## Round-up

The structure of the education system still reflects class divisions in society. Processes within schools, such as labelling and setting and streaming, can further contribute to the alienation of working-class children from education. Nevertheless, some schools achieve great success for their working-class pupils, against the odds.

# How can we explain differential achievement between classes?

Can home background factors related to social class influence educational success?

## Intelligence, home or school?

### Inherited intelligence

Intelligence is both hard to define and to measure. Some writers have suggested that middle-class children do better in school because they have inherited intelligence from their parents, who, it is assumed, must have been intelligent to be middle class. However, intelligence is the product of both inheritance and environment, and the potential to do well is probably equally distributed across all social classes.

 **Much of the research on class and educational achievement was carried out between the 1950s and 1970s. More recently, the emphasis has been on gender and, to a lesser extent, ethnicity. However, all these factors are interrelated.**

**Deferred gratification:** Putting off immediate satisfaction in order to get a greater reward later.

**Underclass:** A group at the bottom of the social ladder, said to be characterised by violent crime, illegitimacy, unemployment and dependency on welfare benefits.

**Cultural capital:** The values, knowledge or ideas that parents can pass on to their children, which can then influence their success at school and later in life.

### Home-based factors

#### Material deprivation

Children living in or on the margins of poverty may be disadvantaged by:

- not having a quiet place to work
- inadequate diet, causing problems in concentration
- being unable to afford 'extras'; although education is free, parents are expected to provide uniform and other equipment and to contribute to the costs of trips.

#### Cultural deprivation theory

This suggests that working-class children fail because of the cultural values into which they have been socialised. The following may prevent educational success:

- a fatalistic attitude
- a need for immediate rather than **deferred gratification**
- for boys, a liking for thrills and excitement, which may get them into trouble
- little value put on education by parents
- absence of role models in the family and community.

Recently, New Right thinkers have linked these ideas to the emergence of an **underclass**. They argue that in the underclass, failure at school is one negative factor among others (such as illegitimacy and dropping out of the labour force) that lead to the same values being passed on to the next generation, who in turn will be unable to break away from the limitations on their potential.

One criticism of the cultural deprivation approach is that differences between middle-class and working-class culture do not necessarily show that the latter indicates deprivation. The assumption that aspects of working-class culture are negative is made by academics and researchers who are middle class.

#### Learning to be poor

Children in low-income families become aware of their family's financial problems at an early age and scale down their hopes and aspirations for the future. They are more likely than other children to want jobs that require few qualifications and little training, and less likely to aspire to a professional career (Shropshire and Middleton, 1999).

# Important studies

Research by Brynner and Joshi (in Denscombe, 2000) showed that class remains a strong influence on educational achievement. They compared the experiences of 9000 people born in 1970 with those of 11 000 born in 1958. They found that the two cohorts experienced similar inequalities of opportunity. For the cohort born in 1970, there had been improvements; for example, they gained more qualifications and a higher proportion went to college or university. But the gap between those with professional backgrounds and those from unskilled manual backgrounds remained as wide as ever.

Bourdieu's theory has been applied in Britain by Sullivan (2001). To operationalise the concept of cultural capital, she looked at reading and television-viewing habits, music, participation in cultural activities such as going to art galleries and museums, knowledge of famous cultural figures and vocabulary. She found that cultural capital was transmitted within the home, was closely related to social class and did have a significant effect on achievement at GCSE. However, social class in itself, regardless of cultural capital, also had an effect. So, cultural capital only explains part of the difference in educational attainment.

## Think it through

Social class is one of the key factors that determine whether a child does well or badly at primary school, according to new research. The study... compares last month's key stage 2 league table results with the information on social class taken from the 1991 census. It shows that local education authorities with the lowest proportion of household heads in partly skilled or unskilled occupations are those with the best key stage 2 skills.

From: Dean, C. (1997) 'Social class linked to results', *Times Educational Supplement*, 18 April

1 What factors might contribute to the pattern of underachievement at primary level revealed by this research?

2 What questions should be asked when evaluating the methods and findings of this research?

3 Suggest and describe other ways in which the effects of social class on education could be investigated.

## Language

Based on research done in the 1970s, Basil Bernstein (1990) argued that language could be described as having two codes. The 'restricted code' is used in everyday communication with people we know well; its vocabulary is limited and meanings are not always made explicit because the two parties share knowledge and assumptions. 'Elaborated code' makes meanings explicit and can be used to express complex and abstract ideas. This is the code used by teachers and in textbooks, and which is required in written work. Bernstein suggested that working-class children were, because of their different exposure to types of language, less likely to be proficient in using the elaborated code. It is important to note, however, that the restricted code has its own strengths and uses, and that everybody uses it – it is not simply working-class speech.

## Cultural capital

The concept of **cultural capital** was developed by the French sociologist Pierre Bourdieu (Bourdieu and Passeron, 1977). This refers to how the advantages of middle- and upper-class pupils derive not only from financial capital (the ability of their parents to buy education) but also from cultural capital, which includes such things as tastes, values and behaviour. The advantages parents can give to their children in terms of cultural capital include familiarity with books and reading, museums and art galleries and a sense of the importance of education. Each class has varying amounts of cultural capital. Pupils with high cultural capital will be judged favourably by teachers and will be likely to be among the most high-achieving students.

## Positional theory

The French sociologist Raymond Boudon (1974) stresses the importance of considering the class position of pupils when assessing the costs and benefits to them of choices about education. For example, a boy from a middle-class background may see himself as a failure if he does not go to university; his parents may well have assumed all his life that he would enter a profession. On the other hand, a student from a working-class background might well be the first person from their family to go into higher education, and might have to loosen ties with their community and move away socially from friends who do not go on to higher education.

## *School-based factors*

The ways in which school-based factors can affect the class-based differences that are rooted in home and social background have been discussed on pp. 90–1.

# Tackling the problem

Many recent government measures to raise standards in schools are trying to address the problem of working-class underachievement, although open references to class are rare. One initiative has been the creation of Education Action Zones (EAZs). These are disadvantaged areas that have been selected for extra assistance. In EAZs, schools and LEAs work with local businesses and other industries. They have received extra funding.

More broadly, the restructuring of the school system to encompass greater choice and competition and different types of schools can be seen as giving greater influence to parents, including working-class parents.

According to Gerwitz *et al.* (1995), most middle-class parents are more active and better informed in choosing a school for their children, and making sure their children are accepted, than are working-class parents.

# Round-up

**Despite the overall rise in attainment, there are still significant class differences. The lower levels of attainment of working-class children in schools can be explained by a variety of factors. Some explanations emphasise how inequalities outside school inevitably affect performance in school. Others emphasise the ways in which schools themselves contribute to class differences in attainment.**

# How have political decisions shaped schooling? Part One: 1870–1979

Education for the mass of the population in Britain is relatively new. The two ancient universities of Oxford and Cambridge, many public schools and some grammar schools go back hundreds of years, but they only provided an education for an élite.

After the Industrial Revolution of the eighteenth and nineteenth centuries, it was argued that workers needed to learn basic literacy and numeracy, plus respect for authority and the social order. Against this, it was argued that teaching people to read would give them access to the radical ideas that had fuelled the revolutions in the USA and France. Education for working-class children was provided largely by voluntary agencies and was not seen as a way of providing equality of opportunity. However, by the mid-nineteenth century, governments began to consider replacing this haphazard system with a national system.

## The Forster Act, 1870

This Act made elementary education available to all, although this did not become compulsory until 1880. Local School Boards were given the power to start schools in areas where there was no voluntary provision. Many new schools were built at this time.

Early in the twentieth century, School Boards were replaced by Local Education Authorities (LEAs), which were able to start new secondary schools modelled on existing grammar schools. The school-leaving age was raised to 14; children who were selected at age 11 could go a secondary school, while the majority stayed on in elementary schools.

## The Butler Education Act, 1944

This Act was one of a whole range of measures (including a major expansion of the Welfare State, the nationalisation of basic industries and the creation of the National Health Service), which together had the intention of rebuilding a better country.

The Act had the following effects:
* It classified education into three periods: primary for ages 5–11; secondary for ages 11–15 and further and higher for those who chose to remain in education after this age.
* It introduced free secondary education for all, provided in three types of school (the tripartite system), designed to meet the needs of pupils according to their 'age, aptitude and ability': grammar, secondary modern and technical schools. These are described on p. 75.

In addition, the independent-school sector remained for parents who could afford to buy a privileged education for their children. The declared aim of the tripartite system was to provide equality of educational opportunity.

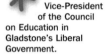

William Forster was Vice-President of the Council on Education in Gladstone's Liberal Government.

R A Butler was Minister of Education in the coalition government led by Winston Churchill during World War II.

### HAVE COMPREHENSIVES SUCCEEDED?

**FOR** – The period of comprehensive schooling has seen a big rise in the number and level of qualifications gained by pupils of all backgrounds and abilities, although significant numbers continue to underachieve. Although comparisons between different periods are problematic, comprehensives appear to have widened access and opportunity.

**AGAINST** – Comprehensives have been accused of teaching towards the middle range, and thereby failing to stretch the most able students.

Comprehensives did not break down class differences. Middle-class pupils continue to do significantly better than working-class pupils. This may have been partly because many schools used setting and streaming as ways of providing a different education to different pupils within the same school. The intended mixing of children from different social classes through attending the same school did not happen either, because comprehensives were based on geographical catchment areas, often mainly inhabited by one class.

The failure to abolish independent schools and to completely eliminate grammar and secondary moderns means that there never was a truly comprehensive system.

## Think it through

One of its [the secondary modern school] main socialising effects is to lower the ambitions of those who pass through it to accord with the opportunities in the labour market... The training and environment of this type of school appear to inculcate into children, directly or indirectly, the realisation that they have been earmarked for the less desirable positions in society. Youthful hopes they might have entertained earlier on tend not to survive the secondary modern experience... The experience of the minority funnelled off by grammar schools... is markedly different... Indeed, there is some evidence that selection for grammar school tends to expand future ambitions; this, as we might expect, is particularly true of working-class children entering grammar school.

Parkin, F. (1972) *Class inequality and political order*, Paladin, St Albans, p. 63

1 How might a child's ambitions have been shaped by the experience of taking the Eleven Plus test?

2 What was the effect of selection and the tripartite system on (a) working-class and middle-class children; and (b) boys and girls?

*Schooling for all – driven by economic needs*

## *Criticisms of the tripartite system*

### The eleven plus

Children were allocated to different types of schools on the basis of Intelligence Quotient (IQ) tests taken at age 11. Inevitably, IQ tests have cultural assumptions built into them, which may lead to some children, such as those from middle-class backgrounds, having an advantage. Eleven is also an early age to test ability; the system did not provide for 'late developers'.

### Gender

Girls tended to do better in the eleven plus exam than boys. However, in most areas there were roughly equal numbers of places in grammar schools for boys, or more places for boys. The result was that boys were able to get grammar-school places with lower scores in the eleven plus test than girls needed. This was clearly unfair.

### Status of schools

Although this was not the intention, grammar schools were seen as better than other schools – partly because their pupils sat examinations. Grammar schools were able to attract better-qualified staff and had better resources.

### The self-fulfilling prophecy

The self-esteem of children who failed to get grammar school places may have been affected. Knowing they had in effect been labelled as failures, their response could be to believe that they were not very 'clever' and not to try hard. The result would be low attainment and would be an example of the self-fulfilling prophecy (see also p. 80).

### Class

The tripartite system perpetuated the class divide in British education: in effect, grammar schools were for the middle class and small numbers of 'bright' working-class children while secondary moderns and technical schools were for the working class.

Middle-class parents could provide coaching for the eleven plus. If, despite this, the child failed, the parents could opt for independent education.

## Comprehensive schools

Dissatisfaction with the tripartite system grew, because it was clearly failing to develop the potential of large numbers of pupils. In 1965, the Labour government asked LEAs to plan to introduce comprehensive secondary education, in which all pupils from an area would go to the same school, have the same opportunities, and mix with children from other social classes. Some LEAs gave this low priority and tried to keep their grammar and secondary modern schools.

Over the next 15 years, progress towards comprehensives depended on which party was in power, both at local and national level. Labour pushed for comprehensives on social justice grounds, while most Conservatives preferred the old system, believing it suited the abilities of different types of children. However, by 1979 about 80% of pupils were in comprehensive schools.

*Many secondary schools now have their own websites. Find out the names and website addresses of schools of different types, e.g. a comprehensive school and a grammar school. Visit their sites and compare them.*

# Round-up

**One of the most striking features of the history of schooling in Britain is the persistence of different types of education for children from different social classes. Schooling for all is relatively new, and the main reason it was introduced was to improve the efficiency of the workforce, rather than for reasons of social justice. The comprehensive ideal, which was driven by social justice and equality, was never put fully into practice.**

## Watch out

**In an exam, note carefully what time period you are being asked about, and keep to it.**

Grammar schools still exist in some areas (e.g. Kent), often affecting neighbouring comprehensives by 'creaming off' some of the brightest pupils.

## Coursework advice

**Your parents, grandparents and other older people will have experienced the schools and changes described here. You could find out more about education in the past using informal interviews with any of these people.**

# How have political decisions shaped schooling? Part Two: 1979–1997

## New Right thinking

The Conservative governments led by Margaret Thatcher and John Major moved all areas of social policy decisively away from the post-war 'consensus', whereby neither party had attempted to fundamentally alter the systems created in the late 1940s by Labour. Instead, the Conservatives implemented policies based on New Right thinking.

New Right thinking on education included these aims:

- to introduce market forces into education, through encouraging competition between schools and parental choice
- to reduce the power of local education authorities
- to enhance the role of business in schools
- to ensure that schools could not be used for political purposes by opponents of Conservatism. Some Conservatives believed that radical teachers and LEAs were spreading propaganda through the curriculum and also through progressive teaching styles.

### *Support for private education*

The first major change was the introduction of the Assisted Places Scheme, by which the government provided funding for some pupils to attend independent schools, subsidised independent schools, implying that the government believed that independent schools provided a better education than state schools. Almost all the senior Conservative politicians of this period had attended private schools, and sent their children to private schools.

**The future of schools?**

### *The 1988 Education Reform Act*

 The Act was introduced by Kenneth Baker, Minister of Education in Margaret Thatcher's government at the time.

This Act was the major break with previous educational policies.

#### The National Curriculum

The Act introduced a National Curriculum for all children aged 5–16. Unlike most other advanced countries, Britain had had little government involvement in what was taught in schools; this had been left to LEAs, head teachers and individual teachers.

The National Curriculum does not apply to independent schools, and so 'National' is not an accurate description.

The 1988 Act identified three core subjects (English, maths and science) and foundation subjects (geography, history, technology, a modern foreign language, music, physical education and art), which all pupils had a right to study. Over the next few years, exactly what should be taught within these subjects began to be specified, and also at what stage in education they should be taught. There have been several changes to the National Curriculum, but its essential structure remains intact.

 This is one of the reasons why GCSE sociology is not more widely taught.

The National Curriculum was controversial because it removed the choice schools and teachers had previously exercised over what they taught. Some regarded it as unnecessary interference, though others saw it as enhancing equality of opportunity. The content of the National Curriculum has also been contentious. There was very little room on the timetable for schools to teach subjects that were not part of the curriculum.

EDUCATION

## Competition and choice

### Testing

The 1988 Act also introduced a new national testing system – Standard Assessment Tests (SATs). These were initially at age 14 (the end of Key Stage 3) but have been extended to ages 7 and 11 (the ends of Key Stages 1 and 2), so that, with GCSEs at age 16, there are national tests at the end of each key stage.

SATs were intended to help teachers identify areas where pupils needed to improve. At the same time, because they were national tests, they made it possible to compare levels of achievement across the country. SATs scores have become an important source of information about schools, and about the difference they make to the attainment of pupils.

### League tables

The introduction of national testing produced a wealth of data that can be used to create 'league tables' to compare schools and measure changes within a school over time. The government and local education authorities can use this data to identify schools that are either failing or doing well, and parents can use the data in choosing schools for their children.

The figures may, however, be misleading because they do not take into consideration factors such as the class and ethnic origin of pupils, or the proportion with special needs, which may affect a school's scores. For example, a school in a deprived inner-city area with many social problems achieving modest results may be doing more for its pupils than a school in a pleasant middle-class area with better results – the latter *ought* to be achieving good results. This has led to attempts to produce 'value added' figures, which try to identify the differences schools make by taking into account the nature of their pupil intake.

### School autonomy

A new system of school management was introduced in 1988. This was known as Local Management of Schools (LMS). It involved schools (in practice, heads and governors) having greater control of their budgets, including, for example, whether to employ extra staff or spend money on other areas. This took power away from LEAs, which are elected and democratically accountable.

### Inspections

A new system of inspections of schools was introduced, overseen by a new body called OFSTED (Office for Standards in Education). Schools had been inspected in the past, but the new system was more thorough and rigorous. Published inspection reports are a further source of information about schools for prospective parents and others.

### New schools

Two new types of school, both of which were outside local authority control, were also introduced during the period of Conservative rule:

- *City Technology Colleges* – partly financed by business, located in inner-city areas. They were intended for children of all abilities, but were allowed to select part of their intake.

- *Grant-maintained schools* – which had decided (by a vote of parents) to opt out of local authority control and receive their funding directly from the Department for Education and Science. This allowed schools to choose which areas to put their money and resources into.

## Significance of the changes

The most significant effect of these changes was that the philosophy of creating a meritocracy through providing equal opportunities was reversed. However, the main opposition to the New Right changes focused on more practical issues:

- that too many changes were introduced too quickly, with insufficient planning
- that the changes created an excessive workload for teachers.

The changes can be seen as the beginning of a process of **privatisation** of schools. Schools are opened up to market forces and have to respond to their 'customers' (parents). Proponents of the changes argue that this will lead to a rise in standards. Opponents argue that the outcome will be the re-creation of a two-tier system based on ability, which will fail large numbers of pupils.

Visit OFSTED's website at **www.ofsted.gov.uk** *and read some of the inspectors' reports.*

When was your school or college last inspected? What was the report like? Ask teachers who were there at the time what it was like to be inspected.

Privatisation: A government policy designed to reduce the public sector by allowing a greater role for private companies.

### Think it through

...the policy advisers who gathered around Margaret Thatcher in the 1980s... wanted to see a greater variety of schools at the secondary level, with a corresponding enhancement of parental choice. But their ultimate objective was the break-up of the state education system, with all schools owned by individual trusts and their survival dependent on their ability to satisfy their customers. The 1988 Education Act would be a step on the road to the complete privatization of the service.

Chitty, C. (1993) 'The education system transformed', *Sociology Review*, vol.2 (3)

1 In what ways did the 1988 Act lead to (a) a greater variety of schools; (b) greater parental choice; (c) greater privatization?

## Round-up

Changes driven by New Right thinking transformed British education in the 1980s and early 1990s. The changes led to greater competition between schools, greater choice for (some) parents and a greater role for business and market forces.

# What are the main features of schools today?

## Changes introduced by Labour governments since 1997

During the 2001 General Election, the Labour Government said that it would transform secondary education through creating a greater diversity of types of schools. It wants most secondary schools to have a distinctive character or ethos, rather than being, as the Prime Minister's spokesperson disparagingly put it, 'bog-standard' comprehensives.

This diversity has been encouraged by the designation of more than a thousand 'beacon' schools since 1998 (which had the responsibility of spreading good practice to other schools in their area) and training schools, where new teachers can be trained 'on the job'. However, the main policy since 1999 has been the creation of 'specialist schools'.

### Specialist schools

Specialist schools teach the National Curriculum but also specialise in one area, such as technology, sports, arts or languages.

For schools, there are two advantages to specialist status:
* extra money per pupil per year, adding about 5% to a school's budget
* the right to select up to 10% of pupils by ability in the specialist subject.

The idea of specialist schools appears to be a successful one, with many schools applying for this status. Furthermore, specialist schools are achieving good results, so that the government is able to claim that the strategy is proving successful in raising standards.

However, the move towards specialist schools has been criticised on the grounds that:

* it is a move away from comprehensive education and may lead to a two-tier system, with successful and well-funded specialist schools and struggling schools that have not become specialist (the latter arguably needing more funding)
* the success of specialist schools is only to be expected, given their funding and right to select pupils; better funding for existing schools might have achieved the same outcome
* from parents' point of view, it is unlikely to increase choice – the nearest school will no longer be a comprehensive but a school specialising in a subject that may or may not match parents' wishes or children's abilities.

### Faith schools

The Labour government has also encouraged the creation of faith schools, which are explicitly committed to a particular religion but can admit pupils of any religious background. There are about 7000 faith schools, of which only 40 are not Christian (*The Observer*, 30 Sept, 2001); 6384 of these are primary schools and 598 secondary. Faith schools tend to have fewer pupils with special educational needs or who are from low-income families (as measured by entitlement to free school meals) and have higher educational attainment than other schools. It can be argued that the apparent success of faith schools is due to the characteristics of their intake, rather than to any difference made by the schools.

The government intends that the number of schools that are specialist schools will grow. Find out the latest figures.

There is controversy about whether faith schools encourage racial discrimination by, for example, separating Muslim and Christian children.

**Coursework advice**

Which of the schools in your area are faith schools, and how does this influence the nature of the school and the learning of pupils? This would make a topical and interesting coursework project.

**Research issue**

OFFICIAL STATISTICS ON SCHOOL ATTENDANCE: The DfES's estimate that one million children 'bunk off' lessons or school is based on school attendance records. These are unlikely to record the full extent of truancy; for example, a pupil may be recorded as present at morning registration but then truant a particular lesson later that morning. Surveys of pupils, which may be more accurate, suggest that the figure could be twice as high (Denscombe, 1999).

## Competition and standards

### The testing regime

The number of tests sat by pupils in British schools has grown considerably. Pupils sit national tests at the end of each of the four key stages. This is a remarkable change from the mid-1980s, when the only national tests were at the end of compulsory schooling. Although in those days schools often set internal tests and exams, the results were not public and could not be used to compare schools – nor, probably, did they put pupils under as much pressure.

### Do we test too much?

Testing provides a wealth of information that can be used to help teachers raise standards. While many people would accept the need for some testing – and perhaps that pupils in the past were 'under-tested' – the 'testing regime' has been accused of going too far, on the following grounds:

- Tests put pressure on pupils, and on parents who push their children.
- Teachers already have a good knowledge of pupils' abilities; tests confirm what teachers already know.
- Britain now has far more testing than other industrial countries.
- Tests are being used for the sake of testing, rather than being used to help individual pupils attain higher standards.

### Government targets

Just as the Labour Government has set targets for schools and made teachers set targets for themselves, so also, in 1998, it set targets for itself to:

- increase the proportion of pupils gaining five or more GCSEs at grade C or above. This target had been met by 2001.
- improve the performance of the lower achieving students by reducing the proportion getting no passes at all at GCSE to less than 5%. At the time of writing, the proportion had fallen from 6.6% in 1998 to 5.5% in 2001.

## Truancy and expulsions

Part of the effort to raise standards has concentrated on those who miss out on part of their schooling through truancy or expulsion.

The DfES believes that about one million school children (15%) truant from lessons or from school. The government is keen to reduce truancy, not just to raise school standards but also because research has shown that truanting school children are responsible for a significant amount of crime. The government has made parents take more responsibility for ensuring their children are in school. In 2002, the government's determination to crack down on truancy resulted in a mother of two girls who had been absent from school without good reason being sent to prison.

Another factor in low achievement, and also for crime, is expulsions. The number of pupils permanently excluded from schools went up dramatically in the 1990s. Boys make up 83% of those permanently excluded (Denscombe, 1999) and African-Caribbeans are about six times as likely to be excluded as any other group.

Cracking down on truancy by making parents responsible – Mrs Amos was jailed for her daughters' truancy in 2002

How would functionalist sociologists view the setting up of specialist schools able to select some of their pupils?

## Important studies

Osler *et al.* (2002) stated that only about 17% of the pupils excluded from schools each year are girls – about 1800 in all. Almost all of the attention and the policies to deal with excluded pupils have been concerned with boys. Even when schools recognise that girls are having problems, their problems receive less attention because boys 'act out' their problems in ways that demand greater attention. Girls respond less visibly, by physical and emotional withdrawal, including anxiety and depression. They also exclude themselves, by truanting or pretending to be ill, losing out on their education in a similar way to excluded boys.

### Think it through

'We were under-testing in that we only had an exam at the end of compulsory education, and really no national testing in between, so we didn't know what was happening. But since tests were introduced at 7, 11 and 14 things have moved on. We decided that as the tests we put in were probably benefiting the education system we have just started adding more and more and now it looks as though the whole concept has gone away from tests as an indicator of student progress to becoming the main purpose of education... We have got into a testing frenzy at the moment.'

Professor Alan Smithers, quoted in Woodward, W. (2002) 'Testing... testing... testing', *The Guardian*, 20 May

1 Why have recent governments brought in more testing in schools?

2 What are the advantages and the disadvantages, to schools, pupils, parents, and government, of having regular tests throughout the years of compulsory schooling?

## Round-up

Labour's educational policies have been driven by a concern to raise standards, and a range of methods have been used to try to achieve this. This system – based on competition, choice, a greater role for business and frequent testing, all with the stated aim of raising standards – has considerable continuity with the changes introduced by the Conservatives.

# What is 'the new vocationalism'?

The emergence of an education system in Britain was closely linked to the needs of the economy (pp. 94–5). In the nineteenth century the sons of the wealthy were trained to become the administrators of the Empire on which Britain's economy was based, while the sons of the working class were trained to be obedient workers and soldiers. Different schools catered for these different needs.

This class-based division is still reflected today in the divide between academic education (high status) and vocational training (low status). Successive governments have regarded this divide as a problem, because, as they have seen it, schooling has not been preparing students adequately for the world of work. Sociologists, however, have noted a strong relationship between schooling and work.

### Coursework advice
If your school or college has vocational courses as well as academic ones, you could investigate and compare students' backgrounds, qualifications and reasons for choosing courses.

New vocationalism: A view of education that sees the meeting of the needs of the economy as being very important; it also refers to the policies connected to this view.

## The New Right

The ideas behind the new vocationalism fit well with the ideology of the New Right. They represent an attempt to instil a belief in entrepreneurialism and individual effort in business. Some of the policies created new roles for business people and industrialists, allowing them some say in the education and training of young people. From a New Right point of view, this is positive in itself, but also because it reduces the role of the educational establishment, which is seen as being too liberal and anti-business.

## The academic/vocational divide

The term 'vocational training', or 'vocational education', is normally used to mean education for non-professional work. It has been assumed that training for professional work need not begin until after the completion of academic education at age 18 or later.

In the period of the tripartite system (from 1944 until the 1960s) academic education was provided by independent and grammar schools, mainly for the children of upper and middle-class parents, plus a minority of working-class children who had been identified as having academic ability. They took O and A levels and many progressed to university. In secondary-modern and technical schools, children from mainly working-class backgrounds were given a more vocational education. They took no exams, or took CSEs (see p. 75) or work-related tests such as shorthand and typing for girls. The more successful pupils (usually boys) from these schools would aim to find work as apprentices for skilled manual jobs. Higher level vocational qualifications were almost all provided in colleges outside the university system.

The comprehensive system broke down some of the barriers between academic and vocational education. Streaming, however, often meant that only those in lower streams took vocational courses. The introduction of polytechnics in the 1960s (see p. 102) expanded the provision of vocational courses at higher education level, but, despite the intentions of governments, the 'polys' were seen as being of lower status than universities.

In 1976, the drive towards improving vocational education was given a considerable boost following a speech by the Labour Prime Minister James Callaghan, which launched what became known as 'the great debate'. Callaghan argued that schools were out of touch with the needs of a modern economy, and that, as a result, Britain was unable to compete effectively with other countries. Education should produce young people able to take their place in both the workplace and society at large. The teaching of subjects such as science and maths should, he said, be more related to practical applications in industry.

### The new vocationalism

The Conservative governments of 1979–97 brought in a series of initiatives that aimed to transform education so it would better meet the needs of the economy.

#### In schools

The introduction of the National Curriculum in 1988 ensured that all children received some vocationally related education. Craft, design and technology (CDT) became a core subject, and ensured that even the most academic children had a chance to develop skills in this area. However, CDT courses involve a lot of planning and writing, which can become more important than actually making things, and this put those with less academic ability at a disadvantage. There was also a

**Is the main purpose of schools to produce a workforce?**

greater emphasis in secondary schools on careers advice and on work experience and work-shadowing.

In the 1990s a range of new qualifications were introduced, designed to provide vocational education for those aged 16–19, and to provide a non-academic route into higher education. General National Vocational Qualifications (GNVQs) were introduced in 1993, available at foundation, intermediate and advanced level. They were general qualifications for broad areas of work, such as health and social care or leisure and tourism. They were designed to have equal status with academic qualifications, but in practice continued to have lower status.

Recent attempts to match schooling to the needs of the economy include:

- key skills qualifications for 16–19-year-olds
- the literacy and numeracy hours in primary schools
- the introduction of Advanced Vocational Certificates of Education (ABCEs), equivalent to A levels.

### Work-based learning

Training schemes for school-leavers who did not find employment were introduced in the 1980s and 1990s. The Youth Training Scheme, for example, provided broad-based training for school leavers. School leavers were no longer counted as unemployed, and welfare benefits to which they had been entitled were withdrawn.

Modern Apprenticeships offer young people jobs with guaranteed training leading to National Vocational Qualifications. Government policy is that they will be available to all school-leavers who want them.

## Effects of expanding training

The introduction of new courses and training kept growing numbers of young people in education after the school leaving age. Critics of the new vocationalism would point out two less obvious effects of this.

1 The new schemes and courses were a way of occupying young people for whom A levels were not suitable.
2 Because young people on these schemes and courses were no longer counted as unemployed, the unemployment figures were kept artificially low.

### *The continuing divide*

Although the many initiatives have dramatically increased the options available to school and college students, they have not succeeded in getting rid of the divide between academic education and vocational training. The number of students who attain the GCSE standard needed to begin A levels, but who opt for vocational courses instead, remains small.

The most recent development is the launch of new GCSEs in vocational subjects, which students can begin to study at age 14. Although these new qualifications are described as GCSEs in an attempt to put them on an equal basis with other GCSEs, there is still a risk that there will be a divide at age 14 between those who opt for some vocational GCSEs and those who do not.

There is, however, a hugely increased emphasis on vocational qualifications in universities, though (with the familiar exceptions of medicine and law) these still tend to have lower status.

**Think it through**

1 Identify and briefly explain two reasons why vocational courses have a lower status in schools than academic courses.

2 Identify and briefly explain two ways in which governments have tried to overcome the divide between academic and vocational education.

* NVQs are related to specific occupations rather than broad areas of work.

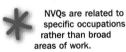

# Round-up

Although sociologists from different perspectives have described ways in which schooling is related to the world of work, the perceived failure of the school and university systems to prepare students for the world of work has been a cause of concern to both Conservative and Labour governments. There have been a long series of initiatives both within and beyond school to prepare more young people more effectively for work.

# What is the role of post-16 and higher education?

### Education for 16–19-year-olds

Introduced in the early 1950s, A levels were originally intended only for a small minority of students. However, the numbers taking A-level courses has risen considerably, both in absolute numbers and as a proportion of the age group. The total entry in all subjects at A level rose by around 20% between 1970 and 1995 (Elwood, 1999). About 750 000 students took A levels in 2001. Syllabuses and exams have changed over the years but the basic qualification has remained the same.

However, a new structure of AS and A2 courses (Curriculum 2000), was introduced in September 2000. The government aimed to reconcile the need, as they saw it, to have higher numbers leaving education having gained advanced qualifications with the need to maintain the standard of A levels (often referred to as 'the gold standard'). In 2002, the new system and examination results at AS and A level caused considerable controversy, and led to proposals to further change the system.

There has also been an increase in vocational courses and qualifications available to this age group. You can find out more about GNVQs and other qualifications on pp. 100–1.

### Further education

Sixth-form colleges and further education colleges (which provide the great majority of work-related training) were taken out of local authority control by the Conservative government in the early 1990s and made into independent corporations. They now receive most of their funding directly from the government-appointed Learning and Skills Council. The purpose of this reform was to introduce greater competition, with the aim of raising both standards and the proportion of students staying in education beyond 16. The representation of businesses on college governing bodies was increased, and funding was linked to the colleges' success in recruiting.

Today, further education colleges are essential to the Labour government's aim of increasing the total numbers of young people in education, especially by attracting people from those groups that are under-represented, and those that are socially excluded.

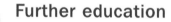

The road to a professional career?

| Main periods in the development of university education in England | |
|---|---|
| 1830s | Founding of the universities of London and Durham, breaking the Oxbridge monopoly. Later, colleges were founded all over the country, teaching for University of London degrees. |
| Late nineteenth century | Founding of 'red brick' universities in major towns and cities, e.g. Birmingham, Liverpool. |
| 1960s | The Robbins Report (1963) established the principle that higher education should be available to all those who could benefit from it.<br><br>Founding of polytechnics*, focusing on technological education.<br><br>New universities founded, e.g. York, Sussex, Warwick.<br><br>Student numbers trebled in 25 years. |
| 1990s | Polytechnics and some other colleges redesignated as universities. |
| 2000 | About 30% of 18-year-olds in higher education.<br><br>The government's target is that 50% of 18–30-year-olds should study in HE. |

\* The founding of polytechnics was an attempt to put right what was seen as the bias against technology and applied science in universities – which was thought by some to be contributing to Britain's inability to compete internationally. The creation of polytechnics set up a two-tier system because polytechnics were seen, perhaps inevitably, as second-class compared with universities.

## Important studies

Connor and Dewson (2001) found that only one in five higher-education students are from working-class backgrounds. This partly reflects lower attainment at GCSE and A level, but many suitably qualified working-class students do not go into higher education. A telephone survey of 2000 young people found that working-class students were more concerned with (and better informed about) employment and financial matters than middle-class students. The most common reasons for not considering higher education were:
- wanting to start work
- wanting to train and work at the same time
- wanting to be independent
- aiming for a job that did not require a higher qualification
- concern about cost, taking out a student loan and not being able to pay off debts.

EDUCATION

# Higher education

## History

Oxford and Cambridge Universities were founded in the Middle Ages and are among the oldest educational institutions in Europe. However, university-level education developed very slowly in Britain, with smaller proportions of university students in England than in other Western countries, even in the mid-twentieth century, and far fewer women than men taking up places.

## Effects of expansion

*Universities* – Between the 1960s and 1990s, the number of students grew, but funding from government did not keep pace with this growth. Universities were unable to maintain staff–student ratios or to maintain resources and buildings at high standards. Universities had to raise money through recruiting more overseas students (who pay higher fees), and developing more postgraduate courses and distance-learning courses. They also had to look for more private sponsorship – for example, to fund chairs and research.

*Students* – The value of student grants fell, and more and more students worked (some for long hours) to pay their way through university, or took out student loans. Students argued that their education was affected by larger classes and pressure on libraries, on accommodation, and so on.

> **Coursework advice** How important are financial considerations for your fellow students thinking about higher education? Are their decisions related to their class background? Exploring questions like these would make an interesting and topical project.

## The role of the State

Although universities still retain considerable freedom, they are now subject to greater control by the State in similar, though less restrictive ways, to schools. The teaching of university departments and their research is regularly inspected, the results being published in an equivalent of school league tables.

## Who goes to university?

University students are far more likely to be from professional and middle-class backgrounds than from working-class backgrounds. This is particularly marked in the case of the older universities and those that are highest in the league tables, which have strong links to independent schools. State-school students account for about two-thirds of the top A-level grades yet Oxford University, for example, takes a large proportion of its students from the independent sector. Even when grades at A level are taken into account, pupils at independent schools take a disproportionate number of places; the Sutton Trust calculated that on the basis of exam results independent-school pupils should take 28% of places at the top 13 universities, but in fact took 39%, while pupils from the less affluent social classes (50% of the population) should have had 17% but got only 13% (cited in Woodward and Ward, 2000).

Women take more places in higher education than men. This partly reflects the higher achievement of girls in entrance qualifications. Once on a degree course, women are less likely to drop out than men.

The proportions of higher education students from minority ethnic groups in Britain grew in the 1990s. Black students comprised 3% of those accepted on to degree courses in 2000, and South Asian students 9%.

**\*** It should be noted that about one in five undergraduate students fails to complete their course (News.bbc.co.uk, 'Fifth of students become university dropouts', posted 9 August 1999).

**\*** Higher education has a considerable impact on future life chances for most students. At the age of 33, men with first degrees earn 15% more than contemporaries with similar backgrounds and similar A level results but who do not have degrees; for women, the difference is 35% (Carvel, 1997).

# Think it through

### Participation rates[1] in higher education: by social class (%)

|  | 1991/2 | 1992/3 | 1993/4 | 1994/5 | 1995/6 | 1996/7 | 1997/8 | 1998/9 |
|---|---|---|---|---|---|---|---|---|
| Professional | 55 | 71 | 73 | 78 | 79 | 82 | 79 | 72 |
| Intermediate | 36 | 39 | 42 | 45 | 45 | 47 | 48 | 45 |
| Skilled non-manual | 22 | 27 | 29 | 31 | 31 | 32 | 31 | 29 |
| Skilled manual | 11 | 15 | 17 | 18 | 18 | 18 | 19 | 18 |
| Partly skilled | 12 | 14 | 16 | 17 | 17 | 17 | 18 | 17 |
| Unskilled | 6 | 9 | 11 | 11 | 12 | 13 | 14 | 13 |
| All social classes | 23 | 28 | 30 | 32 | 32 | 33 | 33 | 31 |

1 The number of home domiciled initial entrants aged under 21 to full-time and sandwich undergraduate courses of higher education in further education and higher education institutions expressed as a proportion of the average 18 to 19 year old population. The 1991 Census provided the population distribution by social class for all years.

From Denscombe (2001), p. 10; original source: *Social Trends 30* (2000)

1 What have been the percentage changes in the numbers of children from different classes entering higher education between 1991/2 and 1998/9?

2 How can these differences be explained?

# Round-up

**Compulsory education ends at age 16 in Britain. The government wants to encourage more young people to stay on in education, and has opened up both the further and higher education sectors to market forces and competition in the hope of achieving this. However, access to higher education still seems to be easier for white, middle-class students.**

# How does education in Britain compare with education in other countries?

## Britain and the rest of Europe

All countries in the European Union are strongly committed to schooling but differ in the approach they take. According to Macionis and Plummer (1977), some of the main differences are as follows:

- The length of time there has been a national education system – while England and Wales have had primary education for all since 1870, compulsory education was only introduced in Italy and Greece in the 1950s, Spain in the 1960s and Portugal even later.
- The age at which children are required to start school – this is 5 years for England and Wales (although subsidised pre-school education is available); in most countries it is 6 and in Denmark it is 7 years.
- The number of years of compulsory schooling – in England and Wales children can leave school at 16; in Italy they can leave at 14 while in Germany they cannot leave until aged 18.
- The numbers and proportions of students staying in education after the end of compulsory schooling – in 1996 the proportion of 18-year-olds in full-time secondary education was under 40% in the United Kingdom but over 75% in Sweden, Germany, Finland and Denmark (OECD, from *Social Trends 30*, 2000, p.55)

(Macionis and Plummer, 1997).

**These children from Malawi even have to buy their own desks and carry them home for the holidays**

✳ The developing world includes many different countries, and most of the world's population. There are enormous variations in education between and even within countries, and the discussion here inevitably involves generalisations that do not apply in all cases.

## Britain and the developing world

When comparing education in Britain and other developed countries with education in developing countries that are considerably poorer there are several important differences.

- Schooling in developing countries is often not free. Parents or guardians have to pay fees. The fees may be modest, and subsidised by government, but they mean that some families cannot afford to educate their children.
- Related to the first point, many families rely on children to work and bring in money. For example, in subsistence-farming communities children often help with sowing, scaring birds away, harvesting and so on. Children who are enrolled in a school will miss a lot of lessons at times when their families need them to help in these ways.
- Schools often lack basic resources. Teachers are often not well paid, and may not have been trained as teachers.

### The legacy of colonialism

Most developing countries adopted a model of schooling closely based on the Western-European model, involving the transmission of knowledge through reading and writing. This is a legacy of **colonialism**, when the colonial powers (such as Britain and France) built schools modelled on their own systems. The curriculum was often inappropriate; students learned about European geography and history from donated textbooks, or learned English literature but not the literature, oral or written, of their own culture. There was no place in schools for the traditional education that had always taken place, such as young people in Africa preparing for adulthood by learning about their society and

## SOME BASIC FACTS

- 125 million of the world's children aged 6–11 in 1995 did not go to school.
  Two-thirds of these were girls.
- A further 150 million leave school without learning to read and write.
- The total number of illiterate people in the world is growing: 872 million in 1995.
  Two-thirds of these are women.

(Brazier 1999, quoting figures published by Oxfam International)

'Cultural imperialism' is a term, usually used by Marxists, to describe how American or Western culture dominates the cultures of many developing countries.

culture, with acceptance into the community marked by a rite of passage. In recent years, this pattern has begun to change in some countries, especially those in the Islamic world, where the colonial influence is being shaken off.

Some countries continue to spend a lot of their education budget on tertiary and university education. Higher education is expensive and benefits only a few, so this lop-sided spending increases inequality. Education encourages people to aspire to white-collar jobs, of which the system can only provide a very few. The sociologist Ronald Dore (1976) called this 'diploma disease' – educational qualifications are so sought after, because jobs are few, that it is easier to select candidates just by qualifications rather than by relevant abilities or skills.

### Education and development

Functionalists and modernisation theorists argue that education is essential to modernisation and development. The theory of human capital argues that investment in education, provided it is tied into developing the skills necessary for industry, can be a basis for modernisation and that human capital can to some extent make up for shortage of money capital.

These views are not accepted by Marxists and dependency theorists, who see education as **cultural imperialism**. Copying developed countries has led developing countries to concentrate on higher education rather on mass literacy; this suited the owners of business and industry, who were happy for workers to have only minimal education. They believed that literacy would lead to a better critical understanding of an individual's situation in society, and would therefore lead to discontent, strikes and rebellion. This view of the potential of literacy was

advocated by the Brazilian educationalist Paolo Freire (1972). Dependency theorists argue that education was one of the main ways in which colonial powers exercised control over their colonies – existing education systems were replaced by new systems that enabled a small élite to obtain jobs.

### Education of girls

Globally, girls are less likely than boys to go to school, to complete their schooling and to become literate. In many countries, the education of boys is seen as more important than that of girls, so a family is more likely to invest in a son's education than in a daughter's.

Over the past few years, education of girls has been increasingly seen as essential to development and the improvement of living standards. According to the World Bank, each year of schooling a girl receives reduces the child mortality rate by up to 19% (Brazier, 1999). Girls who have been educated so that they have an understanding of health, sanitation and nutrition are able to improve the lives of their children, families and communities considerably. Educated girls marry later, have fewer children and can look after them better. They are also less likely to tolerate an oppressive family or social situation.

## Looking ahead

The United Nations has set a target of having all the world's primary-school age children in school by 2015. This recognises the importance of education, and achieving it would be a huge step towards meeting the rights of all children. However, goals like this have been set before, and not achieved. Furthermore, it is also not simply a question of getting all children into school, but also of the quality and relevance of what is taught and learnt.

I wake up very early... I sweep the compound, wash last night's dishes. Then I go to the well, but the natural wells are all dry now and we have to walk very far to the artificial wells. We have to wait in a long queue as there are many people. Then I go to the farm to dig or pick cashew nuts. I prepare the day's relish and make ugali for the family. I sometimes get a few hours to play with my friends in the afternoon. I pound cassava or maize for the evening and next day's meal. I then cook supper. After meals I play or listen to adult conversations, especially when there's moonlight. I go to bed when adults go to sleep. Maybe I could go to school, but it is expensive, and my mother will be alone to do all the work.

12-year-old Amina Hassan of Chikunja village, Tanzania

Brazier, C. (1999) 'Gender canyon', New Internationalist, No. 315, August, p. 16

**1** Examine some of the reasons why girls in developing countries are less likely to go to school than boys.

**2** Examine some of the benefits of educating girls in developing countries.

Colonialism: With only a handful of exceptions, the countries that are now referred to as 'developing' were in the recent past ruled by European countries. Britain and France had the largest empires, made up of colonies. This contributed to great inequalities in wealth and power that continue today.

There are many excellent resources about developing countries on the Web. Try, for example, the New Internationalist magazine www.newint.org.uk and www.oneworld.net/uk.

# Round-up

Although there are differences between the school systems of the countries of Europe, there is agreement on the importance of schooling. In developing countries, there is also a strong belief in the importance of schooling, but lack of money and resources means that many children do not have an adequate education.

# Education: summative review

## Education and schooling

Although the sociology of education at AS level is mostly about schools, it is important to remember that education means far more than just what happens in schools. Education is an essential component of all human cultures. The process of socialisation, by which we all learn to be members of a cultural group, is part of the process of education. In every society there will be ways in which children (and others) learn and are taught. Many of these are informal; modern societies are different only in that a large part of education takes place in formal settings such as schools and universities. However, a great deal of education takes place outside such formal settings. You learned some of the most important things, such as how to speak a language, long before you went to school. Nor is it the case that all school age children go to school. Many in poorer countries do not have the opportunity.

## Functionalism and Marxism

Sociologists are particularly interested in two ways in which education is linked to other aspects of society. These are the transmission of norms and values, and the relationship between education and social stratification. Functionalists and Marxists have very different interpretations of what happens.

- For functionalists, education is essential to ensure the continuity of society over generations; education's function is to help build and maintain consensus. The formal education system also sorts people according to ability, and aims to ensure that we have the right number of people with appropriate skills to fill occupational roles.

- For Marxists, the same processes are ways in which the ruling class maintains its power. Schools instil values that ensure that the working class accepts its subordinate position and see the system as fair. Marxists argue that education is not meritocratic; success depends more on social-class background than on intelligence or ability.

## Interactionism

A very different approach to studying education is taken by interactionist sociologists. Here the emphasis is on researching what actually happens in schools (using ethnographic methods), especially at the 'micro' level of one school or one particular class or social group within a school. This focus on the small scale has led to the formulation of concepts that have come to play an important part in explaining what happens in schools: the hidden curriculum, labelling, the self-fulfilling (and self-negating) prophecy, and so on.

There has also been a focus on studying the subcultures of pupils. Groups of working-class boys have been identified as having anti-school subcultures, based on a simple reversal of the school's values. Such subcultures seem to be a recurring problem in every generation for teachers and schools, but much of the sociological research has been ethnographic and has aimed to give 'the pupils' side of the story'. There are, of course, other (often less visible) subcultures within schools, including those that value learning and within which hard work and high marks bring status. The 'anti-school' boys do not have it all their own way. Researchers on the whole, however, seem to find pupils who conform most of the time – the majority – less interesting than those who get labelled as troublemakers.

## Selection

Another aspect of schooling that has attracted attention is the issue of selection and its consequences. Some schools select some, or their entire intake, by ability. Grammar schools (created as part of the tripartite system in 1945 and still surviving in some areas) select on the basis of intelligence tests at the age of eleven plus. Specialist schools, founded only in the past few years, can also select pupils. Selection is a form of labelling, which can lead to the self-fulfilling prophecy.

### Stratification: identities and differential attainment

Sociologists have also been interested in the relationship between aspects of social stratification and education. In this book we have considered

- gender,
- class, and
- ethnicity.

Other aspects of social stratification (which might form the basis of a coursework project) include disability and sexuality. Schools help to shape how pupils perceive their identity – by conveying ideologies of masculinity and femininity through what is taught and how, by who teaches what and who has positions of authority within the school, through classroom organisation, teaching resources and so on. Feminist research in the 1970s and 1980s highlighted ways in which girls received messages that lowered their self-esteem and ambition. Schools have consequently taken action to try to ensure gender equality of opportunity.

Schools also transmit ideas about national and ethnic identity. The main focus here has been on the experiences of pupils from minority ethnic groups in British schools. Researchers have found strong evidence of racism within schools, including discrimination in allocation to sets and streams, different treatment by teachers and inappropriate teaching resources.

Much research has focused on the reasons for differential attainment and on strategies for reducing the differences. Despite the ways in which girls have been disadvantaged, girls now do better than boys on almost all indicators. This has led to widespread concern, even panic, in the media about the underachievement of boys. However, boys are doing better now than they did in the past, so this level of concern can be seen as misplaced. In considering why girls do better, we need to look at a range of factors, some starting in early childhood and reinforced by schools.

Differential attainment between ethnic groups is complex; some minority groups do better than the national average, others significantly worse. In trying to understand what is happening here, we need to be aware of how ethnicity is interlinked to both gender and class, and to look at various factors including home, family and cultural background, as well as school-based processes.

Social class is sometimes less visible than gender and ethnicity, yet is at the heart of the school system. From the beginning, different schools catered for children from different social classes. The repercussions of this continue today; independent schools continue to exist (although incompatible with the philosophy underlying the comprehensive system, which dominated much of the mid- to late-twentieth century) and to cater for those who can afford to opt out of the state system. Social class has been of particular concern to Marxist sociologists. Amongst the theories and concepts developed in this area have been

- cultural capital
- correspondence theory
- positional theory.

To explain why working-class pupils do less well than middle-class pupils, we need, as with ethnicity, to look at home, family and cultural background, as well as school-based processes.

## Changes and policies

In surveying government educational policies since 1944, it is possible to make out four periods. However, there is not always a clear dividing point, and there has always been considerable continuity, especially at primary level. The first period, introduced by the 1944 Butler Act, was that of the tripartite secondary system-based on selection by ability. This gave way, in a piecemeal fashion, in the 1960s and 1970s, to the period of comprehensive education, which had as its goal a meritocratic system, with the same education available to all. In the 1980s, reforms by the Conservative party began to undermine this and to bring market forces, choice and competition into schools. Finally, since 1997 under Labour governments, some of the Conservative reforms have been continued and others have been scrapped – often to be replaced by similar but less divisive changes.

## Vocational education

The divide between academic and vocational education continues to be a feature of the system. Despite the efforts of successive governments, vocational education (with the exception of training for the top professions) continues to be seen as inferior. Industrialists and business people still complain that schools and universities are producing young adults who do not have the skills they are looking for.

## Post-compulsory education

Further and higher education has also been changed dramatically by reforms since the 1980s. At tertiary as well as secondary level, competition, choices, publication of league tables and regular inspections have become inescapable. The opening up to market forces has brought to the fore issues of access, with some students being deterred by escalating costs.

## The international picture

International comparisons also shed light on British education. England, Wales and Scotland have distinctive systems: we came later to the idea of centralised control of the curriculum than most countries; we start our children's schooling earlier than most, and so on. Of particular concern to governments anxious about Britain's ability to compete with economic rivals, is the relatively low proportion of people staying in education after the age of 16.

Looking further afield, the situation is poor and improving only slowly. Many children in the developing world do not go to school, and large numbers of people cannot read and write. The United Nations' admirable target of aiming for universal primary education by 2015 already looks impossibly optimistic. Yet education, especially for girls, is probably the best way forward towards a less unequal, more prosperous, and therefore safer, world.

# Education: self-assessment questions

## Multiple-choice questions

*Questions 1–14 each have one correct answer and three incorrect answers.*

1 **Which of the following was introduced by the 1870 Forster Education Act?**

   a Public schools for the middle classes

   b Grammar schools

   c Primary schooling for all

   d Technical colleges

2 **Which of the following was introduced by the 1944 Butler Education Act?**

   a Comprehensive schools

   b Free secondary education for all

   c The National Curriculum

   d Free primary education for all

3 **Which of the following distinguishes comprehensive schools from other types of school?**

   a Selects some of its pupils on ability

   b Is funded directly by government rather than the local education authority

   c Teaches the National Curriculum

   d Takes all pupils in an area, regardless of ability

4 **Which of the following distinguishes independent schools from other types of school?**

   a Supported by a church or other religious body

   b Do not charge fees

   c Select some of their pupils

   d Charge fees

5 **Which of the following distinguishes faith schools from other types of schools?**

   a Religious education is taught

   b There are assemblies every day

   c Financially supported by a church or religious body

   d Teachers believe in their pupils

6 **Which of the following subjects is not a part of the National Curriculum?**

   a Mathematics

   b Sociology

   c Music

   d Physical Education

7 **Which of the following was not a policy introduced by the Conservative governments 1979 to 1997?**

   a Introduction of GCSEs

   b Abolition of comprehensive schools

   c Introduction of National Curriculum

   d Assisted places scheme

8 **Which of the following was not a new policy introduced by Labour after 1997?**

   a Specialist schools

   b AS and A2 level examinations

   c Grant-maintained schools

   d The literacy and numeracy hours

9 **Which of these Conservative education policies was not continued by the Labour government elected in 1997?**

   a League tables

   b Assisted places scheme

   c The National Curriculum

   d Standard Attainment Tests (SATs)

10 **Which of the following statements is true?**

   a All state schools can now charge fees.

   b All state schools can now choose to become specialist schools if they want to.

   c All state schools can opt out of teaching the National Curriculum.

   d All state schools have to be inspected regularly.

11 **Who studied the 'Lads' in a Midlands comprehensive?**

   a Spender          c Willis

   b Ball              d Mac an Ghaill

12 **Who developed the concept of cultural capital?**

   a Bernstein        c Boudon

   b Bourdieu         d Willis

13 **Who wrote about 'deschooling' society?**

   a Willis            c Bowles and Gintis

   b Bourdieu          d Illich

14 **What type of school is Summerhill?**

   a A traditional public school

   b A specialist school

   c A progressive independent school

   d A grammar school

**16 Which of the following is a description of the hidden curriculum?**

a The planned instructional activities in a school

b The transmission of norms and values through the organisation of the school and relationships within it.

**17 Which of the following is a description of meritocracy?**

a Rewards are gained through ability and achievement

b Rewards are gained through ascribed status.

**18 Which of the following is a description of streaming?**

a Grouping pupils by ability within a school

b A school selecting its intake by ability.

**19 Match the Education Acts to the ministers largely responsible for them.**

| a 1870 | i Butler |
| b 1988 | ii Forster |
| c 1944 | iii Baker |

**20 Match the argument to the theoretical perspective**

a Marxism

b Functionalism

c Feminism

i The hidden curriculum encourages boys to see themselves as more important than girls.

ii The hidden curriculum is essential for learning appropriate behaviour.

iii The hidden curriculum is a way in which ruling-class ideology is passed on.

**21 Match the argument to the theoretical perspective**

a Marxism

b Functionalism

c Interactionism

i Focuses on the role of schools in maintaining capitalism

ii Focuses on small-scale interaction within schools

iii Focuses on how schools can maintain social stability and value consensus

**22 Match the sociologists to their concepts**

| a Boudon | i Correspondence theory |
| b Becker | ii Labelling |
| c Bowles and Gintis | iii Positional theory |

**23 Match the sociologists to their books**

| a Mac an Ghaill | i Learning To Labour |
| b Willis | ii Divide and School |
| c Abraham | iii Young, Gifted and Black |

**24 Which is the odd one out?**

a GIST

b WISE

c NVQ

**25 Which is the odd one out?**

a A level

b GNVQ

c NVQ

# Education: a timeline

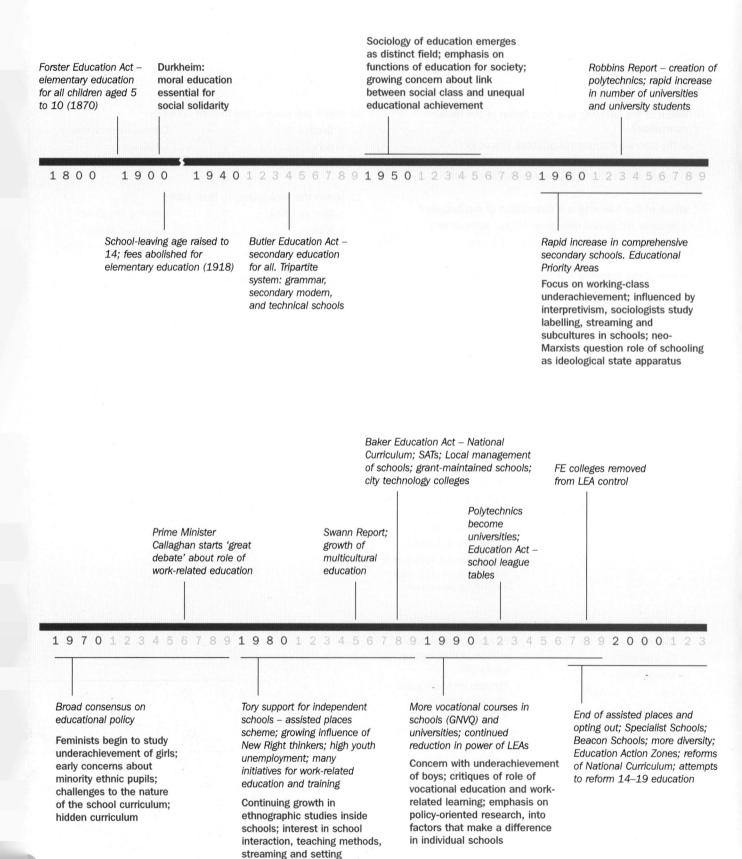

**Forster Education Act –** elementary education for all children aged 5 to 10 (1870)

**Durkheim:** moral education essential for social solidarity

Sociology of education emerges as distinct field; emphasis on functions of education for society; growing concern about link between social class and unequal educational achievement

**Robbins Report –** creation of polytechnics; rapid increase in number of universities and university students

1800    1900    1940 1 2 3 4 5 6 7 8 9 1950 1 2 3 4 5 6 7 8 9 1960 1 2 3 4 5 6 7 8 9

School-leaving age raised to 14; fees abolished for elementary education (1918)

Butler Education Act – secondary education for all. Tripartite system: grammar, secondary modern, and technical schools

Rapid increase in comprehensive secondary schools. Educational Priority Areas

**Focus on working-class underachievement; influenced by interpretivism, sociologists study labelling, streaming and subcultures in schools; neo-Marxists question role of schooling as ideological state apparatus**

Baker Education Act – National Curriculum; SATs; Local management of schools; grant-maintained schools; city technology colleges

FE colleges removed from LEA control

Polytechnics become universities; Education Act – school league tables

Prime Minister Callaghan starts 'great debate' about role of work-related education

Swann Report; growth of multicultural education

1970 1 2 3 4 5 6 7 8 9 1980 1 2 3 4 5 6 7 8 9 1990 1 2 3 4 5 6 7 8 9 2000 1 2 3

Broad consensus on educational policy

**Feminists begin to study underachievement of girls; early concerns about minority ethnic pupils; challenges to the nature of the school curriculum; hidden curriculum**

Tory support for independent schools – assisted places scheme; growing influence of New Right thinkers; high youth unemployment; many initiatives for work-related education and training

**Continuing growth in ethnographic studies inside schools; interest in school interaction, teaching methods, streaming and setting**

More vocational courses in schools (GNVQ) and universities; continued reduction in power of LEAs

**Concern with underachievement of boys; critiques of role of vocational education and work-related learning; emphasis on policy-oriented research, into factors that make a difference in individual schools**

End of assisted places and opting out; Specialist Schools; Beacon Schools; more diversity; Education Action Zones; reforms of National Curriculum; attempts to reform 14–19 education

# Section 4 **Research methods**

# Research methods: a mindmap

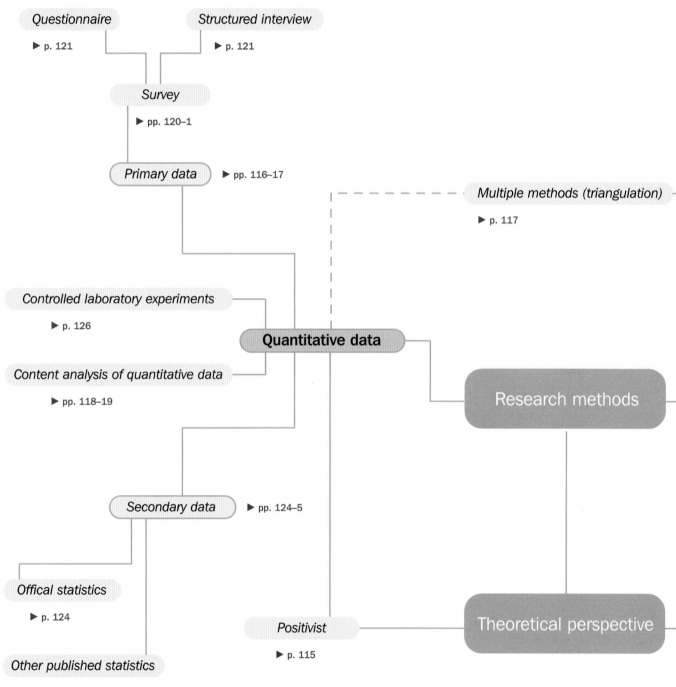

Questionnaire
► p. 121

Structured interview
► p. 121

Survey
► pp. 120–1

Primary data
► pp. 116–17

Multiple methods (triangulation)
► p. 117

Controlled laboratory experiments
► p. 126

**Quantitative data**

Content analysis of quantitative data
► pp. 118–19

Research methods

Secondary data
► pp. 124–5

Offical statistics
► p. 124

Positivist
► p. 115

Theoretical perspective

Other published statistics
► p. 125

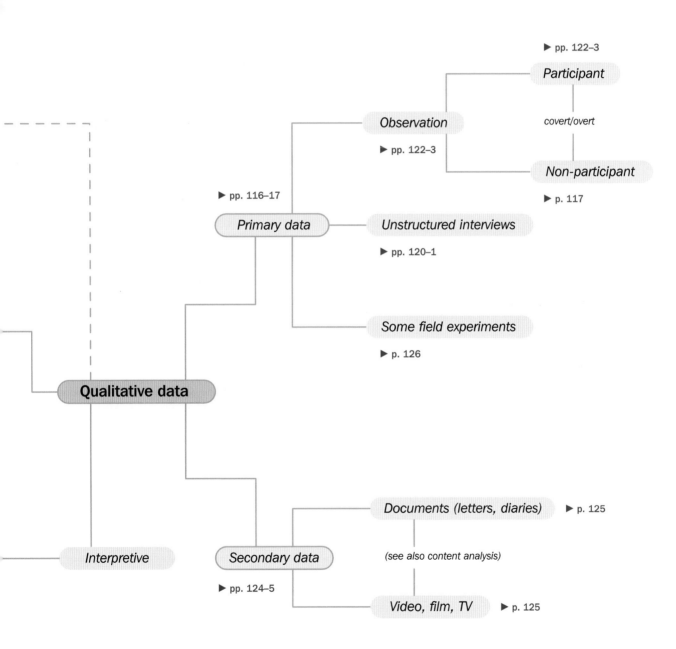

Participant

▶ pp. 122–3

Observation

▶ pp. 122–3

covert/overt

Non-participant

▶ p. 117

Primary data

▶ pp. 116–17

Unstructured interviews

▶ pp. 120–1

Some field experiments

▶ p. 126

Qualitative data

Documents (letters, diaries)  ▶ p. 125

(see also content analysis)

Interpretive

Secondary data

▶ pp. 124–5

Video, film, TV  ▶ p. 125

# What do sociologists study?

**S**ociologists are inquisitive. They want to know and understand about society, social institutions, organisations and how people interact with each other. If we want to find out about something in everyday life we can ask questions about it, read about it, or maybe take part in a social activity. Sociological researchers do much the same but, as social scientists, they do it more systematically.

Good sociology is based on good **empirical** evidence that has been collected using reliable research techniques. The evidence and the conclusions drawn from it are published so that others can judge it.

What's going on here?

**Empirical:** Relating to observation or experiment rather than theory.

## Why do sociologists do research?

### Descriptive research

Some research aims simply to describe what is being studied, to gather information and to increase our knowledge of the social world. It asks questions such as 'How do the exam results of boys compare with those of girls?' or 'How do husbands and wives share household tasks?'

### Explanatory research

**Phenomena:** Anything that can be seen or perceived.

This starts with description but goes on to look for the causes of social **phenomena**, such as 'Why do boys do less well than girls in exams?' and 'Why do women still do most of the housework?' It looks for the causes of problems, which may be social problems or sociological problems.

### Cause and effect

**Correlate:** To show the relationship between two variables; may be positive or negative.

Trying to explain something raises the question of cause and effect. If factors A and B occur together, and B changes when A changes, these factors are **correlated** but it does not follow that A *causes* B. There may be no causal link between them; it may be that B causes A; it may be that a third factor, C, influences them both.

 In natural sciences (chemistry, biology and physics), researchers often use experiments to try to identify which 'independent variables' (causes) result in which 'dependent variables' (effects). See p. 126.

For example, a researcher might find (descriptive research) that young people who watch violent videos (factor A) are violent towards other young people (factor B). It could be that:

- there is no causal link between video-watching and violent behaviour
- video-watching causes violent behaviour
- violent behaviour causes video-watching
- a third factor (e.g. violence in the home) causes both the video-watching and the violent behaviour.

### Action research

In action research, the researcher is actively involved in planning and introducing some change of policy and practice in a particular setting (e.g. a school, a hospital, a social work team) and then in studying the impact of the change as it happens in order to evaluate its effects.

---

## SOCIAL PROBLEMS AND SOCIOLOGICAL PROBLEMS

Sociologists are not only concerned with explaining deviant behaviour or solving social problems such as juvenile crime or family breakdown. Many sociologists are interested in trying to explain 'normal' behaviour. For example, it is just as much of a problem to explain why most marriages last for a lifetime as it is to explain why some end in divorce.

---

## Think it through

For each of the following research topics, identify the concepts that a researcher would need to operationalise. How could this be done and what are the problems?

We have made a start on the first question, as an example.

**1** Why do children from working-class families get in trouble with the police more than children from middle-class families?

| Concept | Operational definition | Problems/ weaknesses |
|---|---|---|
| Child | Person aged between 10 and 16 years | |
| Working-class | | |
| Get in trouble with the police | Receive a formal caution or be convicted of an offence | |
| Middle-class | | |

**2** How does poverty affect educational achievement?

**3** What importance do people of Asian origin attach to their ethnic identity?

## What do sociologists think they are studying?

In studying the natural world, scientists assume that it exists independently of the observer and that stones, weather, chemical elements, etc. have no self-awareness and do not act with purpose. Scientists use observational and experimental techniques that produce objective information.

In this context, 'objective' means 'independent of the scientist'.

But sociologists study social phenomena and people rather than the natural world, and therefore need to ask the question 'What methods are appropriate for studying social phenomena?' The answer depends on how we view social phenomena. If we think they are similar to natural phenomena, then we can borrow the research methods of the natural scientists. But if we think social phenomena are different from natural phenomena, we should use different research methods. This is the basis of the debate between **positivist** and **interpretivist** approaches to sociology.

**Positivist:** The belief that knowledge must be based on observation or experiment.

**Interpretivist:** An approach in sociology that focuses on the meaning that social phenomena have for the people involved.

**Quantitative:** Research that concentrates on collecting statistical data.

**Natural sciences:** These include chemistry, biology and physics.

**Qualitative:** Research where the sociologist aims to understand the meaning of social action.

**Operationalise:** To define something so that it can be measured or counted.

- A positivist approach to sociology argues that social phenomena are as real and objective as phenomena in the natural world. It argues that sociologists should study only what they can objectively see, measure and count and use methods that produce **quantitative** data, aiming to arrive at social laws that can explain the causes of events in the social world – and even to make predictions, as **natural science** has done. The researcher should avoid personal involvement and produce value-free evidence. The positivist view was taken by some early sociologists, mainly in the nineteenth century when sociology was striving to be regarded as the equal of the natural sciences.

Blundell and Griffiths (2002) includes summaries of 25 recent research studies, with commentaries.

- An interpretivist approach to sociology argues that social phenomena are different from natural phenomena. It argues that people are active, conscious beings who act with intention and purpose because of the way they make sense of the social situation they are in. For example, a family is not just a group of people with a biological relationship but a group of people who perceive themselves as a family and act accordingly. Social phenomena do not exist independently of people, as plants or birds do, but are created by people who share an understanding of the situation. Social researchers therefore need methods that enable them to get at these shared understandings. These methods generate **qualitative** data, i.e. data that express how people make sense of social situations. This view, although developed by Max Weber at the end of the nineteenth century and taken up by anthropologists in the 1920s and 1930s, did not become widespread in mainstream sociology until the 1960s and 1970s.

### Operationalising concepts

All researchers have to 'operationalise concepts'. This means defining the phenomenon being studied so that it can be counted or measured in a way that is clearly understood and that can be used consistently. This may be straightforward. For example, if we want to study changes over time in the age at which women give birth to their first baby, it is easy to agree on what is meant by 'age', 'women' 'birth' and 'baby' and to express these in objective, quantitative terms. However, what if we want to study changes in health and illness over time? We have to decide what we mean by 'healthy' – that is, we have to operationalise the concept 'healthy'. Do we mean:

- a state where the individual says they feel well, or
- a state where a doctor can find nothing wrong, or
- a physical condition where the individual can lead the sort of life they want to lead?

And should we include mental health as well as physical health in our definition? Clearly, how we define and operationalise 'health' will affect how many healthy people we find – and, to make comparisons over time, we must always use the same definition.

### Watch out

It is a mistake to suggest that sociologists, or sociological research, fall neatly into one of two camps called 'positivist' and 'interpretivist'. For many years, researchers have recognised that different approaches suit different subject matter and that most social phenomena are best studied using a combination of objective quantitative methods and subjective qualitative methods – see pp. 120–3.

### Round-up

Sociological research takes a systematic approach. It seeks to describe or explain social phenomena using a variety of methods that draw on both positivist and interpretivist approaches. Researchers must be clear about how they are defining and using concepts, especially when there may be disagreement about what they mean.

### Coursework advice
If you do any research yourself, always make sure that you operationalise your concepts.

# How do sociologists conduct research?

## Choosing what to research

The first step is to choose a topic to research. The choice will be influenced by:

- *The interests and values of the researcher* – obviously, any researcher will want to study topics they find interesting but the question of 'values' raises some questions. If a researcher thinks a topic is important enough to research, perhaps because it raises moral or political questions, they may have strong feelings about it and there must be a risk that these feelings will affect how they perceive the situation and do their research.

- *Current debates in the academic world* – sociologists, like anyone else, will be drawn to study topics that are creating interest and controversy among their colleagues.

The choice will also be influenced by practical issues.

- *The time and resources needed* – first-time researchers often underestimate how long it takes to collect data, analyse it, and write the report. A lone researcher, perhaps studying part-time for a qualification, will only be able to do a small-scale study (maybe a **case study**). Large-scale studies need a team of professional researchers and can take years to complete.

- *Access to the subject-matter* – some areas of social life are more available to researchers than others. For example, the private life of a family is much harder to study than the public life of a school classroom. Rich and powerful people can deny access to a researcher more easily than poor and powerless people can.

- *Whether funding is available* – large-scale research projects are expensive: salaries, equipment, living expenses, travel, computer resources, secretarial help and a thousand other items have to be paid for. Individuals and organisations can bid for funds from sources such as the government-funded Economic and Social Research Council, or from charitable trusts, but there is stiff competition for this money. Many researchers have very limited resources.

 Many sociologists are interested in social inequality in all its forms (eg class, gender and sexism, ethnicity and racism). Some critics say that this makes sociology politically biased.

Case study: The study of a single example of a phenomenon

This is one reason why we know more about the lives of poor people than about the lives of the rich and powerful.

## Reading around the subject

The next step in any research project is to read what others have already published on the subject. This saves repeating the same work, and may provide some initial data. It will also give the researcher some ideas about how to approach their own project.

## Formulating a hypothesis or research question

### Hypotheses

It is all very well to be interested in a topic but the research must be focussed on a specific issue. If the researcher already has a hunch about something, or wants to test an idea, they should formulate a hypothesis. This is simply a statement that can be tested. It is a prediction of what the research will find. For example: 'Students who study AS level Sociology watch the TV news more often than students who do not study AS Sociology' is an hypothesis. It can be tested by collecting evidence about the TV news-watching habits of the two categories of student. This will confirm or reject the hypothesis, or suggest what further research is needed.

### Research questions

Researchers doing descriptive research do not usually start with an hypothesis. They will have a general question that has prompted the research but they don't make any predictions. However, they may develop an hypothesis as they learn more about what they are studying.

> **Coursework advice**
> It is absolutely essential that you have a clear focus for your coursework. Be realistic about how much research time you have.

## Think it through

Imagine that you have been asked to produce the outline of a research design to study how A level students decide which university courses they are going to apply to.

1 When would be a good time of year to do this research? Explain your choice.

2 How might you collect primary data?

3 What sources of secondary data would you use?

4 Would you start with a hypothesis or a research question? And what would it be?

5 What problems can you foresee in collecting the data? How would you overcome them?

# Preparing the research design

Primary data: Data collected by the researcher.

Secondary data: Data collected by others and used by the researcher.

## What research methods do sociologists use?

First, there is the choice of whether to base the research on primary data (i.e. data collected by the researcher), or on secondary data (i.e. data that is already available). In either case, the data will have to be analysed and interpreted by the researcher.

 In natural science, hypotheses are tested by experiments. We will consider experiments in sociology on pp. 126–7.

### PRIMARY DATA

The most common methods of collecting primary data are:

- by survey (see pp. 120–1), usually involving questionnaires (perhaps sent by post) and/or interviews; this generates mainly quantitative data
- by observation (see pp. 122–3), which may be participant (where the researcher joins in the life of the group being studied) or non-participant (where the researcher remains detached from the group); this generates mainly qualitative data.

Pages 120–3 examine these methods and techniques but it is helpful to have an overview of how they compare with each other. Figure A provides such an overview.

The Figure shows how the methods vary according to how many people can be studied and how closely the researcher is involved with the people being researched. It also shows how the methods produce more or less quantitative or qualitative data, and are therefore more or less appropriate to a positivist or interpretive approach.

### SECONDARY DATA

Many kinds of data are already available to sociologists:

- Official statistics collected by government agencies (quantitative)
- Reports in newspapers, TV and radio (mostly qualitative)
- Historical documents (quantitative and qualitative)
- Personal letters and diaries (qualitative)

For a discussion of secondary data, see pp. 124–5.

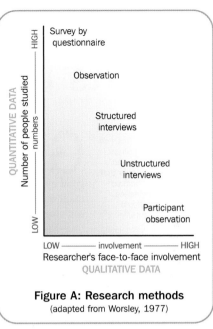

**Figure A: Research methods**
(adapted from Worsley, 1977)

## Triangulation and multiple methods

The *research design* sets out how the researcher will collect evidence and what methods and techniques will be used (see Figure B). Some research designs may use only one method of data collection (for example, a survey using a written questionnaire). Many research designs use more than one method, perhaps combining observation with interviews, together with a study of documents or history, to look at the subject matter from several angles and gain a more complete picture. This is sometimes called 'triangulation' or 'multiple methods' and illustrates how sociologists should not be pigeon-holed into 'positivist' and 'interpretivist' categories.

 **Watch out**

In the exam, don't suggest that triangulation is a method. It is a way of designing a piece of research.

 The Economic and Social Research Council (www.esrc.ac.uk) 'aim to provide high quality research on issues of importance to business, the public sector and government [including] economic competitiveness, the effectiveness of public services and policy, and our quality of life.'

The internet has made it much easier to search for previous publications using sources such as JANET (Joint Academic Network) at www.ja.net . Many FE colleges have links to JANET.

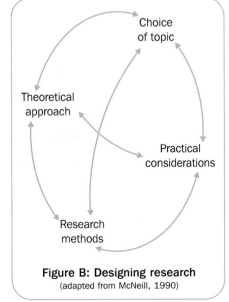

**Figure B: Designing research**
(adapted from McNeill, 1990)

## Important studies

Researchers will, understandably, tend to write up their research as though it had all gone smoothly and in accordance with approved procedures. This is as true of natural science as it is of social science. Of course, life is seldom like that. There are several accounts of what doing the research was 'really like'.

- Bell and Newby (1977) *Doing Sociological Research*
- Hammond (1964) *Sociologists at Work*
- Bell and Roberts (1984) *Social Researching*.

(For full details, see the references list on pp. 158–60.)

## Round-up

Choice of topic, choice of research methods, theoretical approach, and practical considerations are interrelated, as shown in Figure B.

Sociological researchers use whatever technique or combination of techniques is appropriate to the subject of the research, rather than being committed to quantitative versus qualitative data or positivist versus interpretive perspectives. In large-scale studies, many researchers will use one technique to check or confirm the findings of another.

# How can research reports be evaluated?

* The difference between an opinion and a judgment is that a judgment is backed up by good evidence. Sociologists should make judgments.

Good sociology is based on good evidence. That's easy to say but it prompts the question: 'What is the difference between good evidence and poor evidence?' There are three main questions to be asked about any piece of sociological research:

1 Is the method of data-collection reliable?
2 Is the data valid?
3 Are the people or the social setting representative?

But are any of these books any good?

## Reliability

To say that a method of collecting data is 'reliable' is to mean that anybody else using this method (or the same person using it on another occasion) would produce the same findings. Take a simple example from the natural world. If one person measures the acreage of a farm on one day, using surveying equipment that is in good condition, and another person measures it again a week later using another set of equipment that is in equally good condition, the only reason why their results might differ would be that one of them had made a mistake in using the equipment or in doing the calculations. They have operationalised the concept of area by using 'acre' and used this as the unit of measurement. The method is reliable.

A survey using a well-designed questionnaire is reliable. The same results should be gained, regardless of who is asking the questions. By contrast, research that involves a researcher working alone and relying on their own interpretation of what they see, like much participant observation research, must be suspect as to its reliability.

**Reliability:** A reliable method gives the same result when the research is repeated.

**Valid:** Valid evidence is evidence of what it claims to be evidence of.

**Representative:** A sample is representative when what is true of the sample is true of the population from which it is drawn.

## Validity

For data to be regarded as **valid**, it must be a 'true' picture of what is being studied. Or, to put it another way, is it really evidence of what it claims to be evidence of?

For example, suppose we wanted to investigate racist attitudes in the teaching profession. If we designed a questionnaire that asked teachers about their attitude to ethnic minorities, we would certainly get some data that could be expressed statistically. But would this data be a measure of teachers' attitudes to ethnic minorities, or a measure of what teachers will say when they are asked about their attitudes?

A questionnaire may be well designed and produce reliable data but, if the data is invalid, it is no use to the researcher. The data is a product of the research method. Questionnaire-based research may collect data about how people will answer questions rather than about what they actually believe or how they actually behave.

The strength of participant observation is that, when done well, it produces **valid** data that reflects the reality of a situation, unaffected by the research method that is used. In this example, the researcher might get a more valid picture of teacher attitudes to ethnic minorities by joining the staff of a school (see pp. 122–3)

**Objective:** (a) Existing independently of the observer; (b) being free of bias.

**Participant:** Anyone who takes part in research. Some researchers use the term 'subject' but 'participant' is preferable because it suggests that the person is an equal in the process rather than an inferior.

## Representativeness

This is about how far the individual, group or situation being studied is typical of others. If they are typical, then what is true of them is also true of others. We can therefore generalise from this sample.

Researchers who conduct quantitative surveys have developed sophisticated statistical tools to assess how far a sample is **representative** of the whole population (see pp. 120–1). However, very small-scale research must always be questionable as to its representativeness.

## The problem of objectivity

Science should be **objective** – that is, its methods and its findings should not be influenced by the personal interests or bias of the researcher. It is supposed to discover 'facts' and be value-free. There are major debates about the supposed objectivity of natural science but the problem of value-freedom is even greater in sociology. The more that sociologists study topics that they feel strongly about, and the closer they get to the people they are studying, the greater the risk of bias creeping into their research. We will look at the issue of values and value-freedom on pp. 126–7.

### Watch out

**You will often be asked about reliability and validity in sociology exams. Make sure you know which is which and what the difference is.**

In practice, good sociological research makes a trade-off between reliability, validity and representativeness. This is often done by collecting data in several different ways. Thus Barker (1984), in her study of the Moonies, used written questionnaires and face-to-face interviews, joined a group of Moonies (at their invitation) in their everyday life and for religious meetings and ceremonies, and read all she could about their beliefs. She also compared the attitudes of the Moonies she worked with to the attitudes of a group of non-Moonies.

## Watch out

**Be careful to observe these ethical principles when you are planning research of your own.**

*The ethical research principles of the British Sociological Association can be found on their website at* www.britsoc.org.uk/about/ethic.htm

### EVALUATING RESEARCH REPORTS

You should always evaluate (weigh up the strengths and weaknesses) of research reports and evidence. It may help to ask the following questions.

• What were the aims of the research?

• Why was the topic chosen?

• What were the theoretical and practical issues? How might these have affected the methods or the findings?

• Who paid for the research to be done? How might this have affected the choice of topic, the methods, or the findings?

• What research methods were used? Why were they chosen? Were they appropriate to the topic?

• What are the key concepts? How are they operationalised?

• Are the methods reliable?

• Is the data valid?

• How was the sample or group selected? How far is it representative of the wider population?

• What ethical problems are raised by the research? Were they properly dealt with?

## Ethics in sociological research

Ethics is the study of what is morally right or wrong. There are ethical issues in social research just as there are in the natural sciences.

The main ethical principles of social research are that:

• no one should suffer any harm as a result of the research
• participants' rights to privacy and confidentiality should be protected
• researchers should be honest and open about what they are doing.

### Harm

Obviously, sociological research should not risk physical harm to anyone. This is seldom a problem. However, there may be a risk of harming someone:

• emotionally – for example, by asking insensitive questions
• socially – for example, by damaging their reputation, or exposing them to ridicule or punishment.

Ethical research is designed to avoid these risks.

### Think it through

**A student made the following coursework proposal.**

For my research, I want to study the effects on families of a father serving a long prison sentence. To do this, I will interview some mothers with husbands in prison and then go to the prison to interview the fathers. I will then compare their answers. I can get in touch with some families like this because my father works at the magistrates' court.

**Write a response to this proposal, paying particular attention to problems of:**

• ethics
• operationalising concepts
• reliability
• validity
• representativeness.

### Privacy and confidentiality

All research **participants** have a right to their privacy. They have a right to know what the research is about and to refuse to take part in it or to answer particular questions. If they do take part, they must be sure that whatever they say cannot be traced back to them as individuals.

Confidentiality means that the information an individual gives to the researcher cannot be traced back to that individual. Ethical researchers are careful to disguise the identity of individual participants when they write up their research. This is easy in the context of a survey, where individuals may be anonymous in the first place and where individual responses are merged into totals. It is more difficult when a small group of people have been studied through participant observation and where particular characters are described or quoted. Simply changing the name of a location or an individual may not be enough to preserve their anonymity.

### Honesty and openness

Ethical researchers seek the informed consent of participants, ensuring they know:

• that the research is going on
• who is doing it
• why it is being done
• how the results will be used.

It is not always a simple matter to gain informed consent. For example, very young children or people with learning disabilities may not be able fully to understand what the researcher is doing.

## Round-up

**Good sociology is based on good research methods and good evidence. Evidence and methods can be evaluated in terms of their reliability, validity and representativeness. Sociological research should be free from bias and should follow ethical principles, particularly that of the informed consent of participants.**

# Social surveys

The survey method is widely used in sociology because it can obtain large amounts of data:
- in a statistical form
- from a large number of people
- over a wide area
- in a relatively short time.

A survey is sometimes used on its own as the complete research design and sometimes in association with other methods, as part of a larger design.

Survey research is about asking questions. The researcher has first to decide:
- who to ask
- what questions to ask
- how to ask the questions (e.g. by post or face to face).

> ### HOW TO CARRY OUT A SURVEY
>
> - Formulate the research question or hypothesis.
> - Identify the population.
> - Draft the questionnaire/ interview schedule.
> - Pilot the questionnaire/ interview schedule.
> - Finalise the questionnaire/ interview schedule.
> - Select the sample.
> - Collect the data.
> - Process / analyse the data.
> - Write the report.

## Who will be included in the survey?

Surveys are usually carried out on a sample (i.e. a small proportion) of the **population** in question. The first task therefore is to identify the population, which may be made up of individuals, or households, or schools, or whatever other social unit is being studied. The next step is to select a sample, which should be representative of the population – what is true of the sample should be true of the population as a whole.

### Random sampling

In random sampling, every member of the population has an equal chance of being included in the sample. For this, a **sampling frame** (i.e. a list of the population) is needed.

Once the sampling frame is known, the sample can be drawn randomly (e.g. by taking names out of a hat, or using random numbers generated by a computer), or quasi-randomly (e.g. by taking every tenth name from the list). Statistical checks can then be made that the sample is representative of the population.

### Stratified random sampling

If the researcher has a sampling frame that shows the main characteristics of the population, it is possible to ensure that the sample includes the right proportions in each category. For example, if the researcher knows that of 1000 pupils in a school, 55% (550) are boys and 45% (450) are girls, a sample of, say, 10% can be drawn from each group (55 boys and 45 girls).

### Quota sampling

In this case, rather than identifying individuals and then contacting them, the researcher establishes how many participants are needed in each category and goes looking for them. For example, if a researcher wants to interview 50 men aged 40–55 who have mortgages and live in Hertfordshire, he or she can go to where such people are likely to be found and ask each one if they are willing to be interviewed until the quota is filled. It does not require a sampling frame and is not truly representative.

### Purposive sampling

In this method, the researcher selects individuals or cases that appear suitable for the research. The sample is not statistically representative. For example, when Goldthorpe and Lockwood wanted to research whether highly paid working-class people were becoming more middle class, they studied a group of workers in a car factory (Goldthorpe and Lockwood, 1969).

### Snowball sampling

Here the researcher interviews an individual and then asks them to suggest who else might be interviewed. The sample can grow as large as the researcher wants. It will not be representative in the statistical sense.

Population: All the people, or other unit, relevant to the research.

Sampling frame: The list of people, or other unit, from which a sample is drawn.

## Methods of asking questions

| | Questionnaires (by post or telephone) | Structured interviews (face to face) | Unstructured interviews (face to face) |
|---|---|---|---|
| Potential advantages | • can reach large sample <br> • relatively quick and cheap <br> • personal influence of researcher is slight <br> • produces quantitative, reliable and representative data | Similar to questionnaires, but: <br> • higher response rates <br> • can 'probe' the participant's responses by asking follow-up questions <br> • can assess truthfulness of participant | • can create rapport with participant <br> • can follow up responses in depth <br> • produces valid qualitative data |
| Potential disadvantages | • response rates may be low <br> • answers may be incomplete <br> • data may not be valid, or even truthful <br> • cannot be sure who completed the questionnaire <br> • limits possible answers the participant can give | • 'interview effect, e.g. participant may wish to impress or please the interviewer <br> • 'interviewer effect': age/gender, etc. of interviewer may influence participant's answers <br> • time-consuming, so fewer participants and less representative <br> • limits possible answers participant can give | • personal bias of interviewer <br> • data may be less reliable <br> • time-consuming |

## Asking questions

### Questionnaires

These are simply lists of questions written down in advance. They can be administered face to face, by telephone, or by post (when the respondent will write the answers).

Questions may be:
- *Closed* – the range of possible answers is fixed.
  Example: Did you vote at the last general election? Yes/No
- *Open-ended* – the respondent can answer however they like.
  Example: Why did you vote at the last general election?
- *Multiple-choice*
  Example: Did you abstain from voting because:
  - you didn't think it would make any difference
  - you thought none of the candidates were worth voting for
  - you forgot
  - you were away from home
  - other reason?
- *Scaled*
  Example: How do you rate Tony Blair's performance as Prime Minister?
  Excellent – Good – Satisfactory – Unsatisfactory – Poor

Closed, multiple-choice or scaled questions can produce statistical data but limit the answers the respondent can give. Open-ended questions enable the respondent to express themselves but produce data that is difficult to express statistically.

### Interviews

In a structured interview, the researcher reads out a list of questions (the **interview schedule**) and writes down the respondent's answers. An unstructured interview is more like a guided conversation, where the talk is informal but the researcher asks questions to ensure that the participant keeps to the subject of the research. Many sociological interviews are a mix of the structured and the unstructured. Responses in structured interviews can be expressed quantitatively; responses in unstructured interviews have to be analysed.

### Piloting

Questionnaires and interview schedules should always be tried out on a small group of people to check that the questions asked are clear and unambiguous, that they don't upset or lead the participants, and that they will produce the kind of data that is wanted.

### Response rates

However carefully a sample is identified, the results will be unrepresentative if not enough people agree to take part in the research. Postal questionnaires tend to have low **response rates**.

## Longitudinal surveys

Most surveys provide a snapshot of the social context that is being studied. They do not provide a sense of change over time. Longitudinal surveys are a way of addressing this problem. They can be panel surveys (where the same group of people is interviewed at intervals over a period of years) or can be surveys that are repeated at intervals with different groups of respondents. (e.g. the British Social Attitudes Survey, the British Crime Survey and the Census).

## Important studies

Most published reports of sociological surveys, including government-sponsored surveys, include a description of how the sample was drawn and of the questionnaire. The following may be of particular interest to AS-level Sociology students.

- Edgell (1980) *Middle class couples*
- British Crime Survey 2000 downloadable from www.crimereduction.gov.uk/statistics12.htm
- Park *et al.* (2001) *British social attitudes*; the 18th Report
- Mack and Lansley (1985) *Poor Britain*

Interview schedule: The list of questions used by the researcher.

Response rates: The percentage of the sample who return completed questionnaires.

### Think it through

A researcher is interested in how success at school influences the early stages of a person's career. This is the first draft of their face-to-face interview schedule.

1  What is your name?
2  Are you male or female?
3  Are you aged: 15–20; 20–25; 25–30; 30–35; over 35?
4  When did you leave school?
5  What exams did you pass when you were at school?
6  What exams did you fail when you were at school?
7  What jobs have you had since you left school?
8  Do you think doing well at school has affected your career so far?

For each question, ask yourself:

1  Does the question make assumptions about the participant?

2  Is the question asking for information that is necessary to the research?

3  Is the question worded so that it will gain exactly the information the researcher needs?

4  Could the question be understood in more than one way?

5  Will it be easy to group the answers into categories for analysis?

Whenever the answer to one of these is 'No', draft a better question for the interview schedule.

## Round-up

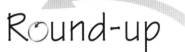

The survey method is widely used in sociology and other kinds of social research. It can be used on its own or as part of a wider research design. Using a questionnaire or an interview schedule, a survey produces quantitative data about a sample of the population. The data should be reliable and representative but may lack validity. Longitudinal surveys can track social change over a period of time.

# Participant observation

Participant observation is the main research method used in ethnographic sociology. '**Ethnography**' simply means 'writing about a way of life'. Many writers do this, of course, but the ethnographic tradition in sociology is rooted in the work of **anthropologists** such as Malinowski, Evans-Pritchard and Radcliffe-Brown who worked mainly in the 1920s and 1930s.

Malinowski studied the people of the Trobriand Islands. He believed that the only way to get a valid picture of their way of life was to study them at first hand by living among them and learning their language, taking notes and recording his observations on a day-to-day basis. This is the research method that has become known as 'participant observation'.

Ethnographic research is sometimes called 'field research'.

Anthropology: the study of the culture of small pre-industrial societies.
Macro: Large scale.
Micro: Small scale.

It is important that the participant observer is as inconspicuous as possible

## Participant observation

The method of participant observation took a while to be adopted by sociologists who, in the 1920s and 1930s, were still mainly concerned with studying the structure of societies from a **macro** perspective rather than looking at the intricacies of everyday life from a **micro** perspective. The Chicago School of researchers in America in the 1930s was the exception to this. The leader of this group, Robert Park, encouraged his colleagues to take part in all aspects of the life of the city and to 'go get the seats of your pants dirty in real research' (Park, 1927). This approach was continued in the 1950s and 1960s by Howard Becker and his Chicago colleagues.

In a participant observation study, the researcher joins the group or social situation that is being studied. The aim is to understand what is happening from the point of view of those involved, to 'get inside their heads' and to understand the meaning that they give to their situation. The research is 'naturalistic': it is done in the natural setting and is not based on the artificial situation created by an interview or questionnaire. The research may take many months, or even years.

### STRENGTHS AND WEAKNESSES OF PARTICIPANT OBSERVATION

*Strengths*
- Participants behave as they normally do, so evidence is valid.
- It takes the viewpoint of the participants rather than the researcher.
- It can 'dig deep' into social interaction.
- The researcher is open to new insights (questions are not fixed in advance).

*Weaknesses*
- It studies small groups, so may not be representative.
- It cannot be checked or repeated, so may not be reliable.
- It is time-consuming.
- The researcher's presence may change the behaviour of the group.
- The researcher may be biased, or even 'go native'.

If covert:
- It raises serious ethical issues.
- The researcher may be 'at risk'.
- The researcher may not be able to ask questions.

### How participant?

How far the researcher participates varies from one research project to another, and at different stages of the same piece of research. The researcher may be a:

- complete participant – concealing the fact that they are doing research
- participant as observer – actively involved with the group but known to be researching
- observer as participant – present in the group but taking little active part.

### Covert or overt?

If a sociologist conceals the fact that they are doing research, they are doing 'covert' research. If they tell group members who they are and why they are there, the research is 'overt'.

Covert research goes against the principle of informed consent (*see* p. 119), and so may be considered unethical. A researcher might argue that the research would be impossible if the group members knew they were being studied (for example, if they are involved in criminal activity), but this may simply mean that some sorts of sociological research should not be undertaken.

## Important studies

Whyte (1955) is still the classic participant observation study. It contains a clear account of how the research was done.

Other studies of interest to AS sociology students include:
- Sewell (1997) Black masculinities and schooling
- Hey (1997) The company she keeps: an ethnography of girls' friendships.

In some studies, the researcher is only an observer, watching a group and recording their activities in an 'observation schedule' to produce quantitative data. This is an important research method but is not participant observation.

# The stages of participant observation

## Choosing the topic and group

The reasons for choosing a topic will be much the same as those listed on p. 116. However, participant observation is particularly appropriate for studying deviant groups such as street gangs who would be unlikely to respond to a questionnaire (not truthfully anyway). There are also several studies of occupational groups (e.g. police, factory workers), many of whose activities are invisible to the general public.

## Joining the group

Occasionally, the researcher is already a member of the group being studied (e.g. Holdaway, 1983, on the police). The researcher may be invited to do the research (e.g. Barker, 1984, on the Moonies). If the group has a formal membership, the researcher can join it (e.g. Festinger, 1956, on religious sects). Very often, the researcher has to find a way of joining the group they want to study. This is usually done by befriending an individual who then introduces the researcher to the group. This individual typically becomes the researcher's 'key informant' (e.g. Tally in Liebow (1967) or Doc in Whyte (1955)).

## Taking part in the life of the group

In the early stages, the researcher will tend to keep quiet, listening to and observing what is being said and done and gaining the trust of the group until their presence is taken for granted. From the start, the researcher will take notes and keep a field diary, as inconspicuously as possible.

After a while (sometimes a long while), ideas will begin to crystallize in the researcher's mind and it will be possible to start asking questions, particularly of the key informant. How far this is possible will depend largely on whether the group members know that the research is being done, i.e. whether the research is overt or covert.

Towards the end of the research, there may be an opportunity to conduct unstructured interviews.

The researcher must strike a balance between getting involved with the group and remaining an observer. If the researcher gets too involved ('goes native'), they will lose the detached perspective (objectivity) that a researcher must have.

## Leaving the group

Eventually, the researcher must leave the group and begin writing up and analysing the notes and other material they have collected. Leaving the group may raise ethical questions. Will friends feel let down? Has the group come to depend on the researcher for advice or help? Has the researcher simply been using the group for their own ends?

## Writing the report

The research report should describe the group's behaviour, suggest reasons (hypotheses) for this behaviour, and, crucially, show how the evidence supports these suggestions. The researcher will have developed some tentative hypotheses about the group throughout the research, but the report must show how far the evidence supports these hypotheses.

## Think it through

The participant observer gathers data by participating in the daily life of the group or organisation he studies. He watches the people he is studying to see the situations they ordinarily meet and how they behave in them. He enters into conversation with some or all of the participants in these situations and discovers their interpretations of the events he has observed.

Becker, H.S. (1958) 'Participant observation and interviewing: a rejoinder', *Human Organisation*, vol. 17(2)

1 Why is participant observation considered to produce valid evidence?

2 Why is participant observation considered to be unreliable?

3 Imagine that you have decided to do participant observation research of your own group of sociology students. What practical, theoretical and ethical problems would you have?

# Round-up

Participant observation is the method most commonly used in ethnographic or field research. The researcher, to a greater or lesser degree, joins in the day-to-day life of the group and learns to understand their social world from their point of view. Properly done, participant observation produces valid data but it may be regarded as unreliable and unrepresentative, and it raise important ethical questions.

*The British Sociological Association has produced ethical guidelines on all these questions at www.britsoc.org.uk*

## Ethics in participant observation

We have already considered the ethics of overt or covert observation and the question of informed consent. However, participant observation raises particular problems in relation to the other ethical principles outlined on p. 119.

- How can the researcher protect the confidentiality and anonymity of the people who have been researched? Simply changing names and locations may not be enough.
- If the group or individuals can be identified, is there a risk of any harm to them, whether of ridicule or, more seriously, of arrest or reprisals?
- Is there any risk to the researcher if certain information is published? Is this a good reason for not publishing it?
- Are there any circumstances when a researcher should breach confidentiality (e.g. where a serious crime is being planned)?

# Secondary data

econdary data is data that is available to the sociologist because it already exists. There is a huge amount of this material, both quantitative and qualitative, about the present, the recent past, and the more distant past. The sociologist's task is to identify, select and analyse what is relevant to their research.

**There is a mass of evidence already available to sociologists**

## Official statistics

Official statistics are the statistics that are produced and published by the government and its agencies. These are collected in three main ways.

### Government surveys

The 2002 edition of *Social Trends* lists 26 major surveys regularly carried out by the government.

For details about the Census, look at the official website **www.statistics.gov.uk/census2001**

The best-known government survey is the Census of Population, which is carried out every 10 years. By law, every household in the United Kingdom has to complete a census form. The main questions (e.g. how many people there are in the household, their age, sex, relationships, occupation) are much the same for every Census. Other questions (e.g. about housing, ethnic origin, travel-to-work details) may vary from one Census to the next.

### Registration

What effect might target-setting have on the validity and reliability of official records?

By law, all births, marriages and deaths, and certain illnesses, must be registered when they occur. The resulting data is published at least annually and provides a record over time.

### Record-keeping

All government agencies, and many private organisations, are required to provide certain information to government at regular intervals.

- Schools have to keep records of their pupils and their achievements for the league tables.
- Doctors and hospitals have to keep records of how many patients they have treated and for what conditions.
- Employers have to keep records of how many employees they have and to make returns to the Inland Revenue (about income tax) and Customs and Excise (about VAT).

In recent years, many of the records kept by public bodies have been geared to assessing whether they have hit the targets they have been set by government.

### Publications

The government publishes hundreds of booklets and leaflets containing official statistics. Of these, the most easily understood is the annual *Social Trends*, which contains statistics drawn from every area of public life.

*The printed version of* Social Trends *is quite expensive but the contents of it are available on the internet at* **www.statistics.gov.uk**

**Coursework advice** **Copying and pasting pages from the internet does not count as research and will earn no marks for coursework unless it is accompanied by a discussion or explanation of your own.**

## Think it through

### ITEM A

Reporting rates vary according to the crimes committed. For example, a high proportion of car thefts are reported to the police as police involvement is required for insurance purposes. There is some evidence to suggest that shop theft is less likely to be reported to the police, with some thefts being absorbed by the businesses as overheads, and some shop owners either not wishing to attract publicity or else believing that reported crimes are unlikely to be detected.

Crime data collected by the police is a by-product of the administrative procedure of completing a record for crimes which they investigate... many crimes are never reported to the police and some that are reported are not recorded.

Police recording rates – whether a reported crime is considered of sufficient seriousness to go 'on the record' – depend to a certain extent on the discretion of the police officers concerned and will vary from force to force.

### ITEM B

The official statistics list record crime in these categories:

- Theft and handling stolen goods, including theft of vehicles and theft from vehicles
- Criminal damage
- Burglary
- Violence against the person
- Fraud and forgery
- Drugs offences
- Robbery
- Sexual offences, including rape

Adapted from *Social Trends 32* (2002)

**1** How likely is each of the crimes described in Item B to be:
(a) reported to the police?
(b) recorded by the police?

**2** What factors will affect the reporting and recording of each type of crime?

## How can sociologists use official statistics?

Some official statistics (for example, the number of babies born in a year) can be taken at their face value as valid, reliable and as accurate as can reasonably be expected. Other official statistics need to be treated with more caution, since it may be in the interests of the people who supply the data not to be entirely truthful (for example, data about income that is supplied to the Inland Revenue).

However, official statistic are of special sociological interest, because they are the result not of counting or record-keeping but of the social process that created them. For example, the chart on the right is reproduced from *Social Trends 32* showing how many people committed suicide in the years between 1974 and 2000 per 100 000 of the population. The figures show how the trends vary between men and women and between age groups, and are based on suicides registered in each year. But, whereas a death is relatively easy to define, and a person's age and sex are usually known, for a death to be registered as a suicide requires a series of decisions to be made by:

- a doctor (whether or not to refer the death to the coroner)
- a coroner (whether or not to hold an inquest)
- perhaps a coroner's jury (what verdict to arrive at).

All these people will base their decisions on the information available to them (e.g. the age of the dead person, their circumstances, the cause of death), which they will interpret in the light of what they 'know' about previous suicides. The same kind of interpretive process produces health statistics, crime statistics and others. The point is not whether the statistics are right or wrong, but that they result from people making sense of, and *interpreting*, events. Sociologists can research this process using participant observation and interviews. The important point is that a suicide (or a crime, or a day off work through illness) is a different sort of 'fact' from the fact of a birth, or a three-bedroom house, or the number of 11-year-olds in the population.

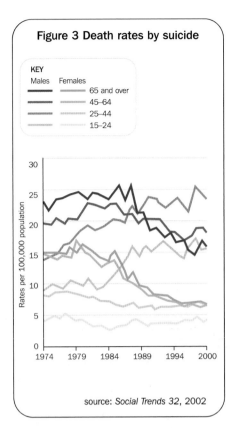

**Figure 3 Death rates by suicide**

KEY
Males  Females
65 and over
45–64
25–44
15–24

Rates per 100,000 population

source: *Social Trends 32*, 2002

## Documents

### Personal documents

Sociologists can also make use of personal documents such as letters and diaries. These are likely to be used by sociologists who take an interpretive or qualitative approach and want to understand more about the experience and world-views of people in the past. Such documents have not usually been produced with research in mind, though some researchers ask participants to keep diaries while the research is in progress. Care should always be taken to check the authenticity of personal documents (i.e. were they really written by the person who is claimed to have written them?). There may also be doubt about their representativeness. Extended writing is likely to be more popular among educated people, who may not be typical of the group being studied.

### Public documents

These include school records, parish records, social work records, court records, hospital records, reports of government enquiries and a host of other resources. Published autobiographies may also fall into this category.

### Mass media

Films, television programmes, TV news, newspapers, and even novels are rich sources of evidence for the sociologist. It is essential to remember that these accounts of events have been created by an author or journalist, rather than being factual objective descriptions of events. This is not the same as saying that they are biased (though they may be) but means that the account is an interpretation from a particular perspective.

### Earlier research

Some sociologists revisit the data collected by earlier sociologists, either to add to what they have collected themselves or to check, and perhaps question, the conclusions drawn by the earlier research.

### Content analysis

Most documentary data is qualitative, but it is possible to convert this into quantitative data using content analysis. Using this technique, the researcher classifies the content of the document into categories (e.g. in a newspaper, 'political news', 'economic news', 'sports news', 'advertisements') and then counts how much of the content falls into each category. This makes it possible to make quantitative comparisons between documents. Jagger (2001) used this technique to analyse lonely-heart adverts in newspapers.

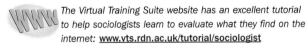

*The Virtual Training Suite website has an excellent tutorial to help sociologists learn to evaluate what they find on the internet:* www.vts.rdn.ac.uk/tutorial/sociologist

# Round-up

**Sociologists make use of a wide range of secondary data in their research. This may be quantitative or qualitative, private or public, official or unofficial. All this data should be assessed in terms of its validity, reliability, representativeness and objectivity. Official statistics can be used as a source of information or as a subject for research.**

# Is sociology more than just common sense?

RESEARCH METHODS

ociologists would accept that there is good sociology and bad sociology (just as there is good and bad in any other subject) but would claim that good sociology is superior to common sense. As we saw on page 114, good sociology is based on good evidence that results from good research and draws logical conclusions based on that evidence. That is what makes sociology a social science rather than just common sense or journalism.

The question of whether sociology is a science like the natural sciences (e.g. physics and chemistry) was more important in the nineteenth and twentieth centuries than it is now. At that time, it was thought that natural science could be objective and unbiased, discovering the 'facts' about causes and effects in the world, and that it would be possible to develop a 'science of society' by, as far as possible, copying the positivist research methods used by natural scientists.

The best-selling sociology textbook for A-level students in the 1960s was called *The science of society*.

## Laboratory experiments

The classic scientific research method is the laboratory experiment, based on an hypothesis. Typically, this involves setting up a 'control group' and an 'experimental group', treating these groups in different ways, and then comparing the results.

Let's imagine a psychology experiment to test the hypothesis 'Having classical music playing in the background is a more helpful aid to students' exam revision than having pop music'. The scientist might:

- start by identifying the other variables that could affect the revision process, e.g. the age and sex of the students, the light, the temperature, the volume of the music, and what is being learned
- set up two groups (the control group and the experimental group), which are matched for variables such as age and sex. In other words, the scientist 'controls' these variables
- give the members of each group the same learning task in the same circumstances but with one variable (the independent variable) changed for the experimental group (e.g. playing pop music, whereas the control group is listening to classical music)
- measure the learning of each group.

If there was a difference in how much each group had learned (the dependent variable), the scientist might conclude, after many other experiments and changes to the variables, that the type of music affects learning.

### How useful are laboratory experiments in sociology?

Laboratory experiments are widely used by psychologists but they have the following serious limitations in sociology.

1 The laboratory is an artificial situation; what happens there may have little relevance to the 'real world' (a validity problem).
2 Experiments can only be on a small scale and for a short time.
3 If the subjects (participants) in an experiment know that it is being done, they may not act as they usually do (the experimental affect – a validity problem).
4 If the subjects are misled about the nature of the experiment, they cannot give informed consent (an ethical problem).
5 It is not possible for a researcher to control all the variables that might affect the subjects' behaviour.

## Field experiments

Although sociologists make very little use of laboratory experiments, there are several well-known examples of 'field experiments', where the researcher sets up a situation to observe in the 'real world'.

While field experiments may reduce some of the problems of laboratory experiments:

1 the researcher has even less chance of controlling all the possible variables
2 there may be greater problems about participants giving informed consent
3 the experiment may have adverse effects on participants' lives.

See p. 81 for a description of Rosenthal and Jacobson's experiment about the effect of teachers' expectations on pupils' performance.

### MAKING COMPARISONS

Experiments are of limited use in sociology but the basic principle of comparing one situation with another to try to identify causes (see pp. 114–15) lies behind a lot of explanatory research in sociology. For example, many attempts to explain why working-class children do less well than middle-class children in education have compared the variables in their home backgrounds.

126

# Sociology and values: the problem of bias

Everyone has values – beliefs about what is morally right or morally wrong, but is it possible to keep these values out of the research process?

Sociologists have argued for years about whether sociology

- is value-free
- can be value-free
- should be value-free.

Values and bias can enter into sociological research at every stage of the research process:

- choosing what to research
- who pays for the research
- deciding what research methods to use
- deciding which questions to ask and which to leave out
- deciding who, what, where and how to observe
- deciding what secondary data to study
- choosing what data or information to record (from questioning, observation, or reading documents)
- interpreting data and observations, and reaching conclusions
- deciding what to include in the research report
- whether the report is published.

Most sociologists today would agree that sociology cannot be completely value-free but there is disagreement about how to respond to this.

- *Some would argue* (following Weber) that, while values will inevitably affect what topics a sociologist chooses to study (for example, a sociologist who feels strongly about domestic violence will be interested in studying it), the research methods should be as objective and value-free as possible. Personal bias and opinions should not affect the questions that are asked, the observations that are made, or the explanations that are offered.

- *Others would argue* that some degree of bias and value is inevitable and that value-freedom is a myth. The important thing is for the researcher to be open and honest about their values so that the reader can take this into account when assessing the work.

- *Yet others would argue* that sociologists should take a committed approach to their work, using it to defend the interests of the poor and the powerless and to challenge the authority and power of dominant groups. Feminists argue that sociology should challenge patriarchy. Marxists argue that sociology should reveal how the ruling classes maintain their power.

- *Some, including postmodernists, would argue* that there are no facts or objective truth anyway and that there is no way of deciding whether one 'account' is any better (more accurate, more objective) than another.

In theory at least, natural science is unbiased. Supposedly, natural scientists take an objective approach to their work and do not allow their personal feelings or values to affect their work. It is 'value-free', in contrast to sociology – which is accused of being 'biased'. In practice, there is considerable argument about whether natural science really is, or should be, value-free.

## Think it through

'A feminist sociology is one that is for women, not just or necessarily about women, and one that challenges and confronts the male supremacy which **institutionalizes** women's inequality. The defining characteristic of feminism is the view that women's **subordination** must be questioned and challenged... feminism starts from the view that women are oppressed.'

Abbott, P. and Wallace, C. (1990) (2nd edn, 1997) *An introduction to sociology: Feminist perspectives*, Routledge, London

1 Do you think it would be possible for a sociologist with these views to conduct unbiased research? Explain your answer.

2 What research methods do you think such a sociologist would prefer to use? Explain your answer.

3 What other social groups might claim that sociology should 'question and challenge' their 'subordination'?

Institutionalise: To reinforce something and make it permanent.

Subordination: Being in an inferior or powerless situation.

## Watch out

**In the exam, don't just say that a piece of research is biased. Always explain why you think this. Was the sample biased? Or the questions? Or the conclusions drawn by the researcher? Or what?**

 Many sociologists hope that their work will influence social policy in areas such as education, crime, or social welfare. Do you think this makes their work any more biased than the work of a natural scientist hoping to find a cure for disease?

## Avoiding bias

Sociological research is at risk of being biased and lacking objectivity. Research reports must therefore give a full account of how the research was done and the data collected must be available for other sociologists to check, along with the conclusions. Bias is not necessarily a bad thing; what *is* wrong is to claim to present 'objective facts' when in practice the work has been influenced by personal values or opinions.

## Round-up

**What makes sociology superior to common sense is its research methods; these should aim to keep personal bias to a minimum. Natural scientists use laboratory experiments to control variables and minimise bias but they are not appropriate for sociology. Most sociologists would agree that it is important to keep personal values out of research as far as possible but that total objectivity is impossible.**

# Research methods:
# summative review

Most sociologists would claim that what makes sociology superior to common sense or journalism is that it draws relatively reasoned and rigorous conclusions from reliable, valid and representative evidence about its subject matter – people, social facts, social institutions and social processes. Furthermore, the evidence, how it was collected, and the conclusions drawn from it are all made available for others to check and scrutinise.

Whether interested in describing the social world or in trying to explain it (or both), sociologists have used, and continue to use, a variety of methods for obtaining evidence. In the past, particularly in the 1960s and 1970s, there were lively disagreements about theoretical perspectives in sociology and, hence, the merits of different methods. These disagreements were once called 'sociology's wars of religion', meaning that they aroused very strong and sometimes irrational feelings among the people involved. Today, however, it is generally agreed that it is sensible to use a variety of research methods, and sometimes a combination, according to the topic that is being studied.

However, this does not mean that the range of research methods can be treated as a kind of 'lucky dip' and that a researcher, whether an AS student or a full-time professional social researcher, can choose whichever methods they take a fancy to. It is important to take a systematic approach, to consider some of the issues that underlie the research process, and to understand why some methods, or combinations of methods, are more suitable in particular situations than others.

## What is being studied?

This is the question that underlies the debate between positivism and interpretivism in sociology. Positivist approaches take the view that the only valid and reliable evidence is what we can observe, count and measure. Researchers should not speculate about processes that they cannot observe – for example, people's motives for behaving in a particular way. Positivism is a perfectly sound way of approaching most research in the natural sciences, where we can assume that the things being studied (e.g. plants, minerals, chemicals) are not self-consciously aware of their actions and do not choose to behave as they do. It is possible to observe them, to make comparisons between one situation and another (perhaps in a laboratory experiment) and to uncover the 'laws of nature'.

The positivist approach dominated nineteenth-century sociology. It was argued then that, by using the same methods as natural scientists, sociologists could produce objective and unbiased evidence, often in a statistical (quantitative) form, which would enable them to develop a 'science of society'. The quest for objectivity and value-freedom, in the context of 'grand theories' of society, tended to dominate mainstream sociology until the early 1960s.

However, this approach had first been questioned by Max Weber, whose work at the beginning of the twentieth century, though still firmly in the realms of 'grand theory', gave rise to the various forms of 'interpretivist' sociology. Interpretivists argue that the subject matter of sociology – people – is fundamentally different from the subject matter of the natural sciences, because people are self-consciously aware of what is happening in a social situation, give meaning to it and can make choices about how to act. Social reality and social phenomena exist because the people involved share an understanding of them and give them a similar meaning. So, to explain an event in the social world, whether it is two people interacting in the street or a major social change, we have to take account of how the people involved make sense of it and how this influences their actions. This view, developed by anthropologists in the 1930s, became more accepted in mainstream sociology from the 1960s onwards.

## How do sociologists do research?

Today, most researchers would accept that it is sensible to use the research methods that are best suited to the subject matter. Using a combination of methods can help to balance the weaknesses of one method with the strengths of another.

A number of factors, including personal interests and current debates in the subject, will influence what a sociologist chooses to study and what methods to use. These can be summarised as the practical factors, the ethical factors and the theoretical factors. We have considered the theoretical debates above. Practical issues include:

- time (how much time has the sociologist got to complete the research?)
- money (can the sociologist get any financial support?)
- labour-power (is the sociologist working alone or in a team?)
- access (can the sociologist get access to the people or situation to be studied?).

All researchers should also take ethical factors into account, such as ensuring that the people being studied have given their informed consent to the work and that no harm will come to them.

Having taken all these factors into account, the researcher will produce a research design. This may involve a single research method, such as a survey or participant observation, or a combination of methods, and may make use of both primary data (collected by the researcher) and secondary data (already available because recorded by someone else).

Essentially, a researcher has three ways of collecting evidence:

- asking questions
- observing
- reading information that others have already recorded.

Each of these can be used to collect either quantitative data (in the form of numbers) or qualitative data (usually in the form of words, often quoted directly from the people being studied).

Whichever method is used, the researcher will have to operationalise the key concepts they are using. They will have to define these abstract concepts in such a way that valid and unambiguous empirical observations can be made about them.

## Quantitative data

A researcher who wants to obtain primary quantitative data about how people live their lives, or their attitudes or beliefs, will usually carry out a survey on a representative sample of the population being studied. The questions may be in the form of a questionnaire, possibly delivered through the post, or a structured interview, where the researcher asks the questions face to face and notes the responses. The data collected should be reliable but may not be entirely valid.

Laboratory experiments, though they produce primary quantitative data, are seldom used in sociological research (unlike psychological research) because of problems of validity, ethics and scale.

For topics where a survey is not possible or appropriate, the technique of content analysis may be used. For example, a researcher studying the lives of people in the past might analyse in quantitative terms the content of old letters and diaries; similarly, a study of the content of the mass media might analyse how much time or space is spent on each topic in the news media.

A very large amount of secondary quantitative secondary data is available to sociologists from the official statistics that are published by the government and its agencies. Some of these (for example, the number of marriages that take place in a year) can be treated as reliable matters of fact. Others, such as crime or health statistics, are the outcome of social processes that can be studied in their own right.

## Qualitative data

Sociologists who want to collect primary qualitative data, usually in an ethnographic study of the way of life of a group of people, will often use observation, which may be either participant or non-participant and either covert or overt. This ought to produce valid data but its reliability may be suspect and such studies are usually of small groups, which means that their representativeness may be questioned.

Many sociologists also use unstructured interviews, where the researcher has a relatively informal conversation with the research participant but asks a lot of questions and ensures that the discussion focuses on the topic that is being researched. The reliability of this method is often called into question.

Qualitative secondary data takes the form of letters, diaries and other personal documents, as well as film, video and TV. These can be analysed in terms of their meanings, symbols and use of language but also, as we have seen, in order to produce more quantitative data.

## Evaluating research and research data

Some important questions that need to be asked about any piece of sociological research are as follows.

- Is the group or situation studied representative of any larger group or population?
- Is the data reliable? Would another researcher using the same methods, asking the same questions or making the same observations have come up with the same results?
- Is the data valid? Is it a true picture of what is being studied or has it been distorted by the research method used?
- Is the research objective? Does the research report claim to be free of bias? Does the researcher acknowledge how their values may have affected the outcome?
- Is the research ethically correct?
- Is there enough information in the research report for you to be able to answer these questions properly?

# Research methods: self-assessment questions

1  **Who wrote Street Corner Society?**
   a Malinowski
   b Whyte
   c Barker
   d Booth

2  **Which of these approaches to research really existed?**
   a The Detroit School
   b The Washington School
   c The Chicago School
   d The New York School

3  **When was 'Family and Kinship in East London' first published?**
   a 1957
   b 1967
   c 1977
   d 1987

4  **When was the first UK Census of population?**
   a 1751
   b 1801
   c 1851
   d 1901

5  **Which research method was favoured by Howard Becker?**
   a Survey
   b Content analysis
   c Experiment
   d Participant observation

6  **Which of the following should produce a random sample?**
   a Snowball sampling
   b Quota sampling
   c Stratified sampling
   d Purposive sampling

7  **Match the word (a–c) to the correct definition (i–iii).**
   a Covert observation
   b Overt observation

   i observation done without the knowledge of the observed
   ii observation done with the knowledge of the observed

8  **Which of the following provides qualitative data?**
   a The census
   b A structured questionnaire
   c A laboratory experiment
   d A TV news broadcast

9  **Which of the following research methods did Barker use when researching for 'The Making of a Moonie'?**
   a Participant observation
   b Interviews
   c Secondary data
   d All of these

10 **Group these sources of data into 'primary' and 'secondary'.**
   a VAT returns
   b The results of a questionnaire
   c School registers
   d Letters written by soldiers in a war
   e The results of covert observation

11 **Which of the following did Charles Booth study?**
   a The Salvation Army
   b The people of London
   c The Trobriand Islanders
   d Symmetrical families

12 **Match the following (a–e) to their authors (i–iv).**
   a *Suicide*
   b *Family and Kinship in East London*
   c *Social Relations in a Secondary School*
   d *Poor Britain*
   e *The Company She Keeps*

   i Mack and Lansley
   ii Young and Willmott
   iii Hey
   iv Durkheim
   v Hargreaves

13 **Which of the following are ethical issues in research?**
   a Confidentiality
   b Representativeness
   c Informed consent
   d Validity

**14** Which of the following is correct?

  a Content analysis can be used to convert qualitative data into quantitative data

  b Content analysis can be used to convert quantitative data into qualitative data

**15** Match the method (a–c) to its strength (i–iii).

  a Written questionnaires      i Validity

  b Participant observation      ii Reliability

  c Random sample      iii Representativeness

**16** Which of the following influenced the researchers of the Chicago School?

  a Marxism

  b The World War II

  c Statistical techniques

  d Anthropology

**17** Which of the following is funded by public money?

  a The Census

  b The British Crime Survey

  c The British Household Panel Survey

  d All of these

**18** Match the word (a–d) to its definition (i–iv).

  a Population

  b Sampling frame

  c Interview schedule

  d Response rates

  i The list of questions used by the researcher

  ii The percentage of the sample who return completed questionnaires

  iii All the people, or other unit, relevant to the research

  iv The list of people, or other unit, from whom a sample is drawn

**19** Which of the following is a natural science?

  a Psychology

  b Biology

  c Physiotherapy

  d Philosophy

**20** Complete the following sentences.

  a The difference between an opinion and a judgment is that a judgment is _____.

  b To say that a method of collecting data is _____ is to say that anybody else using this method, or the same person using it on another occasion, would produce the same findings.

  c For data to be regarded as _____, it must be a 'true' picture of what is being studied. Or, to put it another way, is it really evidence of what it claims to be evidence of?

  d _____ is about how far the individual, group or situation being studied is typical of others.

**21** Which of the following is correct?

  a When variable A changes as variable B changes, we can say that B causes A.

  b When variable B changes as variable A changes, we can say that A causes B.

  c When variable A changes as variable B changes, we can say that A and B are correlated.

**22** To operationalise a concept is to:

  a change it so that it suits the research you want to do

  b define it in a way that can be measured

  c put it to use in a piece of research

  d change its meaning after the research is finished

**23** What are the main factors that influence how a sociologist designs a piece of research?

**24** What is the principle of 'informed consent'?

**25** Put these research methods in order of how many research participants are likely to be involved, from most to least.

  a Survey by postal questionnaire

  b Survey by unstructured interview

  c Case study

  d Participant observation

  e Survey by structured interview

# Research methods: a timeline

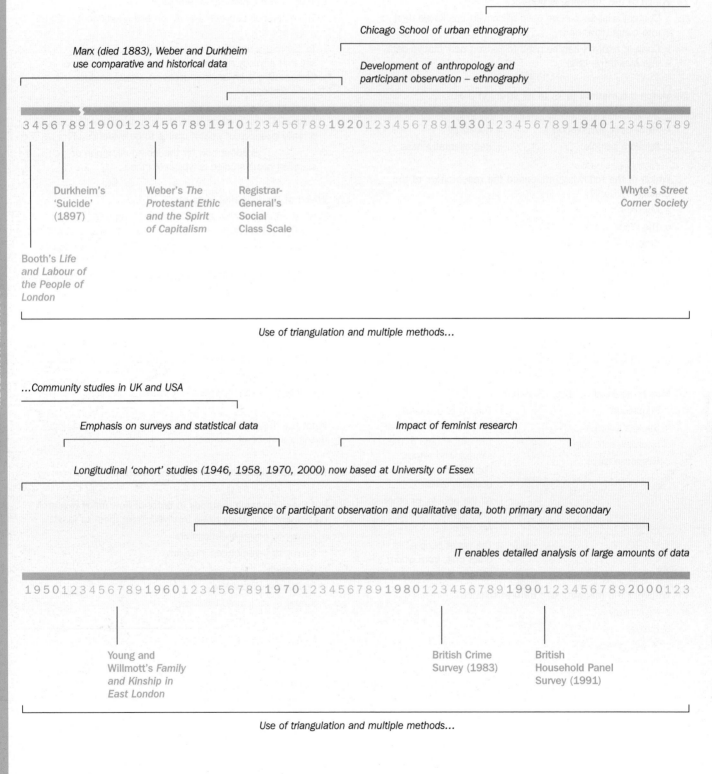

Community studies in UK and USA...

Chicago School of urban ethnography

Marx (died 1883), Weber and Durkheim use comparative and historical data

Development of anthropology and participant observation – ethnography

3 4 5 6 7 8 9 1900 1 2 3 4 5 6 7 8 9 1910 1 2 3 4 5 6 7 8 9 1920 1 2 3 4 5 6 7 8 9 1930 1 2 3 4 5 6 7 8 9 1940 1 2 3 4 5 6 7 8 9

Durkheim's 'Suicide' (1897)

Weber's *The Protestant Ethic and the Spirit of Capitalism*

Registrar-General's Social Class Scale

Whyte's *Street Corner Society*

Booth's *Life and Labour of the People of London*

Use of triangulation and multiple methods...

...Community studies in UK and USA

Emphasis on surveys and statistical data

Impact of feminist research

Longitudinal 'cohort' studies (1946, 1958, 1970, 2000) now based at University of Essex

Resurgence of participant observation and qualitative data, both primary and secondary

IT enables detailed analysis of large amounts of data

1950 1 2 3 4 5 6 7 8 9 1960 1 2 3 4 5 6 7 8 9 1970 1 2 3 4 5 6 7 8 9 1980 1 2 3 4 5 6 7 8 9 1990 1 2 3 4 5 6 7 8 9 2000 1 2 3

Young and Willmott's *Family and Kinship in East London*

British Crime Survey (1983)

British Household Panel Survey (1991)

Use of triangulation and multiple methods...

Note: Except for publication dates, all the dates and periods shown are approximate and open to discussion.

# Section 5  AQA examination advice

# What the examiner is looking for

## How the AQA AS Sociology exam is organised

You will take *either*:
- three exam papers (these are called 'units') *or*:
- two exam papers (units), plus coursework.

The units are broken down as follows.

| Unit 1 | Unit 2 | Unit 3 |
|---|---|---|
| This examination is divided into three sections, each with one question. | This also has three sections, each with one question. | *Exam* |
| Section A: Families and Households<br>Section B: Health<br>Section C: Mass Media. | Section A: Education<br>Section B: Wealth, Poverty and Welfare<br>Section C: Work and Leisure. | This unit has one section, on Sociological Methods. You have one hour to answer all the questions in this. You will find a sample question on p. 144. |
| You have to choose one of section A, B or C and answer all the questions in one and a quarter hours. The majority of students study Families and Households, and this is the topic covered in this book. There is a sample question on Families and Households on p. 136. | You have to choose one of section A, B or C and answer all the questions in one and a quarter hours. There is a sample question on Education on p. 140. | *Coursework*<br><br>You will find full details about this on pp. 148–9. |

### The questions

In each section of Units 1, 2 and 3 (exam) there will be two pieces of written material (Item A and Item B) and six questions. The items are about 10 lines in length. They may include tables of figures, photographs or other illustrations. The items for Unit 3 can be up to about 20 lines.

The six questions will carry the following marks:

Question (a) – 2 marks
Question (b) – 4 marks
Question (c) – 6 marks
Question (d) – 8 marks
Question (e) – 20 marks
Question (f) – 20 marks.

There are 60 marks available on each of the papers.

### What are the items for?

The items are there to help you by prompting your thoughts in the right direction for your answers. Some of the questions will test your understanding of the items; some will ask you to explore concepts or issues that are raised by the items. At least two (and possibly more) of the questions will refer to one or both items. See the sample questions on pages 136, 140 and 144 for examples.

## ASSESSMENT OBJECTIVES

In Sociology, marks are awarded for meeting two assessment objectives (AOs):

- Assessment Objective 1 (AO1) is knowledge and understanding
- Assessment Objective 2 (AO2) is identification, interpretation, analysis and evaluation.

Across the whole examination, the two AOs carry equal marks, but the weighting for each question differs.

### AO1

AO1 tests your knowledge and understanding. You show evidence of this by discussing sociologists' research and theories, sociological concepts and perspectives.

### AO2

The four skills that come under the heading 'AO2' are difficult to separate, both when writing and when reading sociology answers. It is not necessary to show evidence of all four skills. You will be showing evidence of AO2 if you do some of the following:

- show how theories and evidence are linked
- show the stages in the construction of a sociological argument
- show how concepts and ideas can be linked in the construction of a theory or argument
- offer critical points, a concept, theory, perspective or piece of research
- compare and contrast theories or perspectives
- adopt an evaluative approach when a question asks you to do so.

## The nature of each question

### Question (a)

This will ask you to explain a term, usually taken from one of the items.

'Explain' means you need to show that you understand the term. You don't have to define the term. An example may help, but is not essential. Avoid using words in your explanation that are part of the term, e.g. 'Labelling is when a label is applied to someone' is not a good explanation. The following would be better: 'Labelling refers to the ways in which people can be defined by others in ways that can affect their behaviour'.

You will get both marks if you give a reasonably good explanation, and none if you don't.

### Question (b)

This will *either*:
- ask you to identify or suggest two things (for example, two reasons for a particular phenomenon).
  - 'Identify' means simply to state one thing
  - 'Suggest' means the same but implies that it is acceptable to give an answer for which there is no evidence but which is a reasonable possibility.
- You will get two marks for each correct point you make.

*or*
- ask you to explain the difference between two terms.
  - 'Explain the difference' means to show that you understand both terms *and* point out how they differ.

### Question (c)

This question will ask you to identify three things (for example, three reasons for a particular phenomenon). The command word for this type of question will be 'suggest' or 'identify'. (Command word means the word in a question that tells you what to do with the information or ideas you are asked for.) This is the same type of question as the first type explained above for Question (b), but with three answers required rather than two.

### Question (d)

This question will ask you to identify two things, just as in the first type of Question (b), but will also ask for an explanation of each; that is, you have to explain why what you have written is a correct answer. The command words for this type of question will be 'Identify and explain'. The word 'briefly' may be used before 'explain'.

To get the marks for 'explain', say a little more about the answer you have identified, showing the way in which it is an answer to the question. An example can be helpful but is not essential.

### Question (e)

This question will ask you to examine a view or issue, or the reasons or explanations for a particular phenomenon. The command word will be 'examine'. The majority of the marks (14 out of the 20 available) are for AO1, knowledge and understanding. You therefore need to show that you have knowledge and understanding of the topic of the question. You can do this by discussing relevant sociological concepts, theories, perspectives and research findings. To get the six marks available for AO2, your answer will need to include some analysis and evaluation.

### Question (f)

This question will ask you to evaluate a view or theory, or the reasons or explanations for a particular phenomenon. This question will usually refer to one or both of the items. The command word will be 'assess' or 'evaluate' (which mean the same). Of the 20 marks for this question, 14 are available for AO2 skills, so for this question you should concentrate on analysing and evaluating the material you use rather than on demonstrating a wide or broad knowledge and understanding.

### What's the difference between Questions (e) and (f)?
- Question (e) is marked mainly, though not entirely, for the knowledge and understanding shown.
- Question (f) is marked mainly, though not entirely, for the analysis and evaluation shown.

This difference is indicated to you by the command words. The difference relates to the Assessment Objectives (AOs) in Sociology. In sociology, you are being tested on two AOs – AO1 is knowledge and understanding, and AO2 is analysis and evaluation. Across the whole examination, the two AOs carry equal marks, but the weighting for each question differs.

Mark schemes are made public several months after the exam. Your teacher should be able to let you see mark schemes for past papers. They are worth studying carefully because they will give you an insight into how examiners will mark your script. You should also ask to see the Chief Examiner's reports for previous exams.

### Using your time well

For each unit, you need to ensure that the time you spend matches the number of marks available.
- On Units 1 and 2, you should allow 25 minutes for all the first four questions (a, b, c and d) and 25 minutes for each of the other two questions (e and f).
- On Unit 3, you should allow 20 minutes for the first four questions, and 20 minutes for each of the other two questions.

## How exam papers are marked

Your school or college will post your exam paper (known as a 'script') to an examiner appointed by AQA. Each examiner marks several hundred scripts over a period of two or three weeks. Many examiners are sociology teachers. Examiners have to follow a mark scheme that tells them how many marks to award. They meet to ensure that they are all marking to the same standard and some scripts are then marked again by senior examiners, to check that all examiners are marking consistently.

Once the scripts have been marked, there is another meeting to decide how many marks are needed at each grade from A to E, and U (ungraded). They may vary from year to year.

# Unit 1: Families and households
# Sample question and commentary

Time available: 1 hour and 15 minutes
Total marks available: 60 marks

## Item A

The year 1971 is given because the Divorce Reform Act took effect in that year.

At one level, the causes of the rise in the divorce rate since 1971 are the legal changes that have made it easier for couples to divorce – for example, by allowing divorce if both parties consent rather than having to prove an 'offence', such as adultery or desertion. However, sociologists who try to     5
explain the rise in divorce rates also look for changes in society, social values and social structures. The legal changes are not a complete explanation; we still need to ask why so many people – and women more than men – are willing to take advantage of the greater opportunities for divorce. One reason is to do     10
with changes in values; divorce no longer carries a stigma.

## Item B

Until the 1960s the sociology of the family was dominated by one theoretical perspective – functionalism. This way of thinking assumed that the two-parent nuclear family was natural and normal, and functional for society. The nuclear family, it was argued, was ideally suited to modern industrial society. The     5
family needed two adults, one fulfilling the 'breadwinner' role and the other fulfilling a caring and nurturing role. The extended family was seen as not allowing the geographical mobility needed in a modern economy, while the lone-parent family was seen as being a 'broken family', damaged by the     10
absence of one parent, and therefore dysfunctional and sure to create problems for both the children and society.

Although the item begins with functionalism, the main question based on this item (question f) is not about functionalism. Always read items carefully all the way through before starting your answer.

'Stigma' is a term not used only in the sociology of families and households. Questions may be asked about any relevant sociological terms.

(a) What is meant by the term 'stigma'?
    (**Item A**, line 11)                                          2 marks

(b) Identify two ways in which the nuclear family was 'ideally suited to modern industrial society'.
    (**Item B**, line 5)                                           4 marks

(c) Suggest three reasons why the divorce rate has risen in the past 30 years, other than those mentioned in Item A.                                              6 marks

(d) Identify and briefly explain two reasons why women are more likely than men to initiate a divorce.
    (**Item A**, line 9)                                           8 marks

The wording of this question allows you to discuss *any* changes in the law that have affected families. Item A refers to changes in divorce laws; that would be a good place to start. (NB: The question does not say, 'except those mentioned in the items').

(e) Examine some of the effects of changes in the law regarding families in Britain.                            20 marks

(f) Using material from Item B and elsewhere, assess the New Right view that lone-parent families have negative consequences both for the children and for society.                            20 marks

Note that you have to write about *negative* consequences, both for children and for society. If you only write about children, you will not be able to get full marks.

# Grade A answer

Stigma isn't only about divorce, but this answer shows good understanding of what the word means in this context, so gets the marks.

(a) Stigma refers to disapproval by others of those who get divorced.

(b) One way in which the nuclear family is ideally suited to modern industrial society is that we don't need to rely on other family members like uncles and aunts the way people used to.

Another way in which the nuclear family is ideally suited to modern industrial society is that nowadays people need to be able to move easily to where jobs are, and this would be hard if you lived with an extended family.

The answer doesn't explain why we don't need to rely on family members, but the question doesn't ask for an explanation (unlike (d)) so this gets 2 marks.

The answer is too wordy – you don't need 'another way… ' because it will be clear you are answering this question. Nevertheless, this is another good point; the candidate could have mentioned a concept like 'geographical mobility' but the meaning is clear so this gets 2 marks.

So, these two answers would get 4 marks out of 4.

This gets 2 marks – but not for the first sentence. Saying people are dissatisfied doesn't explain why they get divorced; they might take a different course of action instead. The marks are for saying that divorce is 'cheaper and more straightforward than it used to be'; this covers the part of the question that refers to the past 30 years.

(c) Firstly, more people are dissatisfied with their marriage. If they are not getting on well with their partner, they get divorced because this is cheaper and more straightforward than it used to be; they don't have to stay together.

Secondly, in the case of women, they are more likely to be independent and have a career now, so women do not need a man to support them like they used to.

Finally, because so many people get divorced there is no shame or disapproval involved any more. This removes one of the main inhibitions on divorce in the past.

The candidate has realised that the mention of women in line 9 is a helpful hint. They have identified a reason why women may be more willing to start divorce proceedings than in the past. They would therefore get the 2 marks.

Unfortunately, this idea is covered by the mention of 'stigma' in the item, and the question makes it clear that there are no marks for points covered in the item. No marks for this part of the answer.

These answers would get a total of 4 out of 6.

A clear, concise answer, although it does not apply to couples without children. This would get 4 marks.

(d) Women are more likely than men to initiate a divorce because they know that they are more likely to get custody of the children. A man starting a divorce risks losing contact with his children. This means that where both parents want to be with the children, the mother is taking less of a risk if she initiates a divorce.

Women also have greater independence these days and often have careers. So they can support themselves and a family. Men can too, but men lose quite a lot when they separate or divorce. Feminists would say the man loses a domestic servant, the wife who does all the cooking and cleaning. This would make men less likely to start the divorce.

The first two sentences are not promising, but the candidate then recognises that what they are saying would apply just as much to men and makes a specific point about the value of marriage to men. This gains 4 marks.

This gets 8 out of 8 marks.

**At this point, the candidate has 18 out of 20 and, even if their answers on the remaining questions were weak, they would still have a good chance of passing – although with a low grade.**

Some basic knowledge of the law is shown here, but it doesn't go much beyond the item. The candidate needs to move quickly on to effects on families. The question doesn't tell you to use the items, but there is nothing wrong with doing this if it is appropriate. Remember, though, to *use* the items; don't just repeat them in a slightly different way.

By mentioning effects and referring to class, the answer is now becoming more relevant to the question.

(e) Item A refers to changes in the law about divorce. The big change was in 1971, the Divorce Reform Act, because that was when people could get divorced because they both wanted to, they didn't have to prove their partner was wrong in some way. There have since been other changes in the divorce laws – for example, now you only have to wait a certain number of months.

The effect of this has been that more people have been able to get divorced. This includes working-class families who couldn't afford it before (divorce was once only for royals).

Because more people get divorced, there are more lone-parent families (lpfs). So in this way the rise in the number of lpfs is a result of changes in the law. Some sociologists such as the New Right think that lpfs are bad for people and society, especially boys who grow up without a father around. They can become anti-social, involved in drugs etc.

Against this it has been argued, however, that these alleged bad effects are in fact caused by other factors, especially that lpfs are more likely to have low incomes. There is nothing about lpfs as such that leads to bad effects.

The candidate has introduced a theoretical perspective, the New Right, and has made a link to changes in the law. Using abbreviations such as ' lpf' is acceptable in the exam provided that you explain what they stand for.

There are only a small number of marks available for 'evaluation' in this question (unlike question (f)) but the candidate has rightly taken the opportunity to demonstrate this skill.

Three further legal changes are examined, though not in as thorough a way as changes in the divorce laws. The candidate manages to focus clearly on the effects, both for people and for the government.

Overall, there is a range of appropriate knowledge here. There could be more depth and detail, but one needs to bear in mind that there are only about 25 minutes available to do this question. The answers also show some evidence of AO2 skills (analysis and evaluation). This gains 15 out of 20 marks.

There is some good knowledge and analysis of the New Right view here. The candidate now needs to provide some explicit evaluation. Some of the ideas here overlap with those used for question (e); however, this is not a problem, because each of the answers is marked separately.

Another change in the law affecting families has been about marriage. People can now get married in places other than churches and registry offices. This may encourage more people to get married and could affect the trend towards more people cohabiting. Also, the government set up the Child Support Agency to find absent fathers and make them pay money to their ex-wives and children. This has the effect of making men responsible for their families even when they have left them. It also saves the government money because they don't have to pay benefits to support the mother and children. Now the government is considering giving same-sex couples the same rights as married couples. This would change our ideas about what a family is.

(f) The view of New Right thinkers like Charles Murray is that lone-parent families inevitably have negative consequences for both children and for society. In this essay I will examine whether this is true or not.

The reason Murray and others think this is based on the old functionalist idea that the nuclear family is the best kind of family. Murdock, a functionalist, studied families in many different cultures and decided that nuclear families were always best. So a lone-parent family will be seen as a 'broken' family, because one of the parents is not there. The children need a mother to fulfil the expressive role (caring, loving) and a father to fulfil the instrumental role (providing money and food). If one is missing the family will not be able to carry out its functions.

The New Right are responding to changes in the family since the 1960s that they see as disastrous. One of these is the rise of lpfs. Of course there have always been lpfs but in the past this was because a parent had died. Now the cause is people deciding to split up or divorce, or even that girls get pregnant and the boy runs away. The New Right see this as morally wrong; people are not keeping to the marriage vows. Boys who don't have a father figure around will, according to the New Right, not know how men should behave. They won't be able to be good husbands and fathers because they haven't had a role model. They may be unemployed, involved in crime or drugs and so on. So this failing will get passed on to the next generation of boys, which is a problem for the whole of society.

But are the New Right correct about this? Perhaps the negative consequences (crime, etc) are due not to being from an lpf but to growing up in poverty in a bad neighbourhood. Charles Murray was really writing about black American teenagers in cities, so his ideas may not work in this country. There are plenty of lpfs around who manage to bring up the children as well as two-parent families. In any case some of the fathers who the New Right want to stay around to help bring up children would hardly be good role models if they were involved in crime, etc! Feminists would say that a women bringing up children on her own is at least free from being dominated by a male because marriage and the family are patriarchal institutions. She may even be escaping from domestic violence. The New Right seem to be so horrified by what's happened to the family that they believe it must all be bad without looking at the evidence.

It is common to start an essay with an introduction like this, but with only 25 minutes available to write the answer, it is not necessary to include an introduction and a conclusion, even in order to get a high mark.

This is a strong paragraph, showing how the functionalist view has influenced the later New Right view. The focus is on negative consequences.

There is some good, explicit evaluation here. Another perspective – feminism – is briefly covered. The candidate writes in a rather informal style, but this is not important as he or she shows a very good understanding of the arguments and issues.

The total here is 16 marks out of 20.

**The total marks gained by this candidate are 49 out of 60. The answers are not all quite as good as they could be and so do not get full marks. Taken together, however, they are of A grade standard. The candidate demonstrates a very good knowledge and understanding (AO1) and good analysis and evaluation (AO2). Most of the answer is relevant and responds to the questions.**

## Grade C answer

This answer is enough to get the 2 marks.

No marks. Primary socialisation has to happen in all societies, and the candidate does not say why the nuclear family is better for this today than any other kind of family.

(a) Stigma means that divorced people get looked down on and people disapprove of what they've done.

(b) The nuclear family is responsible for the primary socialisation of children which is essential in modern industrial society.

Also houses today aren't built to hold lots of people such as an extended family, so that is why we live in nuclear families.

There is a chicken and egg problem here that the candidate hasn't really addressed. However, it is at least arguable that, for example, some families decide against having an elderly relative live with them because they don't have room. Although the candidate hasn't really explored what is involved, this would get 2 marks.

(c) Divorce has become cheaper because it no longer involves long court cases and hiring a lawyer. So more people can afford it.

There have been many divorces involving famous people like Charles and Diana, and politicians and celebrities, so it has become a more accepted thing to do.

More people today cohabit, so it is easier to split up than before.

(d) Women are more likely to initiate a divorce than men because due to feminism women expect to get more out of marriage than they used to. So if their husbands won't do housework and help with children they don't put up with it any more.

Also women can be more independent than before, they have careers and can support their family.

**So far, the candidate has 12 marks out of 20.**

(e) One change in the law that has affected families has been about making parents more responsible for their children. Last year a mother was sent to prison because she had not made her daughters go to school. And another mother left her child at home on his own expecting him to cook etc for himself. The government wants to have a curfew for teenagers but it would be parents who got in trouble for not supervising their children properly.

So we can see that connecting several government policies is a concern to make parents be good parents. This is from the New Right view, because they say that family standards have declined, people do not do the right things any more. Changes in the law can try to 'stop the rot', make families be like they used to be. But some people would say that this is wishful thinking, because families were far from perfect in the past, in fact there was lots of unhappiness, abuse and so on.

Another change would be about divorce, which is in item A. What has happened is that divorce has become easier, you do not have to prove adultery etc (item A) The effect on the family is that more people get divorced, but also a lot of them get married again and so lots of people have stepparents and stepbrothers and sisters. This in fact means some people have more relatives, which is a bit like going back to the extended family days.

(f) Do lone parent families inevitably have negative consequences for both the children involved and for society? The New Right think so. Writers such as Murray in the USA and Dennis in Britain have argued that it is lone mothers with children who are the big problem. This is because they are worried about boys growing up without a father who behaves in the way the New Right think men should behave – going out to work and supporting the family economically. Boys who don't have a father around are, they say, more likely to not do well at school, not get a job, get involved with crime and drugs and so on. So there are negative consequences for the children, if they are boys, and these then have an effect on society. There will be more social problems, we will need more social workers and police officers and so on.

The New Right say this is part of a much wider moral problem in society, that people do not keep to the same morals as in the past. We need to have men who are good role-models such as David Beckham who helps look after his children.

But are lone parent families as bad as the New Right suggest? Well, some lone parent families do not seem to have any problems at all, in fact they are normal in some societies. It is only some lone parent families who have problems. Also the New Right don't say much about lone fathers, although of course there aren't as many of them.

**Total mark: 35 out of 60. This would usually be a safe grade C. Have a closer look at the answer and work out where you think the candidate could have gained more marks.**

---

*Left margin comments:*

This is a good answer and is succinctly put. It earns 2 marks.

Ending cohabitation does not involve a divorce, so this does not answer the question. No marks for this.

There is a total 4 out of 6 marks for part (c).

Although this could be put more sociologically, the point is a good one. It is also explained, so gains 4 marks. (Notice that you don't have to write a lot to get all the marks as long as you explain as well as identify.)

This is an unusual way to start, and there is a danger of it becoming anecdotal, using any news stories about families that seem relevant. The answer has gained very few marks yet.

A second change in the law, which leaves out some of the obvious points but makes a good one about remarriage becoming more common as a result. Overall, this has become a good answer, although it would be better to cover more than two changes in the law.

The answer gets 13 out of 20 marks.

The mention of David Beckham would receive some credit, because it shows the candidate is able to apply sociological ideas (i.e. role models) to what they see and read about.

*Right margin comments:*

This is close to the idea of 'stigma' given in the item, but by focusing on the idea of an example being set by people in the news, the candidate has added a new angle, so gets 2 marks.

The question asks why women are more likely than men to initiate a divorce. This answer is explaining why women are more likely to initiate a divorce than they used to be, so it does not answer the question. No marks.

This begins to make some good points, and shows a different but relevant and interesting approach. There is a link to a theoretical perspective and some rather undeveloped evaluation of it.

So far this answer shows reasonably good knowledge and understanding. At the end of this section the candidate shows explicitly how he or she is answering the question.

There is evaluation here, but it is quite basic. The points could be developed much more.

Overall this answer shows some knowledge and understanding, but there isn't enough analysis and evaluation for it to score highly. The answer gains 10 out of 20 marks.

# Unit 2: Education
# Sample question and commentary

Time available: 1 hour and 15 minutes
Total marks available: 60 marks

## Item A

Schools teach a formal curriculum. This consists of the National Curriculum, other subjects and courses and extra-curricular activities such as sports teams and school orchestras. However, students also learn, however, through the hidden curriculum. This term refers to the messages students learn through the way that schools are organised and the relationships within them. Interactionists who have used the concept of the hidden curriculum have been interested in, for example, room layouts, routines, rules and the ways in which teachers interact with pupils. Some sociologists have argued that the hidden curriculum helps prepare pupils for the world of work.

5

10

## Item B

A meritocracy is a system that rewards people on the basis of their ability and achievement rather than according to factors such as their sex, age, class or ethnic background. A meritocracy is based on equal opportunities. If the school system were meritocratic, then pupils' success or failure would depend on their ability and effort. Even those from deprived or difficult backgrounds would be able to move up the ladder of success. Functionalists have argued that this is the case, and so those who do not succeed have no right to complain that the system is unfair. Others, however, have pointed to the inequalities that exist throughout the system.

5

10

(a) What is meant by the term 'National Curriculum'?
(**Item A**, line 2)                                     2 marks

(b) Identify two ways in which the hidden curriculum 'helps prepare pupils for the world of work'.
(**Item A**, lines 11–12)                                4 marks

(c) Suggest three ways in which schools can try to provide equal opportunities for all their pupils.
(**Item B**)                                             6 marks

(d) Identify and briefly explain two concepts, other than 'hidden curriculum', that are used by interactionists studying what happens in schools.    8 marks

(e) Examine sociological accounts of how what happens within schools can affect boys and girls in different ways.                                      20 marks

(f) Using material from Item B and elsewhere, assess the view that the education system can be described as meritocratic.                            20 marks

---

*Marginal commentary:*

This item tells you what the questions will be about but you will have to bring in your own knowledge as well.

Questions like this do not ask for an exact definition; it is enough to show that you understand what is meant.

There are many possible answers to this question. One way to approach it is to think about which groups of pupils need positive action from schools if they are to have equal opportunities.

This question requires you not only to explain why some people think the education system is a meritocracy, but also to evaluate this view by criticising it or by presenting alternative interpretations.

The item gives a full explanation of meritocracy so every student should feel able to give at least a partial answer to question (f). If you read the items carefully, they will help you understand what is being asked for.

The term 'hidden curriculum' has been explained, so you are not being tested on this. You have to show how it can be applied to a particular aspect of education – the relationship between schools and work.

The item and the question both refer to interactionists; Item B refers to functionalists. To get a good mark it is essential to know and understand the main theoretical perspectives.

Some questions about gender refer only to girls; this question refers to both boys and girls, so it will be important for your answer to discuss both.

# Grade A answer

This lacks full details (the NC actually only applies to pupils aged 5–16, and only those in state schools) but the candidate shows sufficient understanding to get 2 marks.

(a) The National Curriculum means those subjects which have to be learned by all pupils in British schools.

There are two good, clear answers here: 4 marks.

(b) One way in which the hidden curriculum prepares pupils for the world of work is that in schools they have to learn to do as they are told. In school this is teachers, at work it will be the bosses.

A second way is that schools are organised around times; you have to arrive at the start of school and can only leave when the bell goes at the end of the day. In a workplace the equivalent would be clocking on and clocking off.

Here is an approach that pays off – three good, clear answers. The final one is unusual; many candidates would think first of how schools can address sexism against girls but this candidate is correct in identifying a problem with boys and the type of reading in English, even if the generalisations here are broad.

This gains 6 marks.

(c) In the case of disabled pupils, schools can make sure wheelchairs can get into all classrooms including special rooms like science labs.

In the case of minority-ethnic pupils, schools can crack down hard on racism against them.

In the case of boys, English teachers can make sure that some of what is read appeals to boys and is not just poetry and the kind of books that appeal more to girls.

(d) One concept used by interactionists is labelling. Becker described how teachers labelled pupils in both positive and negative ways. For example, a pupil might get labelled as not very good at maths, and then lose confidence and not do well at maths.

Another concept would be pupil subcultures such as the lads described by Paul Willis.

Here the first concept – labelling – gets four marks, because the example acts as an explanation. The second concept – pupil subcultures – gets only two marks. It is identified but not explained. The mention of the lads and Willis is not sufficient.

The marks gained here are 6 out of 8.

**So far, this candidate has earned 18 marks out of 20, which is excellent. Most candidates should be able to get high marks for these short answers.**

The list here can act as the equivalent of an essay plan, for which there is otherwise little time.

(e) This question is asking me to write about processes in schools. This is what interactionists like Becker have looked at, that is, labelling, the self-fulfilling prophecy, subcultures, streaming and setting and banding.

Becker said that teachers have an idea of what an ideal pupil is like. This is usually described in terms of class (middle-class pupils tend to be more like the ideal than working-class ones) but the concept can also be applied to gender. Girls tend to be more conformist in school. They do what they are told and are usually polite and eager to please the teacher. They are less likely to be disruptive. Teachers are likely to label girls positively (although feminists say teachers don't pay as much attention to them anyway) and boys are more likely to be labelled as a problem. This can lead to the self-fulfilling prophecy although it doesn't have to. Those who are labelled can also reject the label by acting differently and trying to get the teachers to change their minds.

Good use of concepts describing processes within schools, focused on gender differences.

The candidate is not quite sure how what they have learned about setting and streaming applies to gender, but they know this is what they need to look at.

Overall, the candidate discusses a range of processes, shows knowledge of concepts and cites two studies. However, the answer is still generalised in places. Note that there are still six more marks available for an even better answer.

The marks gained here are 15 out of 20.

So the way teachers treat pupils and label them can have an effect. Ultimately it may decide how well pupils do academically. Rosenthal and Jacobson's famous experiment showed the importance of the self-fulfilling prophecy. The children the teachers expected to do well really did do well, because they received more help and encouragement. Perhaps the success of girls in schools is partly because of this.

A general point about labelling is made relevant to the question in the final sentence.

Boys in schools can form anti-school subcultures like the lads Willis researched (but Willis also found a subculture of conformist boys who were called ear'oles). If boys do this (working-class boys) they will behave in ways which make sure they will fail by not working etc. They will also get labelled by teachers as trouble, may even get excluded.

This would have been stronger if the candidate had also commented on girls' subcultures or friendship groups, perhaps on how they are more likely to value academic success than boys' groups.

Another process in schools is setting and streaming. This is how schools put people in different classes according to ability, at least in theory, sometimes it is behaviour too. This is important because it can decide what subjects people do and what GCSE tiers they get entered for. Girls produce neat work and aren't so much a problem so perhaps they are more likely to be put in top sets and this is a reason why they do better.

(f) A meritocracy is when there are equal opportunities for everyone (Item B). In the past educational changes have been designed to try to create a meritocracy because it was seen as a problem that some people were held back. In the days of the tripartite system grammar schools had mainly middle class children and secondary moderns had working class children and did not teach them academic subjects or enter them for exams. So the grammar school children did better and got better jobs. This was not a meritocracy. Only a few bright working class children got into grammar schools. Also some girls were disadvantaged because they got put into secondary moderns although they did better at the entrance exam than boys. This was so there would be equal numbers in grammar schools.

The comprehensive system was designed to stop this and make it fairer. All secondary schools would be similar, taking all the children from their area. Everyone would get a chance to study different subjects and take exams. This seemed more meritocratic but in some ways it wasn't. Independent schools continued, and still do, so some people can buy a better education (supposedly) for their children. Also comprehensives were not all the same, the ones with good reputations in middle-class areas could get better teachers and resources, so working-class children still lost out. And they used setting and streaming and this was not always based just on ability. Today we have tiered GCSEs, and pupils go to many different kinds of schools like specialist schools, so how can everyone get the same chance? Some people even say that the New Labour changes are taking us back to a two tier system with some schools being really good and others failing and unable to get good staff and resources. Working class people are now disadvantaged even if they do well at school because it is harder for them to get the money for university, they are being put off. Overall, we can say that the system allows some people from disadvantaged groups like ethnic minorities and the working class to succeed, but the white middle class still have a head start. We know this because they still get the best qualifications and jobs. They are helped by their background and how their parents can provide cultural capital (Bourdieu). There is still not a lot of upward social mobility. So the system is not meritocratic and recent changes do not seem to be making it more meritocratic.

*Although the material is historical, the candidate has already raised issues of class and gender.*

*Towards the end, the candidate is remembering some points that could have been covered earlier. There are references to the current situation, to different groups, to higher education as well as schools and to why privilege survives. There is only one reference used, but there is clear evidence of good understanding and evaluation through making a case and considering other views.*

*The marks here are 15 out of 20.*

**The total marks gained by this candidate are 48 out of 60. This candidate's answers to (e) and (f) are not of the highest possible standard, but he or she still just gained an A overall through accumulating marks in the earlier questions.**

## Grade C answer

(a) The National Curriculum is what all pupils have to learn in school, it is English, maths, science and some other things like PE and RS.

*As with the other candidate, we might have hoped for greater precision, but this is good enough to get the two marks.*

(b) In school you get careers lessons and can do work experience so this helps you get ready for working.

At school you are with all different sorts of people and you have to get on with them. This is useful for work because you might have work colleagues and customers from all different backgrounds.

*This is not about the hidden curriculum. No marks can be awarded here.*

*An unusual answer, but a good one. It earns 2 marks.*

(c) People who need it can have learning support assistants to help them, so they don't get too far behind.

Schools can encourage girls to do well in science (which traditionally girls didn't like), for example, they can have female teachers and make sure the girls get to use the lab equipment.

*There are two good points here – but the candidate misses two marks by not including a third point. The total gained here is therefore 4 marks.*

(d) One concept interactionists used is labelling. This is when teachers use stereotypes and think of pupils as being in categories like bright, clever, disruptive and so on.

A second concept would be meritocracy. This is when there are equal opportunities.

*This is brief, but identifies a concept and explains it – 4 marks.*

*The candidate has recycled material from Item B. Unfortunately meritocracy is not an interactionist concept, nor does the candidate try to show how an interactionist might use it. No marks are gained here.*

**So far, the candidate has 12 marks out of 20. A reasonable start.**

Girls do better on average than boys in schools. They do better at GCSE in all subjects and at A level in nearly all subjects. Sociologists have suggested many different reasons why this is so. They look at the way girls are brought up and how they are more interested in school work than boys, also how girls are encouraged much more than they used to be to get qualifications for a good career.

Feminists look at how girls are treated differently in schools and how this affects how they do. For example, Spender who was a teacher found that she gave more time to boys even when she tried not to. Stanworth found that the careers advice given to girls in colleges did not encourage them to try for top jobs or careers. Also the books and materials used in teaching can be sexist, for example science textbooks show pictures of boys not girls doing experiments. In my school a lot of the science teachers are women and this is good because they show girls that science is not just for boys.

In the past girls were even taught different subjects, they spent a lot of time learning sewing and cooking. The National Curriculum introduced in 1988 changed this but even now, when there are choices, girls choose different subjects. For example, dance and child development are definitely girls subjects. So this may affect how girls do.

But as I said girls are now doing better than boys even if some of the things the feminists found still happen. This is probably because girls have more confidence now and are encouraged to get qualifications more.

(f) Politicians say they want everyone to have a chance to do well. This means that everyone should have the same education, going to schools that are the same quality. For example the National Curriculum (Item A) says that everyone has the right to study certain subjects. Girls used to drop science as soon as they could, now they can't and this is good because it means girls can pass the exams and have the chance of doing science as a career. Also comprehensives were all about everyone going to the same kind of schools and taking exams, because in the old tripartite system pupils who went to secondary modern schools didn't always get qualifications. So this is an example of a policy increasing meritocracy (Item B).

But the politicians also know that there isn't really a meritocracy because lots of them have their children educated privately. They think that state schools are not good enough. They go to independent schools that don't have to teach the National Curriculum. Independent schools charge fees so this means that people with wealth can buy a better education for their children. This is not meritocratic because it means that people from wealthy backgrounds have a head start and are likely to get the best jobs.

This is a very different approach from the first candidate's answer. This is about gender issues in schools generally; the candidate will need to focus soon on what happens within schools.

There is some good sociological knowledge here, but the answer is limited by focusing almost completely on girls and by some over-generalising. There needs to be consideration of boys as well. Although the question does not refer to any time period, it would also have been better to focus more on what happens today; the candidate does acknowledge this but the studies referred to are quite old.

The marks gained here are 12 out of 20.

This sentence will gain credit – it shows that the candidate can take sociological ideas and apply them to what they see around them. That's good sociology. Beware, though, of getting carried away writing about your particular school – use this approach for brief examples only.

This is a brief answer, without references, but it presents the two sides of an argument. There is some analysis and evaluation. Without developing the ideas further and adding more information and examples this answer cannot score very highly but nevertheless gets a reasonable mark.

Again, the mark is 11 out of 20.

**Total mark: 36 out of 60. This would usually be a safe grade C. Have a closer look at the answer and work out where you think the candidate could have gained more marks.**

# Unit 3: Sociological methods
## Sample question and commentary

Time allowed: 1 hour
Total marks available: 60 marks

### Item A

*Warren carried out participant observation research in a drug rehabilitation centre.*

The institution was open to both male and female residents. But as a female researcher and over several months of observation, I found that men were generally much more ready to talk to me than women. Furthermore, I was generally perceived as harmless by the males, and afforded access     5
bordering on trespass. I vividly remember one day deciding to go upstairs, an action expressly forbidden to anyone not resident in the facility. Someone started to protest; the protest was silenced by a male voice saying, 'aah, what harm can she do, she's only a broad'. Upstairs I went.     10

From: Warren, C.A.B. (1988) *Gender issues in field research*,
Sage, Newbury Park, California, p. 18

### Item B

*Allender studied the Labour movement in Sheffield, and how it had responded to the decline of the steel and engineering industries on which Sheffield had depended. He used this study to draw wider conclusions about the Labour movement.*

The main method used for the case study was that of semi-structured interviews of a small, but representative, sample of key participants in the local labour movement... Between the beginning of April and the end of July 1998, sixteen people were interviewed...     5

The main aspect of the methodological approach taken was to have a common set of themes for each interview, to invite interviewees to speak on each of these subjects and to ensure that, in each interview, all of these themes were covered. Thus, all of the interviewees would be asked for     10
their thoughts on, for example, the main reasons for the decline of steel and engineering as sources of employment in the city... They were interrupted only to clarify or expand upon a point. Some interviewees would talk at length on a particular subject and others would give very brief replies.     15
No attempt was made to curtail any of the points being made unless they appeared to be completely irrelevant to the research topic. The interviews lasted between forty-five minutes and two hours, depending on how much the interviewee had to say.     20

From: Allender, P. (2001) *What's Wrong with Labour?*,
Merlin, London, pp. 62–63

As you probably realised, the purpose of this piece is to get you to think about the effect that the researcher's gender can have on their research, and, in this particular case, with regard to participant observation.

You may feel you want to know rather more about what Warren was doing. Don't let this put you off. Ask yourself why this piece has been chosen as an item.

The beginning of Item B makes it clear that this item is about semi-structured interviews and is about a case study. The researcher was studying a political topic. If you don't know much about politics, don't be concerned. The questions will be about research methods, not about what was being studied.

**EXAMINATION ADVICE**

It is important not to repeat the words representative or sample in your answer without showing that you know what they mean.

(a) What is meant by a representative sample (**Item B**, line 2)?
2 marks

(b) Identify two advantages of using a case study. (**Item B**, lines 7–8)
4 marks

Make sure you identify two advantages, as there will be two marks for each.

Note that this question refers to interviews, not specifically to semi-structured interviews.

(c) Suggest three advantages of using interviews in sociological research.
6 marks

(d) Identify and briefly explain two problems which Allender may have faced in carrying out the interviews described in Item B.
8 marks

This question requires you to think about the particular research Allender carried out. Read the item carefully to pick out clues; for example, it seems that some respondents were less eager to talk than others.

The question says 'factors', so you must identify several. Try to include practical, ethical and theoretical factors. Refer to examples from research projects you have studied. Most of the marks in this question are for AO1 skills (knowledge and understanding). If the question had been 'Assess the relative importance of different factors...' your answer would have needed to show your evaluation skills.

(e) Examine some of the factors sociologists need to consider in deciding which method to use for their research.
20 marks

(f) Using material from Item A and elsewhere assess the view that the personal and social characteristics of the researcher inevitably influence the findings of sociological research.
20 marks

The 'clue' in Item A is the researcher's gender, but you will need to consider other 'personal and social characteristics' as well. Note that you can refer to all kinds of research, not just participant observation (the method referred to in Item A).

# Grade A answer

Clear and concise – this gains 2 marks out of 2.

a) This is when the people selected to take part in research have the same key characteristics as the population that the research is about.

b) One advantage of using a case study is that it if you have chosen the case well you will be able to generalise from it. Another advantage is that case studies can be very useful for finding out things that can be followed up in wider research.

The second point could have been made using more sociological language (e.g. 'case studies can generate hypotheses') but this is enough to gain the marks – 4 marks.

Three good, clear advantages are given here. One could argue that they do not all apply to all types of interview, but the question left this open so this gains 6 marks.

c) One advantage of using interviews is that because you are talking directly to the person you have the chance to win their trust which will help get more truthful answers. You can also explain any questions they do not understand and so make sure that you get an appropriate response. You cannot do this with questionnaires. Finally, if you are not sure what someone meant, you can ask them to explain it again in a different way or ask a slightly different question.

d) One problem Allender probably faced was time. These were long interviews, he was asking people to give up a lot of time and some people may not have wanted to do this. This would affect his response rate and the success of his research. A second problem would be where to hold the interviews. People might not want to invite him into their home, but if he didn't do it that way people would have to travel to meet him. Again this might make it difficult to get a good sample.

Two problems are clearly identified and explained here. The explanations are similar but they relate to both the problems identified. This gains 8 marks.

**So far, this candidate has gained the full 20 marks. Most candidates should be able to get at least 15 marks for these short questions.**

This section raises several important issues and discusses them in a way relevant to the question. The answer shows a good understanding of a number of important terms (notice, for example, the clear explanations of generalisation and triangulation).

e) There are a number of different factors sociologists need to consider when choosing a research method. Firstly, they will need to make sure that the method is suitable for what is being studied and that it will get the kind of data needed to prove or disprove the hypothesis or to fulfil the aims of the project. Sometimes sociologists want to have quantitative data, sometimes qualitative data and sometimes both. They may want to be able to generalise from their sample, claiming that the findings refer to the whole population and not just the sample. They may also want their research to be valid (that is, a truthful and accurate account) or reliable (so that another sociologist can repeat it and prove the findings are right). Some methods are better than others, depending on what you want. For example, questionnaires are good for reliability and for quantitative data and for getting data about large numbers of people, but not so good for validity and qualitative data. One solution is to use two or more different methods so that you get different data and can check the findings against each other. This is called triangulation.

Some methods may not be practical. For example, it would be difficult to interview people face to face if they lived a long way away from you. Also participant observation is not practical if the people you are studying are not together as a group quite a lot of the time. There may also be ethical problems that affect the choice of method. Covert participant observation is now usually thought to be unethical so most sociologists don't want to do it even if it is the best method in other ways (for example, people don't change their behaviour if they don't know they are being watched). This method could also put the researcher in danger if people found out they were being studied without being told because they could be angry. This means that the researcher has to use a method to which the respondents can give informed consent. Sometimes there may be problems about what informed consent means; for example, if you are researching in a school should you ask the head or the pupils for their consent? So it can be seen that there are many things that sociologists have to consider when deciding what method to use.

This is an impressive answer covering a range of issues. The candidate has not included anything on positivism and interpretivism, and how they might influence choice of method, but this is not necessary even to get a high mark. Part (e) earns 17 out of 20.

This answer takes Item A as its starting point, and uses it to make a point. The candidate then shows that they are aware of how gender and other characteristics can raise problems, yet can also be useful, and how they apply differently in different situations. This shows good analysis and evaluation, while the references to studies show good knowledge and understanding.

f) The sociologist in Item A was a woman and she is saying that being a woman had an effect on her research, because the men let her see more of what was happening. They thought because she was a woman she couldn't really be important or a threat to them in any way. The characteristics of the researcher are particularly important in participant observation, as in Item A, because the researcher has to be accepted. So for example James Patrick had to be accepted by the Glasgow gang. Fortunately he was able to pretend to be the same age as them but a woman or a black man could not have done this research. Patrick still had to be careful about his accent and the way he dressed, because he wanted to avoid the gang becoming suspicious of him. Patrick was not being honest with the gang, he was concealing some facts about himself in order to be able to do the research. But sometimes a sociologist can use their personal and social characteristics to help them. Holdaway was able to do his participant observation research on the police while he was a police officer. Ann Oakley studied pregnant women and the fact that she was a woman and had children led the women to trust her and so to provide her with more valid data. In this kind of situation the researcher has to be sensitive and avoid betraying the trust people may place in them.

I have already mentioned several personal and social characteristics. In our society gender and ethnicity are probably the most important usually. Women are often chosen to carry out interviews because it is thought that both men and women feel less threatened by women than by men and so female interviewers are more likely to get a high response rate. It can though depend on what the research is about. A man might feel more able to talk to another man about some issues. Ethnicity is important too. In a research project about racist attitudes for example, it might make a big difference. Someone with racist views might feel they could express them to another white person but not to a black or Asian interviewer. Other characteristics that might affect the research include age, appearance (this could include everything from hairstyle to a sign of disability like being in a wheelchair), accent and so on.

Here the candidate brings together the different characteristics that have been mentioned, and briefly mentions others. Again there are explanations of what might happen in particular situations. This answer gains 17 out of 20.

**Overall marks: 54 marks out of 60. This mark is excellent and puts the script in the top 5% of all scripts. However, there could be as many as 10 fewer marks and the script might still achieve an A grade.**

# Grade C answer

The candidate has simply repeated the term 'sample' and has not properly defined 'representative'. No marks.

a) A representative sample is a sample that has been selected randomly

b) One advantage of a case study is that it is less time consuming than studying several different cases. Another advantage is that the findings may say something about other cases which are similar, so you don't have to investigate them separately.

The second point, about generalisation, is not nearly as well put as the first candidate in the Grade A answer, but the idea is clearly understood. 4 marks.

c) One advantage of using interviews is that because you are talking to people face to face you can judge whether they are telling the truth or not. Another is that you may get a better response rate than with questionnaires, because people meet you and will probably want to help, whereas with a survey they may just ignore the form. Finally a third advantage is that it is quite cheap and easy to do.

This earns 4 out of 6 marks, but only for the first two suggestions. The third one is incorrect: interviews are time consuming so they are not cheap.

d) Allender might have had a problem with keeping a record of what people said. In interviews you have to choose between trying to write notes as people talk, or tape recording. Making notes is difficult because you are listening at the same time and you will probably miss out some important things, while a tape recorder may put people off. A second problem would be getting people talking. Some of them might be upset because they had lost their jobs etc and did not want to remember unhappy times. Interviewers have to be sensitive and know when to prompt and when to just listen.

This gains 8 marks for two points identified and explained. The second problem is hinted at in the item; the first is not but is a general problem in interviewing. The wording of the question allows both types of answer.

**The candidate has scored 16 marks out of 20 so far, which is good.**

This answer is limited to discussing the importance of time and money, and so does not cover enough factors to be awarded a high mark. There are some good points though, such as the references to different methods, and to the importance of funding. This gains 11 marks out of 20.

e) The main factor is how much time and money there is. Some kinds of research take a very long time and are very expensive, for example Barker took five years to research the Moonies. She used a lot of different methods including questionnaires, interviews and participant observation. This is only possible if you have lots of time and money. If not, you can really only use one method. Questionnaires are probably the cheapest and easiest because all you have to do is get them printed and send them out. Having said that, even this can be expensive, for example the Census costs many millions of pounds. Participant observation is probably the most expensive, because you may be giving up all of your time for a long period while you are with the people you are studying. It might also take a long time to gain entry (get accepted) before you can start, but this is important if you want to get valid results. A lot of research is funded by government bodies because they can provide grants, but this means that the topics of research get decided by government not by sociologists.

f) Personal and social characteristics of the researcher can affect research in several ways. Who the researcher is is particularly important in unstructured interviews and in participant observation. This is because the researcher is involved in interaction with the subjects of the research, so they will know whether the researcher is young or old, male or female and so on. They may behave or answer differently because of this. Sometimes participant observation depends on how similar the researcher is to the subjects. For example, a girl studying a gang of boys would probably get a different impression of them from a boy because their behaviour would change when she was with them, perhaps showing off more or acting tough.

The researchers' characteristics are less important with surveys or experiments. In fact in experiments it should not matter who the researcher is, the same results should be obtained every time. With many surveys such as postal questionnaires the respondents don't have any contact with the researcher so this won't affect their answers.

Rather like this candidate's answer to (e) this is brief but what it does cover shows a reasonably good understanding. However, the marks in part (f) are mainly for AO2 skills (analysis and evaluation). These skills are demonstrated in the way the candidate differentiates different types of research. This gains 9 out of 20 marks.

**Total mark: 36 out of 60. This would usually be a safe grade C. Have a closer look at the answer and work out where you think the candidate could have gained more marks.**

# Coursework

## The nature and structure of the task

All AS Sociology students following the AQA specification are tested on sociological methods. There are two options: a one-hour examination (see pages 144–7) or a coursework task.

The coursework task is called a Research Proposal. This means that you explain how you would design a piece of research, but that you do not actually carry it out.

The proposal must not be more than 1200 words and must contain the following sections.

| Section | Description | Length | Marks |
|---|---|---|---|
| Hypothesis/ Aim | A single hypothesis or aim with a summary of the reasons for choosing it. | maximum 100 words | 8 |
| Context and concepts | Brief descriptions of two relevant pieces of material that form the context for the research, and two or three major concepts that are relevant to the research. | maximum 400 words | 20 |
| Main research method and reasons | A brief description of the research method chosen with appropriate details of how it would be used in the proposed research. | maximum 400 words | 20 |
| Potential problems | Brief details of problems likely to be met. | maximum 300 words | 12 |
| | | Total marks: | 60 |

The coursework will be marked by your teacher(s) and a sample of marked coursework from your school or centre will then be moderated (checked) by AQA.

## Choosing a topic

It is best to choose a topic that is related to the subject areas that you have studied so far in sociology – probably families and households or education. If you choose something outside the areas you have studied, you may have problems finding relevant context material and concepts.

Choose something you are interested in. You will need to be motivated to do your coursework well.

You might also want to write a proposal for research that you could actually carry out if you do a coursework project for A-Level Sociology. Talk to your teachers about this.

Decide on the general topic you want to study before trying to formulate an aim or hypothesis. Since you don't actually have to do the research, you are not limited to a project that you as a school or college student could do.

## The sections

### HYPOTHESIS OR AIM?

**The importance of the hypothesis/aim**

To get a good mark for your coursework, it is essential you show a clear aim or hypothesis. You will get marks in the later sections by making clear how what you are writing about is related to your aim or hypothesis. In writing the later sections, always bear in mind your aim or hypothesis.

**Hypothesis or aim?**

A hypothesis is a statement. The purpose of your research will be to find out whether this statement is true or false. Formulating a hypothesis and testing it is part of the positivist approach to studying sociology. It is also used in the natural sciences. You will probably have a hypothesis if your proposal involves an experiment or survey and generating quantitative data.

An aim, however, is not as precise; it states the area that you want to find out about, but does not say anything about what you might find. This is more typical of the interpretivist approach to studying sociology. You will probably have an aim if your proposal involves informal interviews or participant observation and generating qualitative data.

Examples of hypotheses:

- Men are doing more housework than they did in the 1960s.
- Girls in single-sex schools do better in sciences than girls in mixed schools.

Examples of aims:

- To investigate attitudes towards teenage pregnancy among young people.
- To find out how teachers decide on punishments for bad behaviour in class.

To get a high mark, you must:

- have a clear aim or hypothesis that is sociological
- give good reasons for the aim or hypothesis

In giving your reasons, try to show why your project would be good sociology. Would it help us to understand the topic better? Would it provide new information, or perhaps test an idea that you have come across on the course but that has not convinced you? Reasons can be personal but avoid saying something bland that anyone could come up with (e.g. 'I found this really interesting when we talked about it in class' would earn no marks).

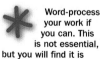 Word-process your work if you can. This is not essential, but you will find it is much easier to edit your work and to count the words you have used if you word-process it.

To save words, don't write 'My first concept is... ' Instead, introduce the concept naturally, by defining it in a sentence and putting it in bold or underlining it.

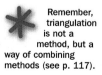 Remember, triangulation is not a method, but a way of combining methods (see p. 117).

EXAMINATION ADVICE

## THE CONTEXT/CONCEPTS SECTION

### Your two pieces of context

These can be books, research studies, statistics, newspaper, magazine or journal articles, or TV programmes or videos. You can use summaries of books or articles that you find in textbooks, provided that these give you sufficient detail. Your pieces of context will essentially be what other people have already said or found out about your topic.

### Your two or three major concepts

A concept means here a sociological term. You therefore need to define your concepts and show how they are relevant to your research and how you would use them. Your concepts may well have been used in your contexts. For example, if one of your contexts is a study of an anti-school subculture, then 'subculture' or 'anti-school subculture' will probably be one of your concepts.

## General advice

- *Use your teachers*
  Your teachers are allowed to give you advice, so ask for it. Make sure early on that they think your aim or hypothesis is one that can work. However, you shouldn't ask for more than advice – they can't write the project for you! The project must be your own work.

- *When you've finished*
  At the end, read through your project, making sure that the aim or hypothesis is followed all the way through.

 The mark scheme for this unit is published in the specification booklet from AQA, which your teacher(s) will have. Ask to see it. Try to ensure that your project meets the criteria for the top mark band for each section.

## THE RESEARCH METHOD SECTION

Your method must be appropriate for your aim or hypothesis. If it won't get the sort of data you need, think again!

You will need to provide details of what you will actually do. This is difficult because you know that you probably won't ever actually carry out this research. This is all the more reason to think very carefully about what would be involved.

For a survey, think about:

- What is the population for your research? (see pp. 120–1)
- How will you select your sample?
- What kinds of questions will you ask?
- How will you give out questionnaires? How will respondents return them to you?
- Where will you conduct interviews? Will you make notes or use a tape recorder?

For participant observation, think about:

- how you will gain entry to the group
- how much you will tell them about what you are doing
- whether there any risks involved
- how you will preserve confidentiality.

This is not an exhaustive list of things you need to consider – try yourself to think of all the practical and ethical details that might be relevant here.

## POTENTIAL PROBLEMS SECTION

Think in terms of practical, ethical and theoretical problems. Try to have at least one of each type.

ACCESS    TIME

COST    ETHICS

OPERATIONALISING CONCEPTS

ANALYSING DATA

PRESENTING RESULTS

Theoretical problems are probably the trickiest. If you're doing a survey, think about how an interpretivist might criticise what you are proposing. If you're doing participant observation, think about what a positivist might say. Think also about problems in operationalising concepts. For example, if you're assessing social class by asking about people's occupations, what are the problems involved in that?

 You only have to point out the potential problems. You don't have to come up with solutions!

### Watch out

**You will only get marked for one method, so there is no point in discussing two. It might be good sociology to use a second method for your research, but it won't get you any marks – and may even cost you some as you won't then have enough words to describe your main method fully.**

# Revision and exam preparation

## Be prepared!

- *For revision you will need the following:*
  - this Nelson Thornes' textbook: *Sociology AS The Complete Companion* (of course!)
  - your file of notes, including any practice exams
  - the AQA specification
  - past exam papers and mark schemes
  - Chief Examiner's reports.

- *You will also need the following stationery:*
  - pens and paper
  - coloured pens
  - highlighter pens
  - index cards.

- *Before you start revising you should:*
  - Check that your file of notes is complete and in order. Use card dividers to separate your notes on different topics.
  - If you think your notes may not be complete (for example, because you know you missed some lessons) check with your teacher(s).

- *Make sure you know the format of the exam*
  - Look back to pp. 136–43 for the format of the Units 1 and 2 exams and to pp. 144–7 for the format of the Unit 3 exam.
  - Remind yourself of the amount of time you have, the number of questions you have to answer, and the likely 'command' words and marks available for each question.

- *Study past exam papers*
  Your teacher(s) should have copies of these. It is a mistake to think that you can predict what questions will come up, but you can use past papers to study the kinds of questions that get asked and to practise exam answers.

- *Ask your teacher(s) for copies of mark schemes*
  These are available from AQA and can help you work out what examiners have to look for. Try marking your own work, or a fellow student's, using a mark scheme.

- *Ask your teacher(s) for copies of the chief examiner's reports*
  These are issued after every exam. These are useful because they tell you the sorts of things students in previous exams did well or badly.

- *How can I use the specification?*
  Your teacher(s) probably gave you a copy of this, or the most relevant parts of it, early on. Now is the time to look at it, if you haven't done so already. The content for Families and Households, and for Education, is set out in four bullet points each; Sociological Methods has five. The specification will also remind you of the Assessment Objectives, which you'll need to understand if you are to do well on (e) and (f) questions.

- *What about textbooks?*
  Keep a textbook beside you when revising but use it only to check when your notes are unclear. You do not want to be taking in new information now; you need to concentrate on fully understanding what you already know.

**\*** It is possible to buy ready-made sets of revision cards, but you will learn far more through writing your own because that way you will have to process the ideas yourself.

**\*** Exam questions can be based only on what is listed in the specification.

**\*** Some people claim to be able to work better if they have music playing in the background. This doesn't work for everyone, and if you choose to have music you should at least avoid music that may be distracting.

# Starting revision

## *Plan when you will revise*

Make yourself a revision timetable, covering all your exams, not just sociology. Do this several weeks (say six) before the exams begin. Divide the days into sections, marking off the sections that you know are not available for revision because of lessons, work, meal-times or other unavoidable commitments. Set aside some time for rest and relaxation. The rest is your revision time. Divide it between your subjects, then between the topics.

For the first three or four weeks (your main revision period) aim to work steadily through all the topics. Cover everything – remember, there is no choice of questions in these exams – but spend extra time on topics you feel unsure about.

Spend the last week or two before the exam re-revising, finally reading over your notes and checking your understanding.

## *Revising*

- *Set yourself a target every time you sit down to revise* – For example, that you will read all your notes on the growing diversity of families and then draw a mind-map of this. The target should be one you can achieve in an hour or so (don't revise for longer without taking a break). Give yourself a reward every time you reach the target – read a magazine, go for a walk, phone a friend, have a cup of coffee or a piece of chocolate.

- *If possible, have a place where you revise at home* – If you're lucky, you'll have a desk or workspace in your room. Keep everything you need there. Tell your family when you're going to be revising and ask them not to disturb you.

- *Revise actively; don't just read* – You will probably find that you read a whole page of notes and then cannot remember what it was about, especially if they are in linear format. Get your mind engaged by always revising with a pen or pencil in your hand.

Try the ideas in the box below.

After revising a topic, always carry out an active task, such as making a summary. If you can find a past exam question on the topic, try answering it. If not, try to write your own questions.

Revision can be a lonely business. You could arrange to revise sometimes with a fellow student. Test each other using your summary notes on index cards.

## Preparing close to the exam

- The best preparation for the exam is to start your revision several weeks before and to work at it steadily so that you feel confident.
- Don't stay up late the night before an exam revising. It is more important to sleep well and have energy available for the exam. In any case, you are unlikely to remember much from last-minute cramming. If you want to do something for the exam, read through those summary notes and index cards again.
- Have enough to eat before the exam. Don't skip breakfast before a morning exam or your blood-sugar level will be too low for you to concentrate properly. Drink some water, and take some into the exam with you – dehydration affects your ability to concentrate.

## After the exam

It's a good idea to avoid talking to your fellow students about the details of what you or they wrote. You will only get worried if someone tells you how he or she answered a question and you did it differently. Your way may have been just as good, or better. Put the exam behind you and start preparing for the next one!

---

# Revision tips

1. When reading your notes, use a highlighter pen to mark out key terms or arguments.

2. Jot down in the margin, in a different colour pen, questions or comments that occur to you as you read.

3. Make summary notes on index cards for each key concept or important name. Cross-reference these to each other and to your notes. You could even colour code them.

4. On a separate piece of paper, convert your notes into a different format, such as a mind-map, spider diagram or flow chart.

5. Don't be afraid to use abbreviations and pictorial representations – they can help make your notes memorable.

theoretical perspective   topic area

main topic of this card

Bourdieu, Pierre        **Education**

French Marxist

Key concept: cultural capital

brief summary of Bourdieu's argument

Argument: That the upper and middle class are able to pass on their privileged position to their children through the education system. Their children then have an advantage through cultural knowledge and skills.

See also: (other Marxists on education) Boudon, Bowles and Gintis

link to other cards on the same or similar subject

# Answers to self-assessment questions

1 a
2 c
3 c
4 c
5 c
6 b
7 c
8 b
9 a
10 c
11 a
12 b
13 a
14 b
15 b
16 a
17 b
18 c
19 a i; b ii
20 a ii; b i
21 a i; b ii
22 a iii; b ii; c i
23 a i; b iii; c ii
24 a iii; b ii; c i
25 Mead is the odd one out because he is an interactionist who is concerned with small-scale interaction. Marx and Durkheim are structuralists. They look at society as a whole.

1 Any of:
   - nuclear family
   - extended family
   - lone-parent family
   - reconstituted family
2 a iii; b i; c ii
3 Any of:
   - looking after grandchildren through babysitting and childminding
   - supporting their own elderly parents
   - through continuing in employment, possibly part-time
   - making financial contributions to children and grandchildren
   - through support with domestic chores and labour
4 a iii; b i; c ii
5 b
6 Household: the person or people who live in a house, such as a family (perhaps with servants), students in a shared home, or people in a community group such as a commune.
7 a in terms of blood or marriage relationships
   b in terms of kinship – that is, a sense of responsibility for family members
8 The term 'extended family' is used to describe those relations who may live close to or with the parents and children. In some cultural groups, brothers and sisters will share a household. This is a 'horizontal extended family'. In other cultural groups, the elderly are very much part of family life, and so there are a number of generations living in the household. This is a 'vertical extended family'. The difference lies in the number of generations who are part of the family group.

9 c
10 a false – it is rising
   b false – the peak year was 1993
   c true
11 c
12 Choose from:
   - an ageing population
   - longer life-spans
   - increased female working
   - the tendency to marry later in life
   - the falling birth rate
   - the rising divorce rate
13 a iii; b i; c iv; d ii
14 • Free communes in which people expressed their individuality and faced issues or made rules as they developed their lifestyle. These communes tended to be characterised by transient living and a short organisational life-span.
   • Structured communes share a basic set of rules and an underlying philosophy. There may be a pooled economic structure and an organised leadership system. This is typical of religious groupings.
15 c
16 a
17 patriarchy
18 a symmetrical family
   b conjugal roles
   c New Men
19 Over 70% of divorces are initiated by women
20 divorce, death, separation or choice
21 b
22 a false – it is 10 years
   b true
   c false – it is 25–29 years
   d false – it is the poorer social groups who are vulnerable to divorce

23  No, nearly three-quarters of never-married, childless people aged under 35 who were cohabiting expected to marry each other. Thus, for most people, cohabitation is part of the process of getting married and is not a substitute for marriage.

24  • Changes in divorce law – divorce law reform has generally made divorce more accessible to larger numbers of people.
    • Secularisation of marriage – fewer people feel bound by traditional Christian teaching with regard to divorce.
    • Changes in the economic status of women – women no longer require marriage as a means of economic support; other sources of income are available to them through work or the welfare benefits system.
    • Changes in women's expectations of marriage – abusive relationships may have been tolerated in the past because people had fewer options; today, people know that they do not have to stay in situations that they find unbearable.

## Section 3
## Education
(pp. 108–9)

1   c
2   b
3   d
4   d
5   c
6   b
7   b
8   c
9   b
10  d
11  c
12  b
13  d
14  c
16  b
17  a
18  a
19  a ii; b iii; c i
20  a iii; b ii; c i
21  a i; b iii; c ii
22  a iii; b ii; c i
23  a iii; b i; c ii
24  c – the others are initiatives aimed at increasing girls' interest in science and technology
25  a – the others are vocational qualifications

## Section 4
## Research methods
(pp. 130–1)

1   b
2   c
3   a
4   b
5   d
6   c
7   a i; b ii
8   d
9   d
10  a  secondary
    b  primary
    c  secondary
    d  secondary
    e  primary
11  b
12  a iv; b ii; c v; d i; e iii
13  a and c
14  a
15  a ii; b i; c iii
16  d
17  d
18  a iii; b iv; c i; d ii
19  b
20  a  backed up by good evidence.
    b  reliable
    c  valid
    d  representativeness
21  c
22  b
23  • choice of topic
    • resources (time, money)
    • theoretical perspective
    • interests and values
    • current debates in sociology
    • access to the subject of the research
24  It is the ethical principle that research participants should be fully informed about the research and should have agreed to take part.
25  • survey by postal questionnaire
    • survey by structured interview
    • survey by unstructured interview
    • participant observation
    • case study

# Glossary

**Agency:** The ability of people, individually or collectively, to take decisions and to act.

**Agencies of socialisation:** Institutions such as the family, education system, religion, mass media, etc. from which we learn the culture of our society.

**Anthropology:** The study of the culture of small pre-industrial societies.

**Ascribed status:** Social standing or status allocated at birth.

**Asymmetrical:** Unequal.

**Beanpole families:** Families that are very small, perhaps consisting of one or two adults and a single child, with the pattern repeated through the generations.

**Birth rate:** The number of live births per thousand of the population in one year.

**Case study:** The study of a single example of a phenomenon.

**Catchment area:** The area around a school. Children living in a school's catchment area are normally given priority when places are allocated.

**Co-educational:** A school attended by both boys and girls.

**Cohort:** A group of people who share a significant experience at a point in time, for example, being born in the same year, or taking A levels in the same year.

**Commune:** A number of families and single adults sharing accommodation and living expenses, usually for ideological and social reasons.

**Conjugal roles:** The roles played by adult males and females within a family; may be 'joint' or 'segregated'.

**Consensus:** Broad agreement on basic values.

**Consumption:** The process of buying and using goods and services.

**Contested:** Debated and discussed, with disagreement.

**Convergence:** The coming together of different types of media, either in one company or one technology.

**Co-parenting:** Where separated or divorced parents take equal roles in caring for children, who spend some time in one household and the rest of their time in the other.

**Correlate:** To show the relationship between two variables; may be positive or negative.

**Correspondence theory:** The view that what happens in schools mirrors (corresponds to) what will happen at work, with different classes having different experiences.

**Couple:** Two adults who share a sexual relationship and a home.

**Crisis of masculinity:** A term describing how the traditional ways of being a man (such as being a breadwinner) are increasingly questioned.

**Cultural capital:** The values, knowledge or ideas that parents pass on to their children, which can then influence their success at school and later in life.

**Cultural resistance:** Ways in which ethnic and other minorities resist pressure from dominant cultures and work to maintain their own cultural traditions.

**Culture:** The accumulated knowledge, norms and values of a particular group; their way of life.

**Custody:** Rules that govern the rights of a parent or other carer with regard to a child.

**Death rate:** The number of deaths per year per thousand of the population.

**Decriminalised:** When behaviour is no longer punishable by law.

**Deferred gratification:** Putting off immediate satisfaction in order to get a greater reward later.

**Demography:** The study of population.

**Deregulation:** The removal of legal restrictions and rules on broadcasters.

**Desensitisation:** Becoming immune to having feelings or to showing emotions as a result of over-exposure to, for example, violent images.

**Determinism:** The view that all events are fully determined (caused) by previous events. In the context of human social behaviour, it is contrasted with 'voluntarism'.

**Deviance:** The breaking of norms, mores, values or rules.

**Digital channels:** TV channels only available via digital, satellite or cable.

**Digital underclass:** People who do not have the material means to access new media technology.

**Domestic labour:** The work of the household, usually known as housework.

**Dual shift:** The work that women do in the home after they have completed paid work outside the home.

**Empirical:** Based on observation or experiment rather than on theory.

**Estates:** The system of stratification in the medieval period, with division between clergy, nobility and commoners.

**Ethnicity:** Shared culture based on common language, religion or nationality.

**Ethnocentrism:** Looking at an issue from one particular cultural point of view

**Ethnography:** The use of direct observation, sometimes combined with other methods, to help the researcher to understand the world view of those being studied.

**Extended family:** Nuclear family plus grandparents, uncles, cousins, etc.; may share a home or keep in close contact.

**Familial ideology:** The view that the traditional family is 'better' than any alternatives.

**Family:** A group of people to whom we may be biologically related and to whom we feel a sense of kinship.

**Feminism:** A theoretical perspective adopted mostly by women, which sees females as being oppressed by a patriarchal society.

**Fertility rate:** The number of live births per thousand women of childbearing age (defined as 15–44 years).

**Fit thesis:** A functionalist theory suggesting that families evolve to suit the needs of industrial society.

**Fragmentation:** The breaking up of class structures and loyalties.

**Free market:** An economic system based on free competition between those willing to invest and/or take risks with capital.

**Function:** A term used by functionalists to describe the way in which a social institution contributes to the survival and well-being of a society.

**Functionalism:** Theories that explain social institutions in terms of the functions they perform for the society.

**Functionalists:** Sociologists who explain social institutions in terms of the functions they perform for the society.

**Gatekeepers:** Media personnel who decide what counts as news.

**Gay families/couples:** These are same-sex individuals who choose to live in a partnership.

**Gendered division of labour:** Work is allocated on the basis of gender, so women do domestic work and men work outside the home.

**Ghettoise:** To imply that a group or issue should not be a mainstream concern.

**Global economy:** Describes the global market in which goods and services are traded across the world, particularly by multinational corporations.

**Globalisation:** The processes by which societies and cultures around the world become increasingly interdependent economically, culturally and politically.

**Grandparenting:** As life expectancy increases and more women go out to work, the role of grandparent is becoming more significant. For example, in many families, grandparents provide childcare for their grandchildren.

**Hegemonic masculinity:** Dominant and traditional ideas about the role of men that stress individualism, competition and ambition.

**Hegemony:** Cultural domination, usually by an economically powerful group.

**Hidden curriculum:** The ways in which pupils learn values and attitudes other than through the formal curriculum of timetabled lessons.

**Homogeneous:** Sharing the same social characteristics.

**Household:** An individual or a group of people who share a home and some meals, e.g. a family (perhaps with servants), students in a shared home or people in a community group such as a commune.

**Icon:** Figure to be worshipped or admired.

**Ideology:** A set of ideas and claims that explains how society is or ought to be. In Marxist usage an ideology is always false (the ideology exists to serve the interests of a class rather than to explain reality).

**Impartiality:** Neutrality.

**Individualism:** An emphasis on individual people – e.g. in terms of happiness and success – rather than on groups, communities or societies.

**Industrialisation:** The set of changes by which a society moves from being predominantly rural and agricultural to being predominantly urban and industrial.

**Institutional racism:** This occurs when the way in which an organisation or institution operates has racist outcomes, regardless of the intentions of individuals within it.

**Integrity:** Trustworthiness.

**Interactionism:** A perspective within sociology that focuses on small-scale social interaction rather than on structures and institutions.

**Interactive relationship:** A relationship in which the parties respond to each other.

**Interpretivist:** An approach in sociology that focuses on the meaning that social phenomena have for the people involved.

**Interview schedule:** The list of questions used by the researcher.

**Kibbutz:** A form of community living that developed among Jewish families in what is now known as Israel before World War II. It involved groups of families sharing childcare and domestic duties, and was often based on farming.

**Kinship:** The sense of duty we feel towards family members.

**Labelling:** The process in which individuals or groups are thought of by teachers, or other agents of social control, in terms of types or stereotypes.

**Macro:** Large scale.

**Marginalised groups:** Groups of people who are excluded from economic and political power, e.g. the poor.

**Media conglomerates:** Large-scale media companies that often have global economic interests.

**Meritocracy:** A system in which the rewards go to those who have talent and ability and who work for the rewards.

**Meta-narratives:** A postmodern term to describe 'grand' theories such as Marxism.

**Micro:** Small scale.

**Misogynist:** Hating, demeaning and devaluing women.

**Modernity:** The period of history from the late eighteenth to late twentieth centuries, marked by a belief in progress through science and rationality.

**Moral panic:** Exaggerated social reaction to a group or issue, amplified by the media, with consequent demands for action.

**Multicultural education:** Education that teaches all children about the cultures of some of the minority groups.

**Multicultural:** The inter-mingling of a number of cultures.

**Multi-ethnic society:** A society in which a number of different ethnic groups live together.

**Nation:** This can mean 'a country' but is used in sociology to define a group of people with a shared common culture and history.

**National identity:** This is a sense of belonging to a particular nation state or cultural group.

**Nationalism:** This is a social and political concept that describes how people feel loyalty to a geographical region or culture.

**Nationality:** This is a legal concept. A person's nationality refers to the country of which they are a legal citizen with rights of residence and voting.

**New masculinities:** This is the change in traditional male roles whereby men are enabled to get in touch with their caring and domestic side.

**New man:** A man who challenges traditional male gender roles and is willing to take on domestic and other traditionally female roles.

**New Right:** A political philosophy that emphasises traditional moral and social values, particularly with regard to the family.

**New vocationalism:** A view of education that sees the meeting of the needs of the economy as being very important; it also refers to the policies connected to this view.

**News values:** What journalists think is newsworthy.

**Norm:** A rule of behaviour in everyday life.

**Nuclear family:** Parents and children in a single household.

**Objective:** (a) Existing independently of the observer; (b) being free of bias.

**Objectivity:** Without bias.

**Operationalise:** To define something so that it can be measured or counted.

**Participant:** Anyone who takes part in research. Some researchers use the term 'subject' but 'participant' is preferable because it suggests that the person is an equal in the process rather than an inferior.

**Patriarchy:** A system where men have social, cultural and economic dominance over women.

**Phenomena:** Anything that can be seen or perceived.

**Pirate radio stations:** Radio stations that transmit illegally because they don't have government broadcasting licences.

**Population:** All the people, or other unit, relevant to the research.

**Postmodernism:** The theory that suggests industrial society has been superseded by a media-saturated society in which the old indicators of identity – e.g. social class – have been replaced by new forms of identity based on consumption of style, fashion, etc.

**Postmodernity:** The period of history after the modern period.

**Power élite:** The minority who control economic and political power.

**Primary data:** Data collected by the researcher.

**Primary definers:** Powerful groups (e.g. the government) that have easier and more effective access to the media.

**Primary socialisation:** The process of learning knowledge, skills and values in early childhood, within the home and usually from parents.

**Private capital:** Financial resources in the hands of private investors.

**Privatisation:** A government policy designed to reduce the public sector by allowing a greater role for private companies.

**Procreation:** The process of having children; the process of creating new members of society.

**Proletarianisation:** A process whereby middle-class people become more working class.

**Qualitative:** Research where the sociologist aims to understand the meaning of social action.

**Quantitative:** Research that concentrates on collecting statistical data.

**Race:** A concept that views human beings as belonging to separate biological groupings.

**Reification:** When the results of human interactions seem to take on an independent reality of their own.

**Reliability:** A reliable method gives the same result when the research is repeated.

**Representative:** A sample is representative when what is true of the sample is true of the population from which it is drawn.

**Republican ideas:** Set of ideas opposed to hereditary power, e.g. arguing that the Queen should be replaced by an elected Head of State.

**Response rates:** The percentage of the sample who return completed questionnaires.

**Rite of passage:** A ceremony to mark the transition from one stage of life to another; for example, marriage ceremonies.

**Role:** The set of norms and expectations that go with a status.

**Sampling frame:** The list of people, or other unit, from whom a sample is drawn.

**Secondary data:** Data collected by others and used by the researcher.

**Secularisation:** The gradual loss of formal religious belief from society.

**Self-fulfilling prophecy:** A predicted outcome that helps to bring about that outcome.

**Sexism:** Discrimination against people because of their sex; most sexism has been against women.

**Socially constructed:** An agreed social definition of how to think or behave.

**Social control:** Social forces and pressures that encourage conformity and punish deviance, either formally or informally.

**Social mobility:** Movement up and down between social classes – for example, from working class to middle class.

**Socialisation:** The process of learning how to behave in a way that is appropriate to your culture or society.

**Status:** A position in society.

**Subculture:** A group sharing values and ways of behaving that are different from the rest of society.

**Symmetrical family:** A family in which men and women have some degree of equality.

**Terrestrial television:** Broadcasting using land-based transmitters.

**Underclass:** A group at the bottom of the social ladder, said to be characterised by violent crime, illegitimacy, unemployment and dependency on welfare benefits.

**Urbanisation:** The proportion of a country's population living in towns and cities.

**Valid:** Valid evidence is evidence of what it claims to be evidence of.

**Values:** The set of beliefs and morals that people consider to be of importance.

**Voluntarism:** The assumption that individuals are agents, with some choice and control over their actions. Usually contrasted with determinism.

**Weberians:** Sociologists who draw on the ideas of Max Weber (1864–1920).

# References

Abraham, J. (1995) *Divide and school: Gender and class dynamics in a comprehensive school*, Falmer Press, London.

Adams, E. (1985) *Television and 'the North'*, Centre for Contemporary Cultural Studies, University of Birmingham.

Adonis, A. and Pollard, S. (1998) *A class act: The myth of Britain's classless society*, Penguin, London.

Akinti, P. (2003) 'This is a message to TV broadcasters: There is a black audience that is sick of the mediocre fare you are feeding it', *The Guardian*, 21 February.

Allen, I. and Bourke Dowling, S. with Rolfe, H. (1998) *Teenage mothers: Decisions and outcomes*, Policy Studies Institute, London.

Althusser, L. (1971) *Lenin and Philosophy and other essays*, New Left Books, London.

Anderson, A. (1993) 'Source-media relations: the production of the environmental agenda' in A. Hansen (ed.) *The mass media and environmental issues*, Leicester University Press, Leicester.

Aries, P. (1962) *Centuries of childhood*, Jonathan Cape, London.

Ballard, C. (1979) 'Conflict, continuity and change' in V. S. Kahn (ed.) *Minority families in Britain*, Macmillan, London.

Ballaster, R., et al. (1991) *Women's worlds: Ideology, feminism and the women's magazine*, Macmillan, Basingstoke.

Barker, C. (1997) 'Television and the reflexive project of the self: Soaps, teenage talk and hybrid identities', *British Journal of Sociology*, Dec, vol. 48 (4), p. 611.

Barker, E. (1984) *The making of a Moonie: Brainwashing or choice?*, Basil Blackwell, Oxford.

Barlow, A., Duncan, S., James, G. and Park, A. (2001) 'Just a piece of paper? Marriage and cohabitation' in A. Park et al. (eds) (2001).

Baudrillard, J. (1985) 'The ecstasy of communication' in H. Foster (ed.) *Postmodern culture*, Pluto, London.

Beishon, S., Modood, T. and Virdee, S. (1998) *Ethnic minority families*, Policy Studies Institute, University of Westminster, London.

Bell, C. and Newby, H. (1977) *Doing sociological research*, George Allen & Unwin, London.

Bell, C. and Roberts, H. (1984) *Social researching*, Routledge & Kegan Paul, London.

Belson, W. (1978) *Television violence and the adolescent boy*, Gower Press, Aldershot.

Ben-Yehuda, B. and Goode, E. (1994) *Moral panics: The social construction of deviance*, Blackwell, Oxford.

Berger, P. and Luckmann, T. (1967) *The social construction of reality*, Penguin, Harmondsworth.

Bernardes, J. (1997) 'Understanding family diversity' in *Sociology Review*, Sept. 2001, Phillip Allan Publishers, Oxfordshire.

Bernstein, B. (1990) *The structure of pedagogic discourse, Vol. 4: Class, codes and control*, Routledge, London.

Berrington, A. (1996) 'Marriage patterns and inter-ethnic unions' in D. Coleman and J. Salt (eds), *Ethnicity in the 1991 Census, Volume one, Demographic characteristics of the ethnic minority populations*, HMSO, London, pp. 178–212.

Bettelheim, B. (1969) *The children of the dream*, Thames and Hudson, London.

Bhatti, G. (1999) *Asian children at home and at school*, Routledge, London.

Bottomore, T. and Rubel, M. (1963) *Karl Marx – Selected writings in sociology and social philosophy*, Penguin, Harmondsworth.

Boudon, R. (1974), *Education, opportunity and social inequality*, John Wiley and Sons, New York.

Bourdieu, P. (1973) 'Cultural reproduction and social reproduction' in R. Brown (ed.) (1973) *Knowledge, education and cultural change*, Tavistock, London.

Bourdieu, P. (1984) *Distinction*, Routledge, London.

Bourdieu, P. and Passeron, J. (1977) *Reproduction in education, society and culture*, Sage, London.

Bowles, S. and Gintis, H. (1976) *Schooling in capitalist America*, Routledge, London.

Braverman, H. (1974) *Labor and monopoly capital*, Monthly Review Press, New York.

Brazier, C. (1999) 'Gender canyon', *New Internationalist*, No 315, August.

Brittan, A. (1989) *Masculinity and power*, Blackwell, Oxford.

Britton, L., Chatrik, B., Coles, B., Craig, G., Hylton, C. and Mumtaz, S. with Bivand, P., Burrows, R. and Convery, P., (2002) *Missing ConneXions: The career dynamics and welfare needs of black and minority ethnic young people at the margins*, JRF/The Policy Press, York.

Broad, B., Hayes, R. and Rushforth, C. (2001) *Kith and kin: Kinship care for vulnerable young people*, Joseph Rowntree Foundation and National Children's Bureau, London.

Buckingham, A. (1999) 'Is there an underclass in Britain?', *British Journal of Sociology*, March, vol. 50 (1), p. 49.

Buckingham, D. (1996) *Moving images*, Manchester University Press, Manchester.

Buss, D. M. (1998) 'The psychology of human mate selection: Exploring the complexity of the strategic repertoire', in C. Crawford and D. L. Krebs (1998).

Butler, J. (1999) *Gender trouble: Tenth anniversary issue (Thinking gender)*, Routledge, London.

Campbell, B. (1993) *Goliath: Britain's dangerous places*, Methuen, London.

Carvel, J. (1997) 'Graduates paid more', *The Guardian*, 22 May, 1997.

Chan, M.Y. and Chan, C. (1997) 'The Chinese in Britain', *New Community*, vol. 23(1).

Channel 4 television (1988) *Baka People of the Rainforest*, produced and photographed by Phil Agland.

Chapman, S., (2001) 'Toffs and snobs? Upper-class identity in Britain', *Sociology Review*, vol. 11 (1).

Charlesworth. S, (2000) *A phenomenology of working-class experience*, Cambridge University Press, Cambridge.

Cohen, S. (1972) *Folk devils and moral panics*, MacGibbon and Kee, London.

Collier, R. (1992) 'The New Man: Fact or fad', *Achilles' Heel*, 14.

Commission for Racial Equality (1992) *Set to fail? Setting and banding in secondary schools*, Commission for Racial Equality, London.

Connell, R. (2002) *Gender*, Polity Press, Cambridge.

Connell, R. W. (1995) *Masculinities: Knowledge, power, and social change*, University of California Press, Berkeley and Los Angeles.

Connolly, P. (1998) *Racism, gender identities and young children: Social relations in a multi-ethnic, inner-city primary school*, Routledge, London.

Connor, H. and Dewson, S. (2001) *Social class and higher education: Issues affecting decisions on participation by lower social class groups*, DfES, London.

Cooper, D. (1970) *The death of the family*, Random House, New York.

Coote, A., Harman, H. and Hewitt, P. (1990) 'The family way: a new approach to policy making', *Social Policy Paper No.1*, Institute for Public Policy, London.

Crawford, C, and Krebs, D. L. (eds) (1998) *Handbook of evolutionary psychology: Ideas, issues and applications*, Lawrence Erlbaum Associates, London.

Cumberbatch, G. (1990) *Television advertising and sex role stereotyping*, Broadcasting, Standards Council Research.

Curran, J. and Seaton, J. (1991) *Power without responsibility (4th edn)*, Routledge, London.

Curtice, J. and Heath, A. (2000) 'Is the British lion about to roar?', in the *British Social Attitudes 17th report*, 2000–01 edition, 'Focussing on Diversity', NCSR/Sage.

Dahrendorf, R. (1992) *Understanding the Underclass*, Policy Studies Institute, London.

Dallos, R. and Sapsford, M. R. 'Patterns of diversity and lived realities' in J. Muncie, M. Wetherell, M. Langan, R. Dallos and A. Cochrane (1997) *Understanding the family* (2nd edn), Sage, London.

Davidson, A. (1997) *From subject to citizen, Australian citizenship in the twentieth century*, Cambridge University Press, Cambridge.

Davie et al. (1972) *From birth to seven*, Penguin, Harmondsworth.

Davis, K. and Moore, W. E. (1945) 'Some principles of stratification' in R. Bendix and S. M. Lipset *Class, status and power*, Routledge and Kegan Paul, London.

de Beauvoir, S. (1953) *The second sex*, (H. M. Parshley, trs & ed.), Alfred A Knopf, New York.

Delamont, S. (2000) 'The anomalous beasts: Hooligans and the sociology of education', *Sociology*, vol. 34 (1), Feb.

Delamont, S. (2001) *Changing women, unchanging men: Sociological perspectives on gender in a post-industrial society*, Open University Press, Buckingham.

Delanty, G. (1995) *Inventing Europe: Idea, identity, reality*, Macmillan, London.

Delphy, C. and Leonard, D. (1992) *Familiar exploitation*, Polity Press, Cambridge.

Denscombe, M. (1999) *Sociology update*, Olympus, Leicester.

Denscombe, M. (2000) *Sociology update*, Olympus, Leicester.

Denscombe, M. (2001) *Sociology update*, Olympus Press, Leicester.

Denscombe, M. (2002) *Sociology update*, Olympus Books, Leicester.

Department for Education and Science (1985) *Education for all* (The Swann Report), HMSO, London.

Dore, R. P. (1976) *The diploma disease*, Allen & Unwin, London.

Dunn, J. and Deater-Deckard, K. (2001) *Children's views of their changing families*, Joseph Rowntree Foundation, York.

Dunscombe, J. and Marsden, D. (1993) 'Love and intimacy: the gender division of emotion and "emotion work"' in *Sociology*, vol. 27 (2), pp. 221–41.

Durkheim, Emile, (1964) *The division of labor in society* (trs. George Simpson), Free Press paperbacks, New York; London: Collier-Macmillan (Originally published by Macmillan (1933), Translation of: *De la division du travail social*).

Easthope, A. (1986) *What's a man gotta do: The masculine myth in popular culture*, Paladin, London.

Edgell, S. (1980) *Middle-class couples*, Allen & Unwin, London.

Edwards, T. (1997) *Men in the mirror*, Cassell, London.

Elkins, M. and Olangundoye, J. (2000) *The Prison population in 2000: A statistical review*, HMSO (http://www.homeoffice.gov.uk/rds/pdfs/r154.pdf)

Elwood, J. (1999) 'Gender achievement and the gold standard: Differential performance in the GCE A level examination', *Curriculum Journal*, vol. 10 (2).

Eversley, D. (1984) *Changes in the composition of households and the cycle of family life*, Council of Europe, Strasbourg.

Eyre, R. (1999) 'The 1999 McTaggart Lecture to the Guardian International Television Festival', *The Guardian*, 28 August, 1999.

Ferguson, M. (1983) *Forever feminine: Women's magazines and the cult of femininity*, Heinemann, London.

Festinger, L. *et al.* (1956) *When prophecy fails*, Harper and Row, New York.

Freire, P. (1972) *Pedagogy of the oppressed*, Penguin, Harmondsworth.

Frosh, S., Phoenix, A. and Partman, K. (2002) *Young masculinities*, Palgrave, London.

Furedi, (1995) 'A plague of moral panics', *Living Marxism*, January.

Galtung, J. and Ruge, M. (1970) 'Structuring and selecting news' in S. Cohen and J. Young, *The manufacture of news, social problems, deviance and the mass media*, Constable, London.

Garfinkel, H. (1967) *Studies in ethnomethodology*, Polity Press, Cambridge.

Gauntlett, D. (1995) *Moving experiences: Understanding television influences and effects*, John Libbey, Eastleigh, Southampton.

Gauntlett, D. (2000) (www.theory.org.uk)

Gerwitz, S., Ball, S. J., Bowe, R. (1995) *Markets, choice and equity in education*, Open University Press, Buckingham.

Giddens, A. (1979) *Central problems in social theory*, Macmillan, London.

Gillies, V., Ribbens McCarthy, J. and Holland, J. (2001) *Pulling together, pulling apart: The family lives of young people*, Family Policy Studies Centre, London.

Gilroy, P. (2000) *Between camps: Race, identity and nationalism at the end of the colour line*, Allen Lane, London.

Glass, D. V. (ed.) (1954) *Social mobility in Britain*, Routledge and Kegan Paul, London.

Goffman, E. (1969) *The presentation of the self in everyday life*, Penguin, Harmondsworth, (first published 1959, Doubleday, New York).

Goldthorpe, J. (1987) *Social mobility and class structure in modern Britain*, Clarendon Press, Oxford.

Goldthorpe. J.H., Lockwood, D. *et al.* (1969) *The affluent worker in the class structure*, Cambridge University Press, Cambridge.

Goode & Ben-Yehuda (1994) *see* Ben-Yehuda and Goode.

Gordon, D. (2000) 'Inequalities in income, wealth and standard of living in Britain' in C. Pantazis and D. Gordon (eds) (2000).

Gordon, D., Adelman, L., Ashworth, K., Bradshaw, J., Levitas, R., Middleton, S., Pantazis, C., Patsios D., Payne, S., Townsend, P. and Williams, J. (2000) *Poverty and social exclusion in Britain*, Joseph Rowntree Foundation, York.

Gramsci, A. (1971) *Selections from the prison notebooks*, Lawrence and Wishart, London.

Greer, G. (1971) *The female eunuch*, Paladin, St Albans.

GUMG (1993) *Getting the message: News, truth and power*, Routledge, London.

GUMG (2000) 'Media coverage of the developing world: Audience understanding and interest' (www.gla.uk/departments/sociology/debate.html)

Hall, S. (1978) 'Cultural identity and Diaspora' in J. Rutherford (ed.) *Identity, community, culture and difference*, Lawrence and Wishart, London.

Hall, S. and Young, J. (eds) (1981) *The manufacture of news*, Owen and Young, London.

Halsey, A. H., Heath, A. and Ridge, J. M. (1980) *Origins and destinations*, Clarendon Press, Oxford.

Halstead, M. (1994) 'Between two cultures? Muslim children in a western liberal society', *Children and Society*, vol. 8 (4), pp. 312–326.

Hammond, P. (1964) *Sociologists at work*, Basic Books, New York.

Hargreaves, D. H. (1967) *Social relations in a secondary school*, Routledge, London.

Harvey, D. (1990) *The condition of postmodernity*, Blackwell, London.

Hattersley R. (2001) 'New Labour's creeping poverty gap' in *The Guardian*, Monday 16 July.

Hechter, M. (1975) *Internal colonialism: The Celtic fringe in British National development*, Transaction Publishers, New Brunswick, NJ.

Hester, M. and Radford, L. 'Contradictions and compromises', in Marianne Hester, Liz Kelly and Jill Radford (eds) (1996) *Women, violence and male power*, Open University Press, Buckingham.

Hey V. (1997) *The company she keeps: an ethnography of girls' friendships*, Open University Press, Milton Keynes.

HMSO (published annually) *Social Trends*, HMSO, London (www.statistics.gov.uk)

HMSO (published annually) *Population Trends*, HMSO, London (www.statistics.gov.uk)

Hockey, J. and James, A. (1993) *Growing up and growing old: Ageing and dependency in the life course*, Sage, London.

Holdaway, S. (1983) *Inside the British Police*, Basil Blackwell, Oxford.

Illich, I. (1973) *Deschooling society*, Penguin, Harmondsworth.

Jackson, P. W. (1968) *Life in classrooms*, Holt, Rinehart and Winston; (1991) Teachers College Press.

Jagger, E. (2001) 'Marketing Molly and Melville: dating in a postmodern, consumer society', *Sociology*, vol. 35 (1) February.

Jones, K. (1998) 'Death of a princess: public mourning, private grief', *Sociology Review*, Sept.

Jones, M. (2000) 'The moral panic revisited', *Sociology Review*, Feb.

Jones, N. (1993) *Living in rural Wales*, Gomer Press, Llandysul.

Kellner, D. (1995) *Media culture*, Routledge, London.

Kidd, W. (1999) 'Family diversity in an uncertain future', *Sociology Review*, vol. 9 (1).

King, A. (2000) 'Football fandom and post-national identity in the New Europe', *British Journal of Sociology*, vol. 51 (3), Sept. p. 419.

Klapper, J. T. (1960) *The effects of mass communication*, The Free Press, New York.

Koerner, Ernst F. K. (1972) *Bibliographia Saussureana, 1870–1970. An annotated, classified bibliography on the background, development and actual relevance of Ferdinand de Saussure's general theory of language*, Scarecrow Press: Metuchen, NJ.

Laing, R. D. (1960) *The divided self: a study of sanity and madness*, (in the series 'Studies in existential analysis and phenomenology'), Quadrangle Books, Chicago, IL.

Langford, W., Lewis, C., Solomon, Y. and Warin, J. (2001) *Family understandings: Closeness, authority and independence in families with teenagers*, Joseph Rowntree Foundation and Family Policy Studies Institute, London.

Lash, S. and Urry, J. (1994) *Economies of signs and space*, Sage, London.

Liebow, E. (1967) *Tally's Corner*, Routledge and Kegan Paul, London.

Lockhurst, I. (1999) 'Men: The silent victims', *S – the A-level Sociology Magazine*, Issue 4, May.

Low Pay Commission (2000) http://www.lowpay.gov.uk/ Low Pay Unit, Manchester.

Lull, J. (1990) *Inside family viewing: ethnographic research on television audiences*, Routledge, London.

Lyotard, J. (1984) *The postmodern condition: a report on knowledge*, Manchester University Press, Manchester.

Mac an Ghaill, M. (1988) *Young, gifted and black: Student–teacher relations in the schooling of black youth*, Open University Press, Milton Keynes.

MacBeath, J. and Mortimore, P. (eds) (2001) *Improving school effectiveness*, Open University Press, Buckingham.

MacIntosh, M. and Mooney, G. (2000) 'Identity, inequality and social class', in K. Woodward (ed.) *Questioning identity: Gender, class, nation*, Open University Press, Milton Keynes.

Macionis, J. J. and Plummer, K. (1997) *Sociology: A global introduction*, Prentice Hall Europe, New Jersey.

Mack, J. and Lansley, S. (1985) *Poor Britain*, George Allen & Unwin, London.

Maclean, C. (1979) *The wolf children: Fact or fantasy?*, Penguin Books, Harmondsworth.

Manning, P. (1999) 'Who makes the news?', *Sociology Review*, September.

Marshall, G., Newby, H., Rose, D. and Vogler, C. (1988) *Social class in modern Britain*, Hutchinson, London.

Marsland, D. (1989) 'Universal welfare provision creates a dependent population', *Social studies review*, Nov.

McAllister, F. with Clarke, L. (1998) *Choosing childlessness*, Family Policy Studies Centre, London.

McNeill, P. (1990) *Research methods*, Routledge, London.

McQuail, D. (1994) *Mass communication theory: An introduction* (3rd edn), Sage, London.

McRobbie, A. (1982) 'Jackie: An ideology of adolescent femininity' in B. Waites (ed.) *Popular culture: Past and present*, Open University Press, Buckingham.

McRobbie, A. (1995) 'Re-thinking 'Moral panic' for multi-mediated social worlds', *British Journal of Sociology*, 46.

Mead, G. H. (1934) *Mind, self and society*, Chicago University Press, Chicago, IL.

Mirza, H. (1992) *Young, female and black*, Routledge, London.

Mitsos, E. and Browne, K. (1998) 'Gender differences in education', *Sociology Review*, vol. 8 (1), Sept.

Modood, T. (ed.) (1997) 'Church, state and religious minorities', *PSI Report No. 845*, Policy Studies Institute.

Modood, T., Berthoud, R., Lakey, J., Nazroo, J., Smith, P., Virdee S. and Beishon, S. (1997) *Ethnic minorities in Britain*, Policy Studies Institute, London.

Morley, D. (1980) *The 'Nationwide' audience*, BFI, London.

Morris, D. (1975) *The naked ape*, Corgi, London, (first published 1967, Cape, London).

Morrison, D. (1992) *Television and the Gulf War*, John Libbey, Eastleigh, Southampton.

Morrison, D. (1999) *Defining violence: The search for understanding*, Broadcasting Standards Council/Institute of Communication Studies, University of Leeds, Leeds.

Mort, F. (1988) quoted in Chapman, R. and Rutherford, J. (1988) (eds) *Male order: Unwrapping masculinity*, Lawrence and Wishart, London.

Mulvey, L. (1975) 'Visual pleasure and narrative cinema', *Screen*, vol. 16 (3).

Murdoch, G. and McCron, R. (1979) 'The television and delinquency debate', *Screen Education*, vol. 30 (Spring).

Murdock, G. P. (1949) *Social structure*, Macmillan, New York.

Murphy, P. and Elwood, J. (1998) 'Gendered experiences, choices and achievements – exploring the links', *Journal of Inclusive Education*, vol. 2 (2), pp. 95–118.

Murray, C. (1984) *Losing ground: American social policy, 1950–1980*, Basic Books, New York.

Murray, C. (1993) 'The time has come to put a stigma back on illegitimacy', *Wall Street Journal*, 14 November.

Nairn, T. (1988) *The enchanted glass: Britain and its monarchy*, Radius, London.

Newson, E. (1994) 'Ordeal by media: A Personal Account, *The Psychologist*, April.

Newson, E. and Newson, J. (1968) *Four years old in an urban community*, Allen & Unwin, London.

Nixon, S. (1996) *Hard looks – Masculinities, spectatorship and contemporary consumption*, UCL Press, London.

Oakley, A. (1981) *Subject women*, Robertson, Oxford.

OFSTED (1999) *Raising the attainment of minority ethnic pupils*, HMSO, London.

OPCS (1994) *OPCS Monitor: National population projections (1992 based)*, HMSO, London.

Opie, I. and Opie, P. (1969) *Children's games in street and playground*, Clarendon, Great Britain.

Osler, A., Street, C., Lall, M. and Vincent, K. (2002) *Not a problem? Girls and school exclusion*, National Children's Bureau.

Pahl, R. E. and Wallace, C. (1988) 'Neither angels in marble nor rebels in red' in D. Rose (ed.) *Social stratification and economic change*, Hutchinson, London.

Pantazis, C. and Gordon, D. (eds) (2000) *Tackling inequalities*, The Policies Press, Bristol.

Park, A. *et al.* (eds) (2001) *British social attitudes, the 18th RSA report: Public policy, social ties*, Sage, London.

Park, R. E, (1927) *Introduction to the science of sociology*, University of Chicago Press, Chicago, IL.

Parsons, T. and Bales, R. F. with James Olds (and others) (1955) *Family, socialisation and interaction process*, Free Press, Glencoe, Ill.

Philo, G. (1997) *Children and film/video/TV violence*, Glasgow University Media Group, Glasgow.

Philo, G. (2001) 'Media effects and the active audience', *Sociology Review*, February.

Pilcher, J. (1995) 'Growing up and growing older', *Sociology Review*, September.

Pilcher, J. (1998) *Women of their time*, Ashgate Publishing, Aldershot.

Reay, D. and Mirza, H. (2000) 'Spaces and places of black educational desire: Rethinking black supplementary schools as a new social movement', *Sociology*, vol. 34 (3).

Redhead, S. (1992) *Rave off and the end of the century party*, Routledge, London.

Rex, J. (1996) 'National identity in the democratic multi-cultural state', *Sociological Research Online*, vol. 1 (2) (www.socresonline.org.uk)

Robinson, M. (1991) *Family transformation through divorce and remarriage: A systemic approach*, Routledge, London.

Rose, S. (1998) *Lifelines: Biology, freedom, determinism*, Penguin, Harmondsworth.

Rosenthal, R. and Jacobson, L. (1968) *Pygmalion in the classroom*, Holt, Reinhart and Winston, New York.

Sarlvik, B. and Crewe, I. (1983) *Decade of dealignment: The Conservative victory of 1979 and electoral trends in the 1970s*, Cambridge University Press, Cambridge.

Saunders, D. G. (1995) 'A typology of men who batter: three types derived from cluster analyses', *American Journal of Orthopsychiatry*, 62, pp. 264–275

Saunders, P. (1995) *Capitalism: A social audit*, Open University Press, Buckingham.

Savage, M., Barlow, J., Dickens, P. and Fielding, T. (1992) *Property, bureaucracy and culture: Middle-class formation in contemporary Britain*, Routledge, London.

Schlesinger, P. (1990) 'Rethinking the sociology of journalism' in M. Ferguson (ed.) *Public communication: The new imperatives*, Sage, London.

Schudson, M. (1994) 'Culture and the integration of national societies', *International Social Science Journal*, vol. 46.

Scott, J. (1982) *The upper classes*, Macmillan, London.

Scott, J. (1986) 'Does Britain still have a ruling class?', *Social Studies Review*, vol. 2 (1).

Selbourne, D. (1993) *The spirit of the age*, Sinclair-Stevenson, London.

Sewell, T. (1997) *Black masculinities and schooling – How black boys survive modern schooling*, Trentham Books, Stoke on Trent.

Shropshire, J. and Middleton, S. (1999) *Small expectations: Learning to be poor?*, York Publishing Services, York.

Slater, D. (1997) *Consumer culture and modernity*, Polity Press, Cambridge.

Smart, C., Wade, A. and Neale, B. (2000) 'New childhoods: Children and co-parenting after divorce and objects of concern?', *Children and Divorce*, Centre for Research on Family, Kinship and Childhood, University of Leeds.

Smith, P. (1991) *Ethnic minorities in Scotland*, Central Research Unit Papers, The Scottish Office, The Stationery Office, Edinburgh.

Southerton, D. (2002) Boundaries of 'us' and 'them': Class, mobility and identification in a new town, *British Sociology Association*, vol. 36 (1), 171–193, Sage Publications, London.

Spender, D. (1983) *Invisible women: Schooling scandal*, Women's Press, London.

Stacey, J. (1990) *Brave new families: Stories of domestic upheaval in late twentieth century America*, Basic Books, New York.

Sullivan, A. (2001) 'Cultural capital and educational attainment', *Sociology*, vol. 35 (4).

Thornton, S. (1995) *Club cultures: Music, media and subcultural capital*, Polity Press, Cambridge.

Tunstall (1983) *The media in Britain*, Constable, London.

Turak, I. (2000) Inequalities in Employment in C. Pantazis and D. Gordon (eds) (2000)

Van Dijks, T. (1991) *Racism and the Press*, Routledge, London.

Warnock Report, The (1984) *Report of the Committee of Inquiry into Human Fertilisation and Embryology*, Chairman of Commission: Dame Mary Warnock, HMSO, London.

Weber, M. (1978) *Economy and society*, vols. 1 & 2, (eds) G. Roth and C. Wittich, University of California Press, Berkeley.

Wedderburn, D. and Crompton, R. (1972) *Workers' attitudes and technology*, Cambridge University Press, Cambridge.

Westwood, S. (1999) 'Girls just want to have fun: Re-presenting gender', *Sociology Review*, September.

Whannell, G. (2002) 'David Beckham: Identity and masculinity', *Sociology Review*, February.

Whyte, W. F. (1955) *Street corner society: The social structure of an Italian slum*, University of Chicago Press, Chicago, IL.

Willis, P. (1977) *Learning to Labour: How working-class kids get working-class jobs*, Saxon House, Farnborough.

Winship, J. (1986) *Inside women's magazines*, Pandora, London

Winston, R. (2002), *Human instinct*, Bantam Press, London.

Wolf, N. (1990) *The beauty myth,* Vintage, London.

Woodward, W. and Ward, L. (2000) 'End bias, élite universities told', *Guardian Weekly*, 8 to 14 June.

Yip, A. (1999) 'Same sex couples', in *Sociology Review*, vol. 8 (3).

Young, J. (1971) *The Drugtakers*, Paladin, London

Young, M. and Willmott, P. (1973) *The symmetrical family*, Penguin, London.

# Index

ability, mixed  81
abortion  37–8
    rate of  36
abuse, domestic  56–7
academic education  100
achievement, differential
    class  92–3
    ethnic groups  88–9
    gender  84–5
action research  114
adoption  40
    by gay couples  43, 59
    rights  59
adult personality, stabilisation of  28
adultery  50
African-Caribbeans  99
    families  44, 48
    pupils  78–9, 81, 86, 88–9
age  16–17
    old  15, 54
ageing  15
    population  54–5
agency  14–15
agriculture  8
A levels  83–4, 100–2
Althusser, L.  11
American culture  7
Anglo-Pakistani families  45
anthropology  122
anti-school subcultures  78
Apprenticeships, Modern  101
ascribed status  6, 16, 28
Asians
    families  26, 44–5, 57
    pupils  78, 86, 88, 103
aspirations  89, 92
assessment objectives  134
Assisted Places Scheme  96
attitudes  6
Baby Boom  35
banding  81
Bangladeshi families  44–5, 47
beacon schools  75, 98
beanpole family  39
benefits, social security  38, 58
bias  127
biological factors  10
birth rates  32, 34
    falling  36–7
black people  44, 81
bourgeoisie  13, 16
boys
    education of  82–5
    underachievement of  78, 83–5

British Asians  57
British Empire  8
Butler Education Act  94
capitalism  13
case study  116
caste  16
catchment area  75, 90
cause and effect  114
census  27, 124
cereal-packet norm  30
Chicago School  122
Child Support Agency  30, 49
childhood  52–3
    changing  52
    mortality rates  35
    poverty  49
    social construction of  14, 52–3
childlessness  36–7
children
    birth rates  34–5
    defined  52
    dependent  27, 44, 48
    feral  70
    number of  32
    relationship with parents  52–3
    rights of  59
    speaking skills of  53
    status of  33
Children Act  31, 57, 59
Chinese  26, 45, 88
citizenship  76
city technology colleges  97
class, social  16, 81, 88, 90, 95
    identities  90–1
    movement between  72
class conflict  16
class dimension  47
closed questions  121
co-educational schools  74
cohabitation  27, 32, 40, 50
cohort, age  17, 93
collective agency  14
colonialism  104
command words  135
common-sense thinking  13, 72,
    126–8
commune  42, 60
communism  13
community schools  75
comparative method  13
comprehensive schools  75, 90, 94–5
Comte, A.  4
conflict theory  72
conjugal roles  46–7

consensus, post-war  8–9
consent, informed  119, 122, 126
Conservative governments  95–7
    see also New Right thinking
consumerism  7
content analysis  30, 125
contraception  36, 38
control group  126
convent  42
co-parenting  39
correlate  114
correspondent theory  90
counter-culture  42
couple  40
coursework  148–9
crime  7, 11
cross-cultural family  40
cultural capital  17, 92–3
cultural deprivation  89, 92
cultural diversity  7
cultural imperialism  7, 105
culture  7, 18, 26, 89
curriculum
    formal  76
    hidden  73, 76–7
    national  71, 74, 76, 82, 96, 100
custody, child  48, 57, 58
data collection  5, 117
    reliability of  118
    representativeness of  118
    validity of  118
    see also secondary data
death rates  34–5
debate, the great  100
dementia  54
demography  34–5
dependency culture  48
dependency theory  105
dependent children, families with  27,
    44, 48
deprivation, material  92
descriptive research  114
determinism  10, 13
    genetic  10
deviance  7
differential achievement  84–5, 88–9,
    92–3
discrimination  82
divorce
    law  50
    patterns of  50–1
    rates  32, 34–5
Divorce Reform Act  50
documents  124